The Apothecaries
Stephen Llewelyn

In days of yore, your days could be quite short.
Short and brutal. Your nights could be even worse...

www.fossil-rock.com

Published by Fossil Rock Publishing 2023
Copyright © Stephen Llewelyn 2023

The author asserts the moral right under the Copyright, Designs and Patents Act 1988 to be identified as the author of this work. All rights reserved. No part of this publication may be reproduced, stored in a retrieval system or transmitted, in any form or by any means without the prior consent of the author, nor be otherwise circulated in any form of binding or cover other than that with which it is published and without a similar condition being imposed on the subsequent purchaser.

ISBNs:
ebook 978-1-915676-07-8
hardcover 978-1-915676-08-5
paperback 978-1-915676-06-1

Download your FREE introduction to the New World Series by Stephen Llewelyn. Your eBook is waiting...

Six people alone in a Cretaceous jungle. Ordered to make a threat assessment of their environment, Corporal Heinz Engel is at a loss where to begin. Between running and hiding from a most irascible spinosaur, his team find that foolish mistakes have bloody consequences, and while their predicament brings out the best in some, others show their true colours. By the end of the mission, Engel seeks only justice.

ENGEL is one of the short stories that form a companion set to the New World Series. ENGEL is set during the early chapters of REVENGE, the New World Series Book 2.

Get a free copy of ENGEL here:
www.stephenllewelyn.com/free-book

Other free eBooks here:
www.stephenllewelyn.com/books/short-stories/engel

For Sally…
Thank you for your unwavering commitment,
support and for everything you do.

I also wish to acknowledge the help and support I've received from Mum, Dad, Bill, Sally-Marie and Fossil Rock, and Melanie at The Chapter House for all the reads, re-reads, marketing, publishing, IT help and on, and on, and on…

To my long-suffering friends, thank you for a lifetime of memories and for offering encouragement with my mad ideas – especially Karl for the music and tech help. Also, to my old school friends, Mark N, and Mark S, for popping back into my life after more than thirty years, and in the most unexpected way – I hope we'll meet up again soon. A special thank you to my lifelong friend in music and knowledge, Dr Nick, who is embarking on an incredible new adventure of his own – *bonne chance!*

My thanks to the White Company medieval re-enactment society, who provided inspiration for Harry-the-Cough's medicinal remedies.

…And last but by no means least, to everyone who reads this book, my sincere thanks.

Stephen Llewelyn

Contents

Map of Warmstirrup Environs viii
Map of Warmstirrup Town ix
Preface xi

Chapter 1 ..... A Cold Day in Warmstirrup 1
Chapter 2 ..... The Pail Hoarse Man 13
Chapter 3 ..... The Dog and Castle 21
Chapter 4 ..... The Price 31
Chapter 5 ..... Every Dog 45
Chapter 6 ..... Fox on the Run 57
Chapter 7 ..... Dave 69
Chapter 8 ..... One Mistress Too Many 79
Chapter 9 ..... Bitching Hour 89
Chapter 10 ... Death, Death or Death 105
Chapter 11 ... Geese and Ganders 115
Chapter 12 ... Dead Men, Tall Tales 125
Chapter 13 ... Matins 141
Chapter 14 ... In the Grey Light, Blackest Deeds 155
Chapter 15 ... In Troubles of Plenty 171
Chapter 16 ... Family 187
Chapter 17 ... There's a Storm Coming 205
Chapter 18 ... Shepherd's Warning 219
Chapter 19 ... Crossed Line 227
Chapter 20 ... Injured Parties 241
Chapter 21 ... Second Wind 253
Chapter 22 ... Playing Chicken 267
Chapter 23 ... The Also Rans 275
Chapter 24 ... Dues 283
Chapter 25 ... A Bad Day in Warmstirrup 293
Epilogue .... Wednesday 303

Author's Notes 319
Also by Stephen Llewelyn 323

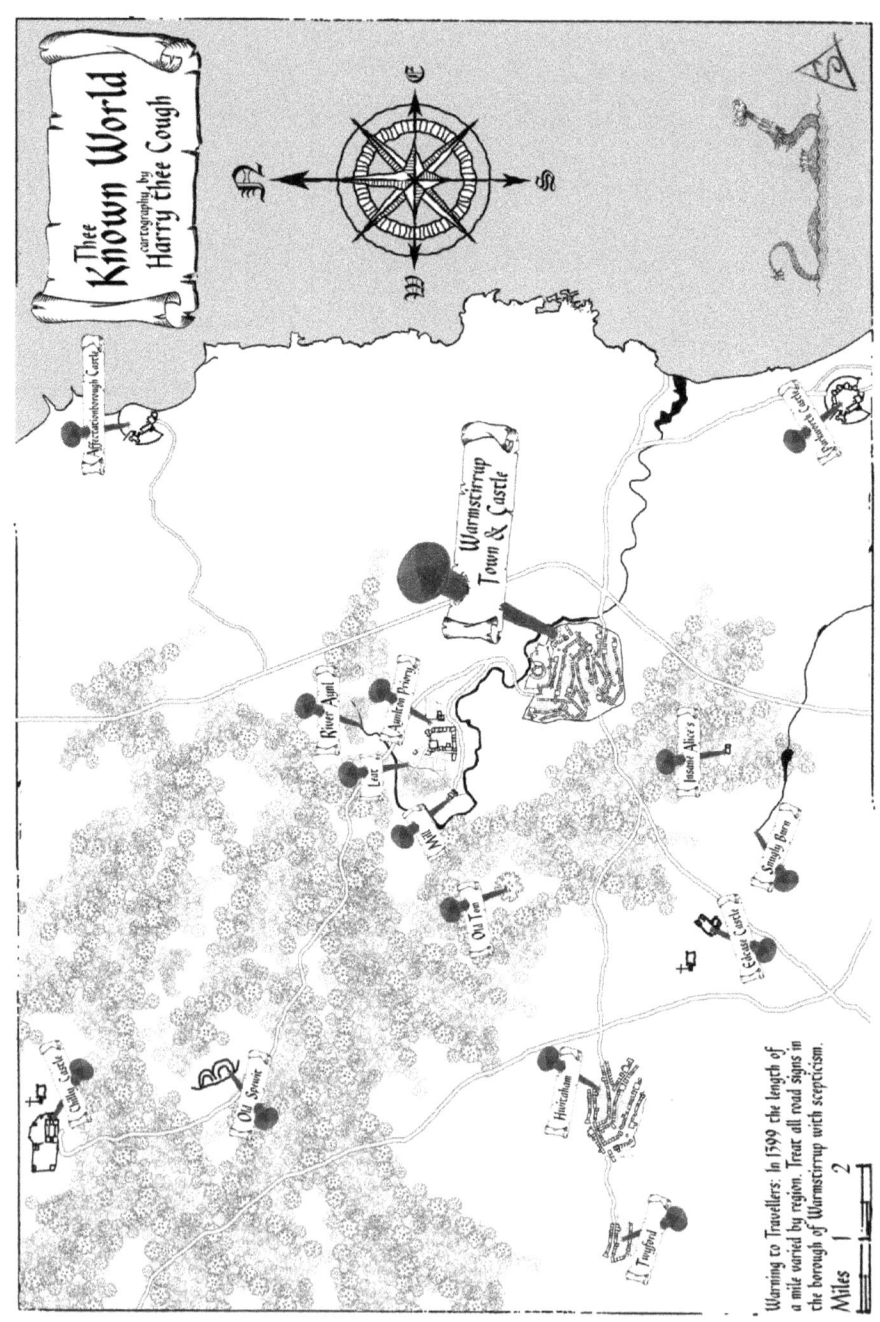

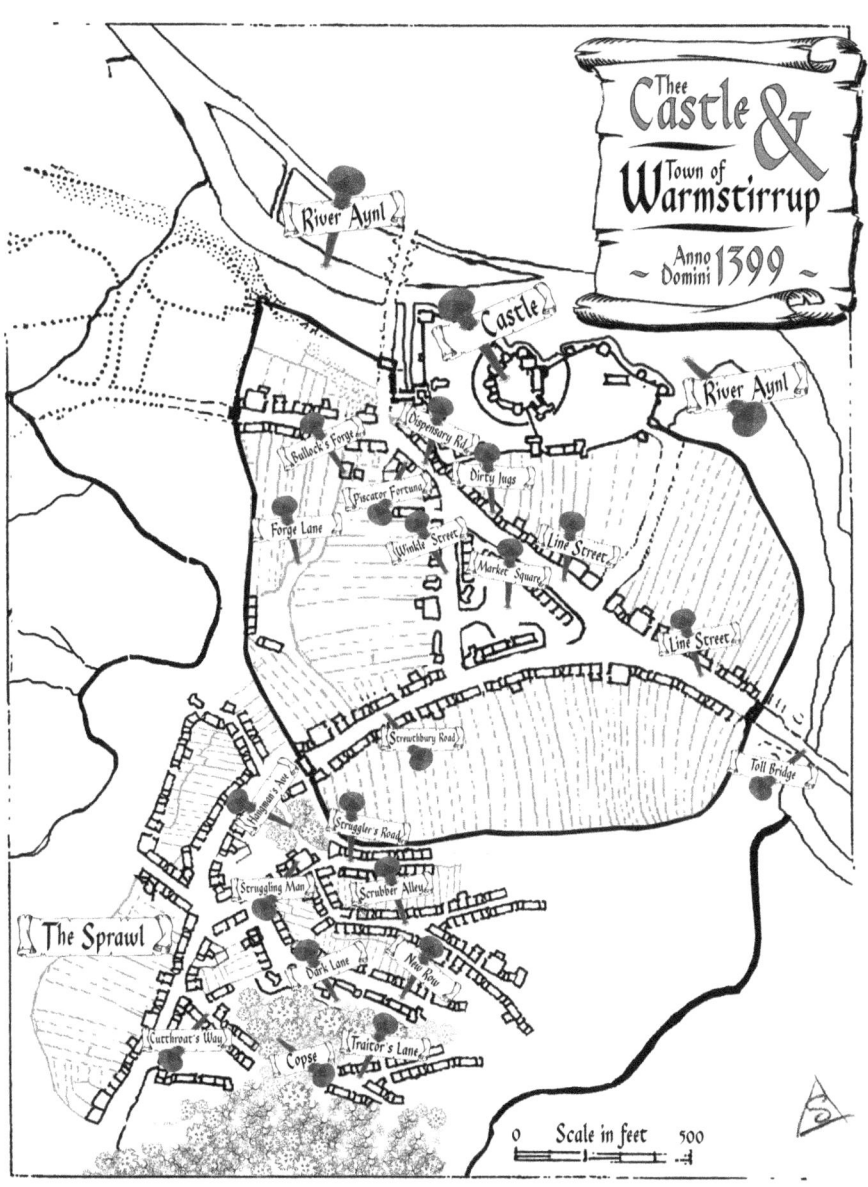

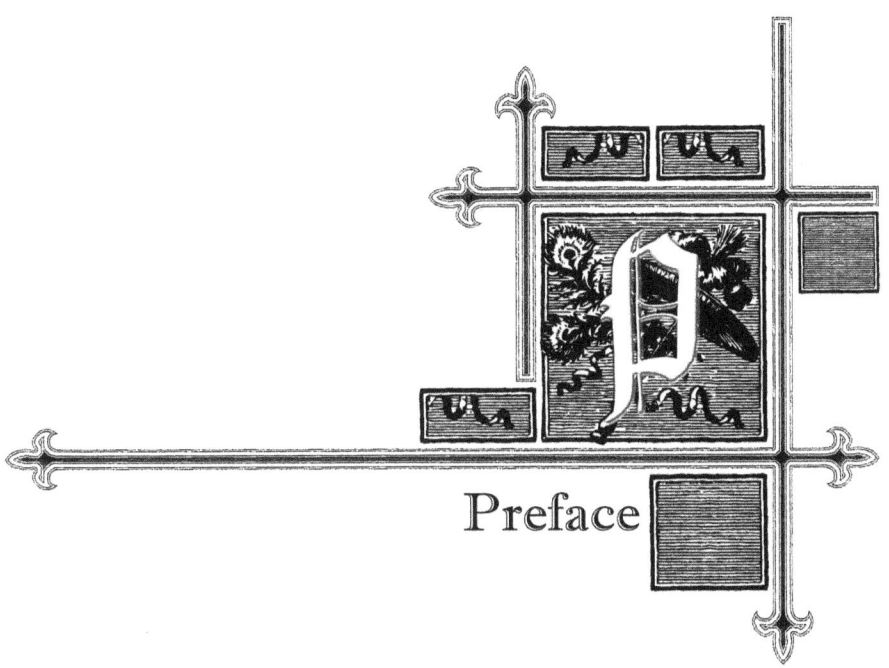

Preface

Dear friends... The setting for 'The Apothecaries' was inspired by the real medieval market town of Alnwick in Northumberland, England. Here in the far North East, the visitor may walk through 8000 years of human history and pre-history, all brimming with wonderful monuments and tantalising legends. Its most hospitable people, and glorious views, make the place meat and drink for a writer; a world where the imagination can truly run wild, and to its treasure trove of stories, I humbly submit one more.

My initial fleshing out of the idea seemed rather grim. As a book takes several months to write, it morphed into a comedy of sorts, all on its own, because I lack the stamina to remain serious for that long.

The beginnings of the tale came to me while standing outside the mighty gatehouse of Alnwick Castle. Alnwick (pronounced 'Annick' – hence the several place name gags throughout the book) was where Harry-the-Cough (the least of the famous Harrys!) was born, so it seemed a fitting tribute and thank you to use the old place as a basic template for the story it inspired. Before that moment, 'The Apothecaries' was little more than a title and an elevator pitch. I'm not sure how long I stood gawping up at the impressive medieval palace and war machine, but during that time came the idea for another Harry's rags-to-riches ride against a backdrop of war, disease and perhaps even a little black magic. I say *another* Harry because Alnwick was, of course, the home of one of England's greatest medieval heroes, Harry Hotspur – and yes, it was also the place where the early Harry Potter movies were filmed.

I always enjoy including a little history within my stories because I believe it gives a grounding in reality – even when history beggars belief! A few notes about the real 14th century Alnwick, and where my novel deviates, may be found in my author's notes at the back of this book. For example, Hotspur (Sir Henry Percy) did not actually live long enough to become Earl of Northumberland and AD1399 was a little before the town walls in the novel were built. I chose it specifically so that my story would fit within Hotspur's lifetime. He was so named because of his penchant for 'hotspurring', that is, riding fast and furious into battle. His courage won him renown among friends and foes alike, and what can I say, I'm a fan.

However, this is Harry-the-Cough's story, a fictional peasant with poor prospects but a good mind and an unusually good education, by the standards of the day; someone who would doubtless have viewed the ruling aristocracy with great suspicion, including the Harry Hotspur-inspired Lord Henry Warmstirrup. Lord Henry does not always come over well within my story – though he has his moments to shine – that is because the narrative is written as seen through the eyes of the medieval poor. Harry-the-Cough and his friends are understandably partisan. This is no commentary on my own part. I believe in humour for all, and at the *expense* of all, highest and lowest, with neither fear nor favour. Apologies, if that sounded like soapboxing. It's simply that, in recent years, one might argue that a trend has emerged for 'trashing' our greatest heroes; this story is by no means intended to reflect that. I love my country and Northumberland especially, and with that said, I hope you enjoy this comedy adventure as much as I enjoyed writing it.

Thank you so very much for reading.
Stephen

Chapter 1
A Cold Day in Warmstirrup

All life, indeed, all things, came from the stars. Aeons passed, alternating between silence and violence, until one day a creature was born to ask why? Throughout meagre human history, this has proved a most dangerous question – at some times, more than others. The European Middle Ages proved one such time.

Some say there is no such thing as bad publicity, but for a 14th century healer, even the good kind could land you in trouble – often fatally – and that was the rub, the mediocre status quo in which the men and women of early medicine became ensnared. Progressiveness with caution, tempered with traditionalism, was the only way to inch forward. To do otherwise was to risk being branded a heretic or a witch. Most cleaved to the belief that there was nothing new to medical science since Galen's charming four humours of black bile, yellow bile, blood and phlegm. It was safer. Consequently, there was often little solidarity and little progress.

The Church saw to that.

One creature born to ask such questions stared up at the stars from which he was made. He often wondered why. In fact, on that occasion, he was wondering why he was lying in the freezing February mud looking up at the stars. The heavenly spectators winked knowingly to one another but offered no explanation, so the young man ignored them.

Confused, he sat up, blearily refocusing his stare towards the door hanging broken from its hinges. Judging by his trajectory, he was surprised how little he hurt – though he suspected the morning might bring a degree of re-evaluation there, along with the more certain pain of a bill for damages.

The frigid night air tasted of hearth smoke, made more bitter yet by the sounds of raucous laughter carried from inside the tavern. However, of more immediate concern was the chilly wetness creeping into his nether regions – despite the insulation provided by a skinful of ale. He groaned, his befuddled mind catching up to realise that, if he wished to stop further numbness pervading downstairs, he should probably get to his feet. Standing stiffly, he swayed with the alcoholiwobbles before eventually turning to totter away home, down narrow streets and dark alleys, back to his workshop.

Perhaps 'workshop' was to overstate his situation. Contemptuously familiar, and always greeted with a sigh, the rented hovel with its rickety door housed all his worldly goods. In the bleak starlight, he read, 'Harry Bones, Apothecary to thee Nobility' – the block-lettering daubed by his own hand in yellow ochre. Faded now, after three years.

In the far north-east of England, nestling within the little town of Warmstirrup, the single room, fronting onto Scrubber Alley, was both workshop and home for Harry. Known locally as Harry-the-Cough, he was famous for his 'Harry-the-Cough's Inside and Out, When in Doubt – The All-in-one Cough Syrup and Ointment'.

It had not always been so.

Harry ran away to Warmstirrup precisely *because* he was unknown there. Scrubber Alley had been all he could get back then. Although far from the more affluent quarters, the back streets and alleyways around Harry's hovel were not completely without their attractions. For instance, there was nowhere better if you were a villain on the run, a mugger or a lady of the night – or looking to hire such tradesmen and women. They led such exciting lives there, too, soaring one day, diving the next. Banally straddling the breadline day after day, Harry often wondered whether he should retrain. Surely, he deserved better.

"Three years..." he pondered aloud. Where had they gone?

When asked why he stayed in Scrubber Alley, he would invariably respond, 'Oh, you get used to it', but it was no answer, not really, and he never did. The cramped alleyways of Warmstirrup had simply been safer than what he left behind.

That was back in 1396, but by the year of our Lord 1399, things were changing. Indeed, some might say, becoming downright perilous. The earl, Lord Henry of Warmstirrup, who ran the entire region and owned most of it, had a hard choice to make – support the king, or his friend, who would *be* king. It was something like a state secret, so naturally the whole town discussed it openly. Opinions flew left and right, but one thing on which everyone agreed was that hard times were coming. When great men like Lord Henry faced difficulty, they usually spread it around to the extent of their greatness, forcing it onto all who lived under their writ. It was ever thus.

Forcing open his sticking front door was about Harry's limit, and he did so keenly aware that his business image left much to be desired, just when he most needed to shine. For though the armed men gathering at Warmstirrup Castle presented a rising concern for the townsfolk, Harry-the-Cough's interest in them was more prosaic. So many men, with more arriving each day, all locked within castle walls – or more specifically, locked in with castle latrines – meant sickness, and sickness was Harry's business. Winning the castle contract to supply his medicines and expert knowledge in wartime could change his circumstances forever. More than the money, it was really about reputation, because with reputation came connections and those would provide the key to unlock his future.

Perhaps it was selfish, but the town's greatest fear was his greatest hope, and had kept him going... until today.

Ale consumed earlier now seemed less medicinal as freezing hands fumbled with flint and candle. Eventually, a yellow glow filled his hovel and was the only warmth he would feel this night. Looking back to the open door, he was tempted to break it up and throw it into the hearth, but knew he would regret it once the fire burned low. Shaking his head, he put his shoulder to it instead, closing out the night with a creak and a scrape. The bitter draught reduced from a numbing wall of cold to several icy blades that probed for him through gaps in the planks.

Earlier that day
Harry's morning started rather well. After selling a family-sized jar of Inside and Out to a wealthy merchant, and customer of some years, he looked forward to an appointment with a master mason later that afternoon – an important man, with two sickly apprentices. However, on the way out, his wealthy merchant imparted some disturbing news.

"You'll have heard about your competitor's latest venture then, young Master Bones?" The merchant was a large, completely bald man named Bavol, whose business was in sail canvas. While his workshops and warehouses were on the coast a few miles east, he retained a large, fashionable townhouse in Warmstirrup.

Bavol also made it his business to know everyone else's, so Harry's ears pricked immediately. With a casual air to hide his concern, he asked, "What's he up to now? I've not caught wind of it."

Bavol tutted and smiled, pleased to convey his knowledge of other people's affairs. "Dear me, Master Bones, you really should stay abreast of your competitors' doings." He leaned in, conspiratorially. "He's got street children running all over town for him, fetching and delivering. Sounds like an impressive new service. You should get into it."

Harry attempted a nonchalant smile. Not sure if his grimace passed muster, he nevertheless thanked Bavol for the advice. '*You should get into it.*' The merchant's words rang around his head again and again. *Get into what, exactly, and even more exactly,* with *what?* Harry barely had the wherewithal to employ a beggar to take away his scraps – not that he could afford any scraps.

Reaching a decision, he shut up shop for an hour. This was no time to sit about. A little investigation was called for. It was a beautiful morning, too, filled with early sun and promise as he set off across town with purpose. Even so, his competitor's latest scheme gnawed at him. Harry knew that man would stop at nothing to get his greedy hands on the castle work he himself needed, if he was ever to escape Scrubber Alley. The weather, tracking his mood, quickly gave way to black clouds and icy rain.

The walk took no more than a few minutes. Just long enough to become soaked through to the skin, as it happened. Casually, he sidled past his rival's prestige establishment, and it became immediately apparent why Harry had fallen upon such especially hard times of late.

The building was impressive, clearly the workplace of a man who already enjoyed reputation – or so it must have appeared to the townsfolk. While rival apothecary, Felix L'Éternuement, organised his storefront, his assistant set up a large sign outside, outlining his new service.

Recently arrived from distant parts, far to the south, L'Éternuement was slick, but Harry was not fooled by the façade. News had already reached him about many of the newcomer's alleged cures making people worse. However, that inconvenient truth did not seem to prevent him from hoodwinking others, or from relieving them of their money, for that matter. Looking at the state of his premises, it must have been a scam ongoing for some years, too – long before he ever set foot in Warmstirrup.

Harry's roots, being of the humbler sort, left him outside in the freezing rain, scratching his head about how anyone ever made that much money. Parents butchered in a Scotch cattle raid across the border when he was little more than a boy, Harry had been taken in by the local wise woman, who taught him his trade, and his letters – he still bore the scars from early failures. Overall, he should have felt fortunate, after being so cruelly orphaned, and yet...

Amabilis was her name. 'Mad Mab' was what they called her. Perhaps it was the misery of standing there in the cold, or the fear of losing what little he had to someone who had so much already, but it all came back to him. Harry found that loss was like that, each instance interconnected, plotting a course backwards through his memories. His mother and father might have been mere peasant farmers, but he had loved them. Yet, strangely, he could no longer recall their faces with any clarity. On the other hand, the fact that their lives were worth less than a stolen cow was something he would never forget. Maud and Hugh. They had simply been Mum and Dad to him, young as he was. He remembered trusting them, and then they were gone.

Bitterness in his heart, he turned towards the castle gatehouse, just opposite his competitor's new premises that were naturally located in the richest quarter – a location the locals had recently been calling Dispensary Street. Harry really had to grit his teeth over that. Anyone of worth demanded more than the protection of town walls. Should push ever come to shove, they wanted to be within a short dash of the castle itself. Harry's hovel was in what was known locally as 'The Sprawl' and not even inside the town walls, let alone near the castle. He harboured no doubts at all that, should Warmstirrup come under siege, his invitation to the keep would be 'lost by messenger'.

It was a scenario growing in people's minds, becoming more acute every day. Meanwhile, Lord Henry continued to build his forces – a natural response to the whiff of civil war in the air. A constant threat in times where over-mighty magnates, discontented with their lot, forever pushed their luck – despite their lot being... well, a lot. However, this time the stakes were higher than usual. This was no wrangling over succession; this was full-on *usurpation,* and it was coming.

When troops began to arrive, in small groups at first, the folk of Warmstirrup had welcomed the opportunity to sell their wares. Although, what often begins as 'sell and barter' often drifts towards petty theft, before invariably ending up at confiscation under threat – or perhaps even worse, promises. Yet, their presence should have been as manna from heaven for Harry. He would have won Lord Henry's business automatically had L'Éternuement not set up shop just a few months earlier.

He blinked against the sleet. The castle was so close, yet so far outside his grasp. A freezing February might well reduce the likely spread of disease, but so many men barracked together could still bring on a second Christmas for any apothecary with his wits about him – especially when you threw in a few companionable ladies – and here was his flash competitor, mere yards from the gates, just waiting to fill his trough. It was sickening.

Worse yet, Harry suspected Lord Henry's personal physician, a bumbling old fool who styled himself *Doctor* Bodges, was already patronising his competition. Another income stream dammed and damned.

With the whole town turning into an armed camp, Harry considered, *how do I get past these imbeciles to speak with the earl himself?* "Or, at least, the castle's quartermaster?" He mumbled the last, teeth chattering almost uncontrollably now. Fellow bystanders, admiring L'Éternuement's new sign, turned in query. Harry touched his forelock, self-consciously. "Good morrow, sir, madam."

The man and his wife responded to Harry's courtesy with glares, clearly distrustful of mutterers – especially when they appeared to have the shakes. Warmstirrup had several, all begging a miserable existence in the streets, and it depressed Harry further that he might present such an impression.

He looked away, pretending to take an interest in the facing masonry of L'Éternuement's front wall. While he had been skulking and spying, a crowd had gathered outside L'Éternuement's shop. Taking advantage of the limited cover the extra bodies provided from the driving sleet, and more importantly, from the shifty eyes of his nemesis, he moved in closer, scowling at the monstrosity on display behind the now-open shutters. Nonchalance did not come easily when confronted with a giant stuffed fish. The shop's main sign read *Thee Piscator Fortuna,* or 'The Lucky Fisherman'. Harry suspected this had more to do with reeling people in than the bloated, half-rotten horror on display in the window. Along with the Latin name, L'Éternuement probably believed it gave him an air of sophistication.

Harry fumed silently, mulling over a few choice names of his own.

L'Éternuement was explaining his revolutionary new service to his young assistant, but loudly enough for the whole street to hear. The apprentice, a sixteen-year-old urchin-turned-beggar, taken on because he knew the town like the back of his hand, was a useful asset for a boss new to the region. His name was Lott, and despite there being virtually nothing to him, the lad was clever, sly even, and he knew everyone.

Bavol the sailmaker may have enjoyed bestowing bad news on Harry earlier that morning, but he had been quite right in his observations. While making his way across town, Harry had spotted several such scrawny urchins posted at strategic locations; each wearing over-ponchos sporting the ghastly fish motif livery he now recognised as *Thee Piscator Fortuna*, embroidered over the wings and serpent emblem of the apothecary.

They had a strong presence on Line Street, which ran almost-straight through the centre of Warmstirrup, connecting the town gates to the castle gates. Much of Warmstirrup's prime real estate adorned its flanks, including its oldest tavern, The Dirty Jugs. Some predated the Norman kings and possibly even the Danes. Many of the finest stone buildings, not to mention the more successful shops and businesses in the town, could be found there, or around the marketplace nearby.

Harry could only dream. Yet despite his circumstances, there were still those who wished to avoid being poisoned by their apothecary, simply because he owned a flash building and a fish. Nevertheless, L'Éternuement's words numbed him more than the cutting sleet. He strained to hear more.

"...'Tis the new business model we're rolling out this very week," the shopkeep extolled loudly and confidently in his outlandish southern accent. "Should any of our customers, our most *valued* customers," he added unctuously, "have an emergency, or perhaps the bustle of business simply makes it impossible for them to find the time to drop in on our emporium of healing – fear not! They may now order direct. That's right! All our miraculous medicines, ointments, potions and salves may now be ordered anywhere on Line Street!"

Such sweeping promises only added to Harry's misery. *What the hell is he up to?* Pulling his hood tight to obscure his face, he drew even closer, listening intently.

"Now customers may simply grab one of our liveried urchins stationed along Line Street – or from one of several other prominent locations about town – to place their orders or repeat prescriptions. Having instructed one of our *specialist* runners, they can then leave the rest to us!

"Their medicaments will be delivered to their very door, as it says on our advertising board, within a daye and a nighte!"

The enthusiastic audience outside *Thee Piscator Fortuna* was growing. Even the appalling weather failed to put them off. L'Éternuement, clearly enjoying the attention, looked around for praise and was rewarded with an appreciative smatter of applause. Harry used the distraction to slip in close enough to read the sign's small print before fading away. At least, that was his intention. Lott spotted him, pointing him out to his master. Harry gritted his teeth. His luck really was at low tide.

L'Éternuement grinned. "This service is offered free of charge simply to give something back to my esteemed customers in recognition of their much-appreciated support." He glanced in Harry's direction once more, checking he was still there as he plunged the knife deeper. "*Other apothecaries in the region can neither offer this prime service, nor provide the comfort you deserve, simply knowing that we're working on your behalf without need to even travel to our shop. Your remedies will arrive by fastest courier, and you pay only when you have the goods in your very hands!*"

Harry slipped away quickly after that, the sound of cheers still ringing in his ears. He remembered little of the journey back as he fought the despair clutching at his heart. His head swam and his belly felt like it was full of eels. How could he fight such big-city ideas?

Home before he knew it, he shoved his way past the rickety door and into his workshop. Leaving the shutters down, he sat behind his bench, deep in thought. Many hours slipped by before he was forced to admit that he had no better plan than to get blind drunk. So, in the failing daylight, he dragged his feet to his favourite alehouse. It was his favourite by virtue of being the closest, yet its draw completely drove the missed appointment with the master mason from his mind.

Never a good idea to let business slide that way, it was an even worse idea to drink his rent. Especially as the alehouse landlord was also Harry's landlord, and so we return to the beginning of our story, with Harry picking himself up from the freezing mud, chucking-out time having come early and lost all benefit of metaphor. He rubbed a new bruise forming on his side from one of several impacts. It was hard to tell which, after the numerous tankards he had downed before and after his money ran out. The barman may have taken a less belligerent stance had Harry owned up to that fact before the last of the ales disappeared.

He looked up at the twinkling stars, swore at them for being so jolly, and staggered home, while he still had one.

Once inside, the first symptoms of sobriety brought on early-stage depression, followed by full-blown desperation – each becoming more acute as he recalled his rent was due in one week. Add to that the side effect of it being dead of winter, and he would need a miracle cure to keep his home and win the castle contract. His business was under siege, L'Éternuement making it clear that he intended to starve him out. It was hardly necessary to catapult faeces over Harry's wall[1] – he was in enough of it already.

Pacing in the yellow light from his lonely candle, as it flickered across his shelves and stock, he sought inspiration. When in need, he often thumbed through his recipe book. Retrieving it from its hiding place within a cubbyhole behind a board in the wall, he sat at his bench, turning the pages thoughtfully. The book contained all he knew, including the notes taken during his time with Mad Mab as a boy.

It also contained one thing he did not know – a passage, written in the back by Mab herself before she gave it to him. He sometimes wondered whether she realised it was there when she handed it over. That had been before her appointment with the Twyford village ducking stool.

Harry had no idea what the scrawled hand was trying to tell him. The language was strange and ancient. Some of the sigils, almost certainly written in blood, had the appearance of being alive – or in mockery of life. He knew for a fact that if the wrong person looked at what could only be a spell, it would mean the fire for him. Yet he could not bring himself to destroy it, or part with it. Instinctively, he knew it was the most valuable thing he owned, and perhaps that sense of ownership had further driven his desire to leave his village – that and the threat of following his mistress to the bottom of the pond. Barely seventeen at the time, youth would not have saved him.

---

1. A quaint medieval siege practice used to spread disease within a fortified enclosure. Other projectile delights included heads and body parts from captives or dead animals. Possibly the first and most reliable airmail service, there being no doubt at all that the addressee got the message.

Learning such as that shared by Harry and his old mistress bordered on heresy in a time when, for a woman at least, even being unmarried attracted all kinds of unwanted attention. Harry was unsure of his exact age, but looking back as an adult of twentyish, he suspected the constant fear of being accused of witchcraft may have driven Mab to her madness – yet she was brilliant, there was no doubt about that. Being a man attracted less attention from the lunatics and zealots, but figuring the village duck pond had enough quacks in it already, Harry erred on the side of caution and left for the sprawling metropolis and brightly lit torches of Warmstirrup.

If only the spell could help him now, for in truth, he had never felt more desperate. He rubbed tiredness from his eyes. The alcoholic fog was not helping, or perhaps it was the worry; either way, inspiration was not forthcoming. He sat in the room's single rickety chair and thought about his future. Willing it to brighten.

The candle guttered and went out. Harry sighed. What had he done to deserve all this? Accepting that he needed help, he decided to outsource, and knowing only one firm that worked for free, whatever the hour, he put the book aside and knelt to pray... and worry... and pray some more, until the tattered wings of hopeless exhaustion wrapped themselves around him, dreams of ruin roosting in his troubled mind.

Chapter 2
The Pail Hoarse Man

Harry awoke tired and stiff the next morning. He was hungover as hell, but weirdly felt a little better, too. He vaguely remembered babbling nonsensically to God for several hours before collapsing onto his crate. The Lord had listened kindly, but left him with the headache as a lesson. Bright sunlight entered through the cracks in the workshop's shutters, the stab of pain through his eyes a gift, reminding him that he was not in fact dead – not yet. He had suffered a setback, that was all. It was all so much clearer in the morning sunshine.

He would just have to rely on his own talents, but then, perhaps it was enough to simply get back up and try. Maybe that very act of defiance against the odds could in itself unlock answers to prayers, albeit on a stage-payment basis.

Munching industriously on stale bread and rock-hard cheese left over from the day before, he was suddenly ready to fight back, realising he had as much right to the castle contract and to service that great body of filthy humanity, all penned in together within those mighty walls, as L'Éternuement – maybe more. Harry drove the broader consequences for Warmstirrup from his mind, focusing on those upright fighting men, striving for a king to remain upon his pew. Of course, he saw them as puking men fighting to remain upright, but nevertheless, they gave him hope.

It occurred to him that he would feel better yet, were he to shed the darkness of his shuttered workshop and take his new, if unexpected, sense of optimism outside into the alley. His throat was on fire from thirst, but with arms thrown wide, he greeted the new day, chest expanding to drink in the morning air as he proclaimed, "Harry-the-Cough is open for business! Aye, and I'll be offering special rates today, an' all!"

Now fully alert, he was ready for anything. Well, almost anything – the bucket of nameless filth emptied over his head came as a surprise.

"Oh, sorry, Harry," the voice of Matilda carried down from above.

He wiped his face, pulling the Lord knew what from his hair. Turning, he looked up, trying his best to smile back at her. She was hardly an angel, but she *was* a friend. Matilda, or Matty as he knew her, was young and fair. She whored out of the room above his shop, and slop bucket aside, it was usually a pleasure to see her. "Thank you, Matty. Your little pot only highlights the plight of small businessmen everywhere – so eloquent, so succinct, and yet not a word spoken!"

"Eh?" She looked down, pretty confusion playing on her face. "Are you alright, pet?"

Wiping the ghost of a hearty meal from his cheek and spitting again, to clear his mouth, Harry managed a real smile. "Indeed, I am! Being covered in this – oh, my God, what *was* that? Sorry, sorry. Being covered in *this*, is something I'd rather forget, if I'm honest. But the message is clear – it's time I stopped allowing people to dump on me from above. I'm a new man, reborn!" Arms wide once more, he punched the air, turning his dynamism on the world. "And on this day, I'm going to... I'm going to——"

Splosh.

"Oh, sorry, Harry," Mrs Pigden called from her upper storey window on the opposite side of Scrubber Alley.

Harry's shoulders slumped as a second bucket of ordure cascaded down his back. "I'm going to... move back indoors," he concluded quietly. Feet dragging, he walked back into his workshop, despondency already threatening to overwhelm him once more, when Matty called him back outside.

He stepped out cautiously; no one could accuse him of being a slow learner. However, this time Matty had good news from above – a client referral. She leaned from her window, speaking conspiratorially behind her hand. "My *gentleman* would like to consult with you, Harry." She straightened to glance back into her room and then leaned back down towards him. "And he'd prefer to use the *back* entrance," she added with a wink.

Standing just a few feet below, directly beneath her, Harry mouthed, "What's wrong with him?"

She leaned out still further, far enough for Harry to glance a freebie – two, in fact – his luck was indeed changing. "I'm very keen for you to help him, Harry."

"Why?"

"Let's just say that, upon spotting his... his *problem*," she whispered, "I felt it necessary to refund his money in full – no questions asked, so to speak. It cost me a night's work, but I couldn't... well, you'll see. The poor man."

Harry shrugged. "Fine. Send him down. Thank you." Just as she pulled back into the window, he called after her, "Oh, by the way, Matty?"

She popped her head back out. "Yes, Harry?"

"Would you mind looking below, before you do what you do first thing every morning? Some of us have to put signs out and may not always be quite as fleet of foot as we normally are – depending on how much we've imbibed the night before."

"Whatever you like, Harry." She grinned and disappeared.

He sighed. Bringing a hand to his forehead, he saw what was on that hand and changed his mind. Instead, he went back inside to clean himself up before Matty's gentleman caller arrived via the back door. Most importantly, he had work. Surely a sign that his fortunes were improving.

The shouting could be heard even outside the castle walls. Lord Henry was angry. Whatever people were doing, they made a point of getting on with it – preferably in a direction away from the castle gates.

The shouting had, just momentarily, been preceded by loud barking from several hunting dogs. They were Lord Henry's pride and joy, so whatever they had done wrong was about to carry a severe penalty for someone. Henry was strict with his hounds, but he never brutalised them – that was what servants were for.

"Fetch my physician!" he bellowed.

Dr Bodges was soon tipped unceremoniously from his sleeping crate by an unimaginative duo who dragged him into his lord's presence, still struggling to slip on his second shoe.

"BODGES!" Lord Henry split the air with his fury.

"Here, erm, lord." Bodges genuflected. "How may I, erm, serve?"

"Isn't it obvious, fool?" Henry slapped Bodges hard about the head, knocking him to the great hall's rush-strewn flagstones.

Used to such treatment, the physician righted himself, almost as if he were on a spring. Whilst down, he noted his lord had already removed one of his riding boots. *If he did that all on his own, he must have needed it off in a hurry,* he thought, uncharitably. Henry's right calf bore the unmistakable marks of a dog bite.

"Put some of that paste on it," Henry demanded. "The stuff that dulls the pain."

"I no longer have, erm, stock of that particular remedy, lord. After last, erm, week's hunt, you may, erm, recall ordering me to treat Sir William's, erm, saddle, erm, sores?" Bodges had gained a facial tic during his years of service to Lord Henry, along with the nervous habit of punctuating his sentences with inappropriate 'erms'.

Henry leaned forward menacingly. "Are you saying your poor stock management is *my* fault, Bodges?"

Bodges shrugged before his wits caught up with him. "Erm, no, lord, erm." He visibly wilted.

"I suggest you get one of those apothecaries here, right now," Henry added dangerously.

"At once, lord. Erm, which one?"

"Either one! Harry-the-Cough's not a complete fool. And what's the other called, the new chap?"

"Felix, erm, L'Éternuement, lord."

"Get Lucky the Sneeze in as well, then." He made to stand, but gasped at the pain in his leg and crashed breathlessly back into his throne-like chair. "Now, damn you!"

"At once, erm, lord." Bodges was already bowing his way from the hall when Lord Henry picked up the riding crop he kept by his great chair and bent it menacingly in his hands.

"Now, where is that dog handler? Guards!"

Bodges closed the great hall's heavy oak doors on the sounds of a young man's screams.

"Now, sir. What seems to be the prob—— Ah." Harry tailed off immediately as Matty's man-friend showed him his pain and his shame. "Right. Er... sore, is it?"

"What do you bloody think?"

"Tetchy." Harry raised his hands placatingly. "I take it you didn't manage to," he made a gesture, "you know... last night?"

"What do you bloody think?"

"Hmm." Harry arranged his features into something approaching sympathy. He could understand the man's lack of vocabulary just now. The poor fellow must have been excruciatingly uncomfortable, in both senses of the word. Adding to his misery, Harry also noted a louse. He took a small pottery jar from his shelf. "You'll need to keep the area clean and free of lice. I'll prepare a powder for you. Any scratching will make things far worse, may even spread the infection to other parts of your body. I'll just rub some of this ointment——" The client's sharp intake of breath forced him to change tack. "I'll just give *you* this ointment to rub onto the, er, problem. Twice daily, until the lotion is all used up. Needless to say, you'll also need to…" His expression slipped slightly, a chuckle creeping into his voice that he immediately disguised with the dignified cough of the cool practitioner. "That is, you'll want to *rest* it, for a while."

The man whimpered as he self-administered the first dose. A huge bang on the front door made him yowl in pain and throw the jar up in the air. Harry jumped to his feet, mind racing. His rent was not due yet; he still had a week before his landlord would evict him. Could he have sent a couple of heavies round to extract the price of a new tavern door? Another *bang* rattled his own door on its hinges. *It'll be two new doors the way they're going!* "Who is it?" he called out, nervously.

"Open up in the name of Lord Henry Warmstirrup!" Unfortunately, the guards had been told to fetch Harry-the-Cough and not to waste any time about it. They were obviously 'to the letter' types, because the middle plank of Harry's door smashed through before he could even move to open it. A second blow fetched the frame out of the wattle and daub wall, smashing the whole structure to the earthen floor of his hovel.

"I was coming to open it!" Harry bawled, anger overriding his good sense.

One of the guards grabbed his arm roughly. "Harry-the-Cough?"

"Maybe."

"Good enough. With me, move it… *ew*. What happened to him?"

Matty's client, now Harry's customer, sat in the hovel's only chair with his breeches around his ankles, a broken door at his feet, the lid of a jar in his hand and an agonised expression on his face.

"You should see someone about that," the guard suggested unhelpfully.

Harry was propelled through the new hole in the wall. "What's all this about?" he asked plaintively.

"Didn't we mention it?"

"No!"

"Dr Bodges wants you up at the castle for a consult. Bring your bag – or whatever."

"And my door?" Fury still radiated off Harry.

The guard shrugged. "Come on. Get moving. Let's not keep Lord Henry waiting."

As Harry stumbled out into the alley, oilskin bag thrown hastily over one shoulder, he heard Matty cry out from above. "Harry! What's happening? Are you alright?"

"Matty, can you mind my shop for a while, please? My door seems to have been kicked in. Oh, and your friend is still in there. He might need his hand held – just his hand, mind you! He's a bit... well, you'll see."

Chapter 3
The Dog and Castle

Harry's heavy-handed escort bustled him through the streets of Warmstirrup and before he knew it, he was once again passing L'Éternuement's house and shop in Dispensary Street. Unthinkingly, he slowed to admire it anew without the crowd outside. Raised near the castle, the development replaced a row of old hovels that burned down during one hot summer's day the previous year. It was held that the fire had been started as a jape to get someone out of bed. When Lord Henry charged out of his castle on horseback to see what was going on, he summarily had the comedian responsible thrown onto his own fire as the final punchline.

Warmstirrup's justice system worked swiftly when Henry was in residence. All process due immediately. A disquieting thought for Harry as he was shoved onwards.

Those were the last hovels to be removed from that part of town. The last blots on the landscape, one might say, and right next to the castle gates, too. Harry grudgingly noted that the approach certainly looked more salubrious these days, though he still wondered if Lord Henry might have been behind the 'realty adjustment', just outside his doors. Conflagrating the man in flagrante delicto left no one to point the finger. A neat solution.

Despite his nervousness, Harry eyed the new-builds with envy. They even came with a ten-year NHBC guarantee.

Noah's House Building Company[1] were very proud of their reputation, their work, easily recognisable. Harry knew that Noah himself came from a long line of carpenters, proudly stating that his family could trace their ancestry all the way back to the man who built the boat that even God was unable to sink. His grandfather and his father had both been named Noah, as was his eldest son, so maybe it was true.

One thing was certainly true – L'Éternuement's premises were so much plusher and more modern than the ramshackle affair Harry rented from his drunken, violent landlord. Shutters down to hide L'Éternuement's hideous fish, it was a fine-looking building. Just a few steps from the nearest well, with the latest in poop-conveyance systems, Felix L'Éternuement was never forced to use a bucket, or stick his backside out of an upstairs window into the street, like most of Warmstirrup's citizenry. The builders had ingeniously included a chute out of the *rear* elevation, straight into the new pigpens included, en suite. Harry could still recall Noah's marketing blurb: Your reare at the reare, for the pigsys to cleare. Such luxury. His desire was only natural, although stopping to ogle proved a bad idea, and he received a slap around the head for his trouble before being hauled away for a forced consult.

---

1. Many centuries into Harry-the-Cough's future, the National House Building Council (NHBC) would be established in 1936; its purpose, to provide oversight for the construction standards of new homes within Great Britain, and, coincidentally, to provide homebuyers with a 10-year Buildmark warranty, too. To that end, Noah's lawyers issued the following disclaimer: Any similarity to actual organisations, live, defunct, or yet to be registered in the far flung future, or actual events, is purely coincidental.

Cold, bruised and more than a little afraid, Harry was pushed to the floor before Lord Henry. Getting shakily back to his feet, he bowed low and immediately got down to work. "You poor lad. My Lord Henry was right to call me in so urgently." The young man's back was a crosshatch of bloody stripes over old scars. Harry vaguely recognised him from around town and tried to recall his name. Jack, maybe?

"What the hell are you doing?" the earl demanded.

"My lord?" Harry stopped and turned to face him. "I assumed I was called to treat this man's brutal wounds?"

"Brutal wounds...?" The magnate looked genuinely mystified. "Never mind that, you damned fool! You're here to treat my leg. Bodges, come here."

Bodges knelt immediately at his lord's feet.

"This oaf allowed us to run out of that unction you make." Henry belted him around the head again.

Bodges sprang back to position *again*. "Yes, lord," he agreed, tonelessly.

Harry began to understand why the man had lost his brains. He had never been called into Lord Henry's presence before, had only seen him out and about, usually on horseback and with an entourage. His first real impression was that of a tyrant.

"Well, get to it, man!" the nobleman bellowed impatiently.

Harry abandoned the whipping boy regretfully, and knelt to examine his lord's dog bite, instead. It was just possible that the earl was tetchy because of the pain. Although Harry doubted it. He knew a bully when he met one – Mad Mab had beaten him every day with a stick as a child 'for his own good'. He looked around for a nearby servant. "Fetch me clean water, and a brazier, please."

The servant standing to Henry's side looked for confirmation. The earl nodded and he disappeared, returning almost immediately with a large pitcher, while two guards threaded a rod from the fireplace through the wrought iron basket of a lit brazier and carried it over between them.

Harry placed a small bowl on the floor and poured a little water. Mixing in lavender procured from a Spanish trader, he gave it a stir before dipping a clean rag and wringing it. "I need to clean the wound before I treat it, my lord. This will sting. If you knock me across the floor, it will hurt more, yes?"

Henry's brows knitted angrily, but he nodded affirmative.

Harry cleaned the wound.

The earl sissed, gripping the arms of his chair, but made no moves of violence.

Content the area was sterile, Harry removed several small jars and leather pouches from his bag. "May I have some wine, my lord?"

Henry nodded again and the servant returned quickly once more, this time with a large jug.

Pouring some into a fresh bowl, Harry mixed marigold with yarrow, elderflower and cinquefoil, placing it over the heat and stirring until it became greasy. He then strained off the excess wine and plant matter to leave a warm lotion. Daubing some of the tincture onto a second clean cloth, he was about to apply it when one of the large double doors at the far end of the chamber swung open with a *boom*.

Everyone turned to see two guards bustling Felix L'Éternuement into the great hall. He also bore a shoulder bag, although Harry noted with annoyance that his was of the finest dyed leather.

"Where the hell have you been?" Lord Henry demanded. "You only live outside my gates."

"My lord, a thousand apologies." L'Éternuement threw himself fully into his role of slimy sycophant. "I was away from my emporium, but came immediately upon receiving your summons."

"Emporium? I always think of it as the bloated fish house." Lord Henry let go a brief bark of laughter. "Looks like the sort of crap they used to fob us off with as a prize, back in my mêlée and tournament days."

Harry watched L'Éternuement's mouth screw up tight with impotent annoyance. "Yes, lord," he agreed quietly. Harry smiled to his competitor before turning back to his work.

L'Éternuement's eyes narrowed spitefully. "My lord, what is this man doing?"

"Cleaning and treating my wound. What's it look like? I thought you were an expert? *He* got here from the other side of town in half the time it took you to arrive, Mr Sneezy."

L'Éternuement tried again. "What I meant, my lord, was that man is hardly qualified to treat such a personage as yourself."

"You doubt Harry-the-Cough's competence?"

"My *lord*," L'Éternuement oozed. "He's hardly at the level where he might be trusted with such august care. I mean, just look at the slum he works from. Let him butcher peasants, if he must, but he should *never* be allowed into your lordship's presence with his soiled oilskin bag of tricks."

Lord Henry looked down at Harry and his bag, pondering the wisdom of L'Éternuement's words. "What say you, Cough?"

"My lord, this ointment will reduce the swelling and draw out any infection before it can take hold within the wound. It has been tried and tested on many patients——"

"*Peasants,* my lord," L'Éternuement interrupted, sanctimoniously. "They don't enjoy the noble humours you yourself possess. No, indeed they don't, my lord. The *noble* humours are more complex – they require more delicate handling to bring into balance. This impostor is no apothecary, my lord. Let him treat the beasts of the field, but not the thoroughbred fighting men of your company, and certainly not you yourself, my lord."

Henry looked to Bodges for a second opinion. "Your lordship is wise," he muttered, head low.

"Hmm. You may have a point, L'Éternuement. Very well. Send Harry-the-Cough home, Bodges. Pay him for his trouble."

"Yes, my lord. This way, Harry."

L'Éternuement caught Harry's eye as he cleaned and packed away his things. The glee on his face made Harry want to ram his giant fish right down his greedy neck. "My lord." Harry bowed and followed Bodges out. What else could he do?

Once outside the great hall, he turned to Bodges again. "That man is a fraud and a fool, Dr Bodges." He used Bodges' bogus title to curry a little favour. "You know my treatments have always been good. Good enough until that, that *fishmonger* rode into town!"

Bodges shrugged. "I cannot gainsay my lord."

"He asked for your judgment. Why didn't you give it?"

"Because if you failed in your treatments, it would have been my head."

Harry knew Bodges was speaking literally. He sighed. "Very well. Here." He handed Bodges a jar containing the lotion he was about to administer before L'Éternuement arrived. "If that idiot makes things worse, try this. But clean the wound thoroughly first."

"Whatever for?"

Harry rolled his eyes. "Trust me. I cleaned the wound well, before that fool came and stopped me from working. It may be enough to allow Lord Henry to heal himself."

"Let's hope so," Bodges muttered without conviction. "Before you go, erm, Harry, perhaps you would complete your, erm, treatment of the dog handler? The castle will, erm, pay."

"Of course. What happened to him?"

"One of the hounds in his care bit Lord Henry. Vicious, erm, things. The earl likes them that way, but of course, when the inevitable, erm, happens, he blames the handlers."

"Poor chap," Harry commiserated. "By all means, take me to him."

Bodges led them out into the castle courtyard and across to a wooden structure leaning against the curtain wall. The howling and snarling from within was most disconcerting, but Harry knew he must show willing if he were to stand any chance of turning his fortunes around. At least he was inside the castle. It was a start. *Favour the bold,* he thought, bracing himself.

"I like dogs."

"You, erm, won't like these," Bodges assured him.

Although Harry was anything but assured, a light came on in his eyes, as the wheels within his mind began to turn.

A wooden bowl thumped into the wall, causing the young scallywag to duck and jump round. "What the... You could have caved my head in!" he roared, scandalised.

"I know. I missed!" Matty retorted. "Maybe next time? Oh, look, here's another bowl."

"No. Stop!" Lott cried, covering his head protectively. Always an anaemic-looking bag of bones with a long, sharp nose like a blade, Matty knew him well. These days, he was more often seen on L'Éternuement's business, skittering about town like a giant, evil-minded, flightless bat.

She paused, arm raised. "What are you doing here, Lott? Harry will go berserk if he comes back to find you in his workshop. Especially now you serve that flash Herbert with the fish."

"It's not what it looks like, Matty."

Matty laughed in his face. "That line's older than Leviticus. And how do you know my name?"

His hawkish features turned furtive. "I've watched you – that is, seen you about a bit... sometimes. What's Leviticus?"

"The bit in the Bible about burning witches. It's best for a single businesswoman to have some knowledge of the law these days. They don't call us solicitors for nothing, you know. Anyway, been spying, have we? Or are you just nosing around Harry's place looking for stuff to steal, hmm? Taking Harry's potions and medicines so your boss can try to work out how a real apothecary brews up actual cures?"

The waif swallowed. "No," he replied sulkily.

She raised the bowl once more. "Empty your scrip[2]."

Under duress, the scrawny urchin unpacked two small pots and three small bags. Matty recognised them instantly as the type of receptacles Harry used to dispense his cures. "And what have you hidden in your tunic?"

"Haven't got anything."

"Did I mention I had this wooden bowl?" Matty explained conversationally, pulling her arm back ready to throw.

Lott scowled, all round shoulders and spots. He turned away and produced another jar from inside his clothing.

Matty took it from him, shaking her head disgustedly. She recognised its contents as the little headache pills Harry sometimes gave her. She had

---

2. A scrip was a small bag or pouch, typically tied about the waist.

once watched him make them by grinding feverfew and honey to a paste and rolling it with beeswax. "Pathetic," she spat. "Felix-the-Sneeze needs to sink to this? He's already doing everything he can to ruin Harry. Now he's got you robbing him, too?"

"No. It's not like that. Honestly, Matty, I came to *see* Harry. My master was summoned to the castle to treat the earl, and I thought——"

"You thought you'd help yourself."

"No. I didn't know Harry-the-Cough wasn't here."

Matty studied him. "Those soldiers must have taken Harry for the same reason, then. That's good. I was worried what he might have gotten himself into. Alright, I'll bite. *Why* did you want to see Harry?"

"'S private."

"Fair enough. Maybe I should call the watch?"

"No. No. Please don't do that. I have a proposition for him, that's all. Please, Matty, don't tell my master." His pallid face showed genuine concern.

She lowered her arm, not exactly feeling sorry for him so much as wondering what he was about. "And when you found Harry gone, you thought you'd help yourself, is that it?"

He looked awkward. "Thought I'd better make it look like I was using my initiative. You know, should Felix ever find out I was here. Can I take just one of these, just in case he catches wind of it?"

"On your pony!" she snapped, batting him about the head with a sheaf of rushes from Harry's workbench and driving him towards the open doorway.

Lott saw his opportunity and ran for it. Matty watched him go before trying to lift the broken door back into place. She struggled and let it fall again. "Oh, Harry," she muttered, her voice stressed, torn between helping her friend and neighbour, and her own business concerns. As it happened, her own *business* turned up at that moment, reeking of ale.

"Allo, Matty. Missed me, have you?"

Matty placed her head in her hands and then a thought struck her. She resurfaced, beaming. "Hello, Allan. Finished work for the day, pet?"

Allan staggered slightly. "Oh, yes. It's happy Friday, *hic!* I finished the joinery on those trusses for Noah. I used some of those new edge... new edge... *hic!* new edge-halved scarf joints, and ho *ho,* you should have seen his face. But it's the, *hic,* it's the, *hic,* it's the future, I told him. He's been trading on that boat job for too long, I, *hic,* told him that, an' all." He grinned, self-satisfied, and belched again. "Any road, he's paid me, and now it's time for——"

Matty sighed internally. "Yes, yes. Of course." She cut off what would surely have been a bawdy joke involving either wood or tools. "Don't suppose you have your tool——, er, *equipment* in that bag, by any chance?"

He straightened with suspicion. "Why?" He let the tool bag drop from his shoulder.

"Perhaps you can keep your penny this week. Let's barter."

He frowned, completely confused now.

Oh, dear. He's really not a bright boy, Matty thought, kindly. *I'd better explain. In really short words.* "Now, Allan, you see this broken door?"

Bodges opened the door with extreme care. There was an explosion of noise from inside as several large dogs launched themselves at it, slamming it shut again.

Harry swallowed. "I can come back. I mean, if they're busy."

Bodges gave him a withering look as the door opened again, just a crack. Enough for the thin young man who had been brutalised by the earl to slip through. He touched his forelock. "Dr Bodges."

"Jack, this is Master Bones."

"I know Harry-the-Cough, sir."

Hearing strange voices, the dogs attacked the door again. Failing to break through, it sounded like they turned on one another instead. "Quiet!" Jack hollered, to limited effect.

Harry looked around the young man, checking the door was secure, or at least, still in one piece. "Do you live in there, Jack?"

"Aye, master."

Harry gave Bodges a succinct look. "Might we go somewhere else?"

Bodges nodded. "Follow me." He led them into another outbuilding with a large wooden vat, full of water. "The women do their washing in here," he explained.

Harry looked around, wrinkling his nose. *Not often enough,* he thought. *That explains a lot. Still, it all helps the spread of disease.* "Remove your tunic, Jack, and lie down on this bench, please. On your belly, naturally." Turning to Bodges, he added, "Can you get someone to wash his tunic? He shouldn't put it back on over these cuts – not in that state."

"*Clean* it?" Bodges seemed almost alarmed by the notion.

"I assume Jack doesn't have another to wear, and that *is* what this vat of water is for, isn't it?"

"Well, yes, but not for cleaning the outdoorsmen's rags. The knights, men-at-arms, heralds and maids get their clothes cleaned twice a year by the laundress – whether they need it or not – but next washday's not until spring."

Harry sighed. "You're not really getting to grips with the importance of keeping wounds clean, are you?"

"Alright, alright." Bodges held up his hands. "I'll get one of the women to *clean* it for him," he agreed bombastically, and turned away to leave.

"Thank you," Harry muttered sardonically. "Now, let's see what we can do for you, Jack. This'll sting a bit, but it'll make you better."

Bodges stopped at the door. "You'll submit a bill?"

Harry paused, mid-treatment. "I'd rather have payment today, please, Dr Bodges."

"Very well. I'll be back anon. With a cleaning woman!" He slammed the door behind him.

What a pillock, thought Harry. "Jack?"

"Yes, master?"

"Those hounds of yours. I was wondering, do they like fish?"

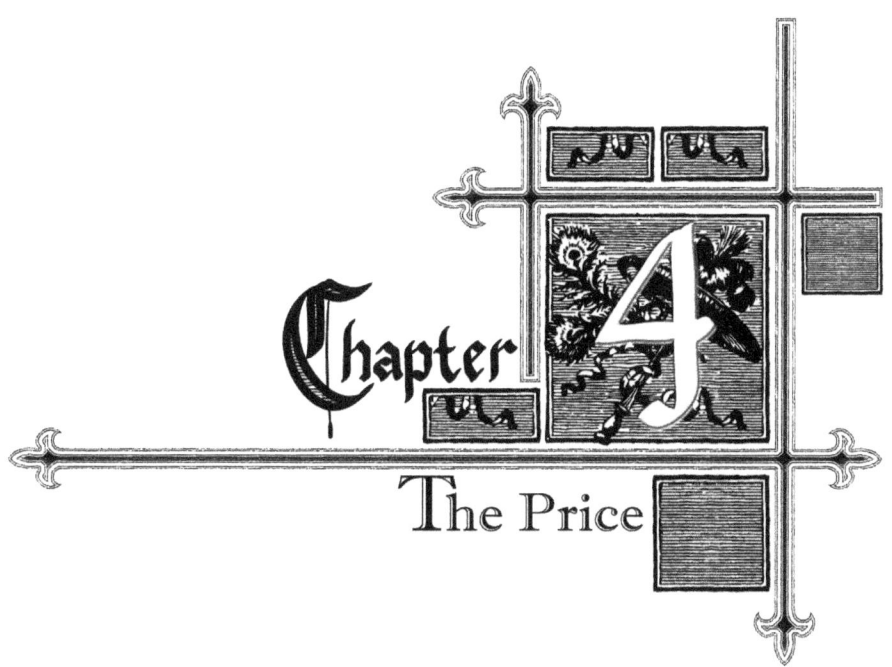

Chapter 4
The Price

Harry opened his front door, placed his bag on the workbench and sat down heavily on his rickety chair before even realising he *had* a front door again. He blinked. Thumps and moans from the room above told him to wait before calling on Matty with questions, so he took the small purse from his belt and poured its few pennies into his hand. Bodges had been generous with Lord Henry's money. The coins represented more than Harry had seen in a while but were hardly life changing. A few weeks' rent or a few weeks' food. What a choice. What a life.

He placed his head in his hands and massaged his temples. Felix L'Éternuement had thwarted him again. The earl was the consummate noble, honestly believing his class were superior beings and L'Éternuement had played him perfectly – Harry had to hand him that. Casting aspersions on Harry's skill simply because he was poor, and therefore no good, was just cruel. Yet, it had worked as intended. *Why do rich customers throw money at businesses and individuals who obviously don't need their patronage?* "Honestly," he continued his internal rant aloud, "can they smell it when someone's struggling?"

Reputation, reputation, reputation, he thought. *It always comes back to looking* successful, *but confidence is only part of it – they really* can *smell it! When things are going well, I could sell sand in Arabia – when my luck turns down, life is just one big fat door in the face.* "How can I find my way forward when I have nothing behind me but my brains and my own two hands?" He snorted, sadly, realising what he had just said. "That's about right, isn't it? Hands behind me – tied behind my back!"

He poured the pennies back into his purse. *More importantly, after today, how can I kick the legs out from under L'Éternuement?* Unfortunately, the only thing he could think of that might shake Lord Henry's faith in the superiority of the wealthy, would be for L'Éternuement to cause his death through incompetence – not much future in that strategy. He needed the earl very much alive if he was to win his patronage, and with civil war brewing that, in itself, might prove easier said than done – especially with L'Éternuement queering his patch.

A knock on the back door brought him out of his reverie. He dragged his feet half-heartedly to answer it.

Matty waited in the back yard, hair a little awry, but once again fully clothed. "Harry, I thought I heard your door slam. Are you alright? May I come in?"

Her intensity of movement and questions only threw his exhaustion into sharper relief. "Of course," he replied tiredly. "By the way, what happened with my door?"

She grinned impishly. "My last caller was a carpenter. I had him fix it up for you. I suspect he'd *really* been looking forward to seeing me, because he had it back up in no time. It doesn't stick any more, either. See?" She illustrated by opening and then closing it smoothly.

Harry smiled, shaking his head wryly. "You can *always* sell sand, Matty."

"Eh?"

"Never mind. Thank you so much. What do I owe you?"

"Oh, don't worry about that. Tell me what happened to you."

Harry described his visit to the castle.

Matty listened, intrigued. "Lord Henry sounds *horrible* when he's riled up. I'm glad I've only ever known him in a good humour."

Harry shrugged. "His kind didn't get where they were by being nice. I was within a hair's breadth of impressing him, though. I know I could have relieved his pain and healed his wound. But that fish-toting fool rolled up and ruined everything!" He spat the last words angrily. "Sorry, Matty. Didn't mean to take it out on you."

"I understand. I was thinking, just a few minutes ago, and I had an idea that might help you."

"You were *thinking?* While your friend was here?"

"Oh, yes. I find it helps to let my mind drift."

He studied her. He had never really considered how awful it must be for her sometimes, but he supposed it was that or starve.

She read his expression and tapped him on the arm. "Silly. I'm alright. Listen, I have a plan."

The messenger wrinkled his nose and Lord Henry could hardly blame him. The stink from the stuff L'Éternuement had pasted all over his leg was alarming. He hardly dared dwell on what might be in it, but the man had charged him a small fortune, so it must be quality material. Pity it stank like pee and poo, and unless he was very much mistaken, there was a whiff of pig about it, too.

"My lord, my master sends greetings from his marching camp in Cheshire and asks, will my lord support him in his bid?"

The man's master was Henry Bolingbroke of Lancaster, son of the late John of Gaunt, grandson to King Edward III, and the man who might very well be the next King of England, if things came to a head leaving him on top. Lord Henry knew him well and had little doubt about that outcome, if events did indeed go that far. Bolingbroke was a fighter, King Richard less so. Many might even welcome the transition. After all, pacifistic kings tended to spend money – warlike kings tended to steal it, increasing the wealth of those behind them with their patronage. Even so, the overall situation for England was perilous.

Before asking Lord Henry's help, the messenger confirmed John of Gaunt's recent death – the very catalyst for their current situation. King Richard II's imperious and unexplained blocking of what should have been Bolingbroke's automatic inheritance of his father's lands, including the Duchy of Lancaster, had left Bolingbroke furious over the denial of his rights. Understandable, but what would it mean for the nation? If Henry had the story straight, Bolingbroke would now have to beg – at least, that was how he would have seen it – King Richard for what was already his own by right. No, Bolingbroke would not take that well. Not well at all, and small blame to him.

Lord Henry of Warmstirrup nodded acquiescence. "I gather forces to me as we speak. Tell your master, he has my support in the north and east."

The messenger smiled. "My lord," he replied simply.

Henry waved him away impatiently; his leg was sorer than when the hound had bitten him. He had no understanding about the anaesthetic qualities of canine saliva, of course; he simply knew the wound now stung like hell – and after the soothing cleansing he had received from Harry-the-Cough, too. His concoction had even smelt pleasant – certain proof it was no good. No, L'Éternuement had been right. He must have been. How could a man of such low standing have superior knowledge to his betters? The ointment L'Éternuement used was disgusting, too. A sure sign of its efficacy.

He rubbed the bite – he could not resist it – forcing L'Éternuement's paste further into the wound. His eyes watered as the pain redoubled. *Apothecaries and physicians!* he pondered, furiously. *Did any of them know what they were doing?*

Henry had more than three hundred men gathered within the castle's curtain walls now, awaiting the arrival of many more. He would soon have to arrange entertainments before they became bored and violent. Bear baiting, cock fighting, perhaps a troupe of mummers, to name but a few. Then there would be hawking for his knights – they would all need women, too. If only he could just put them back in their box until needed, like he had with his toy soldiers as a small boy. Even housing them all was problematic at that time of year. *Damn Bolingbroke and his father. Could they not have waited until spring and the warring months before causing a fracas?*

The smarting from his leg stabbed at him again. He waited for the worst to pass, sighing heavily. "Bodges!"

"I can't ask you to do that!" Harry was shaken by Matty's offer. It would place her in the worst kind of danger for a woman, even one in her line of work.

"Now, don't be silly," she assured him. "I know how to look after myself. Besides, I'll have to go anyway. If I, and the other girls, shy away, those brutes will only start snatching women off the streets of Warmstirrup – *any* women. They won't care."

"So, what are you saying, it's your *duty?*"

Matty shrugged. "In a way. Look, it won't be as bad as all that."

He looked at her askance.

"Seriously. If I know anything about soldiers, it's that the senior officers like to sample the goods first. I have certain, shall we say, charms, as you can see." She twisted her torso, hands on hips, into a pose Harry could hardly fail to notice was *bosominous*.

Momentarily distracted, he recovered quickly and began shaking his head. "Oh, no, no, no. You can't mean..."

"Why not? He's a man, isn't he? Besides, if that cretin, L'Éternuement, has left him in a bad way, his will probably be the safest billet I could visit. It will also give me the chance to, *ahem*, whisper in his ear about how brilliant my apothecary friend is, and tell him that, if he wants the pain to stop, he should sack L'Éternuement."

"That's dangerous, Matty. He's a pompous fool. He trusts L'Éternuement, as much as he trusts anybody, because he's gentry. I'm just a peasant, in his eyes, and so are you. He thinks we're his property. Who knows what he might do if he thought you were trying to advise him – or worse, that you're trying to play him? You may have noticed, the nobility doesn't tend to generate that many healers or craftsmen, so he'll see the gentry as next best thing. They're dispensable, but good for certain tasks. *We* don't even count as people."

"Yes, funny how the sharpest minds come from the gutter, isn't it?"

Harry pulled a face. "What choice do we have? When you own almost nothing, you have to reinvent yourself, and what little you do own, every day, just to stay alive."

"Hmm, true."

"Matty, this isn't necessary. I'm ready to fight L'Éternuement, now. Really, I am."

She stroked his cheek with a half-smile. "Funny, I never had you pegged as the 'death to my enemies' type, Harry."

He shrugged. "I might be."

Her eyebrows shot up, incredulous.

Harry squirmed uncomfortably. "Alright, perhaps not death to my enemies, exactly. But that's only because I've got this mortal fear of being left alone."

She laughed. Such a pretty sound to his ear, and it brought a smile to his own lips. "Seriously, Matty, please don't do this, I…"

She stopped him, this time with a kiss on the cheek. "Don't worry. If you want to protect me, chaperone me through the forest this evening. I need to call on Insane Alice."

"Now there's a name you can trust. Who the hell is Insane Alice?"

"Shh. Keep your voice down. She's a wise woman. And she doesn't need to come to the attention of the watch – or *any* men for that matter. You don't count."

Harry's expression soured. "Thanks."

"Don't worry. She's nothing like Mad Mab. I know how you felt about your old guardian——"

"*Guardian?*"

Matty smiled. "Alice is a good old stick, but you of all people know how careful people in her—— in *your* line need to be."

"Might be easier on them, and all of us, if they didn't live alone in the forest cackling inanely to themselves."

She giggled, slapping his chest. "That's not fair and you know it."

"Well, do we really have to see some old sort in the woods? Can't I help you?"

She thought about it, but then shook her head. "Sorry, Harry. Sometimes a woman needs to…"

"What?"

"See *another* woman, about a problem – or the preventing of one. Don't trouble your little whiskery head about it."

He sighed. "Alright. When do we leave?"

Insane Alice lived in a thatched hovel about three miles south of Warmstirrup. The forest was thick there and Harry would never have found the place without Matty to guide him. Indeed, he clung to her like a limpet, afraid he might never find his way back should they become separated. By the time they arrived, it was getting dark, too.

The cackling seemed a little forced at first, but he supposed the dotty old crone had an image to uphold. After all, reputation was everything in business. He *had* hoped to remain outside, but Alice fairly dragged him through the door. Clearly, she did not receive many male callers, as Matty had alluded.

Money was of little use out here in the sticks, so Matty had visited several traders on Line Street, just before they closed, to procure foodstuffs and other little treats and necessities before they left town. Alice thanked her appreciatively. Indeed, once they were inside, Harry wondered if Insane Alice was actually insane at all. The old woman offered Matty a small clay pot, sealed with a cloth tied around its top, in return for her bartered goods.

"What's in that?" he asked, taking the pot from Matty and sniffing it. It smelt minty – more precisely, of spearmint. He looked up sharply. "Pennyroyal? Oh, Matty."

"Don't worry, it's only in case."

"I've seen women die from this. It's a poison."

"And I've seen women who have been caught out, starve to death!" Her reply was harsh. She softened. "Sorry, Harry. I know you're a good man, but the world is as it is. No one cares about women, at least not women like me. And until that changes——"

"I care," he interrupted chivalrously.

She smiled dotingly. "Thank you. I know you do. Now, listen, Alice may also be able to help us with our little problem at the castle."

He looked doubtful. "Oh?"

"I can make men more *pliable*." Alice grinned, showing a few lonely brown teeth.

"You know, some might call that witchcraft."

Alice cackled again, forcing Harry to re-evaluate – maybe she really did laugh like that. It certainly enhanced her brand. He found himself feeling rather envious and wondering whether he could adopt some outward sign for his own profession – a lantern outside his workshop, perhaps, with a flickering candle fed with copper to make it flash blue? Distracted by the epiphany, his mind began to turn towards the mechanics of building such a device, when Alice drew his attention back to her.

"I can provide you with a magic potion that will bend any man to your will, young Harry."

"You know my name?"

"Matty, and others, have mentioned Harry-the-Cough to me in the past. You recognised the pennyroyal, so you have some understanding of the herbs. We share some of the same patrons, it seems. When describing your abilities, some of my callers have even gone so far as to say that you're not a complete idiot."

"High praise," he replied, deadpan. "You must let me know who they are, so I can thank them."

The cackling began again, ebbing and flowing, giving no clue as to when it might abate. Harry found himself swaying with it. When Alice stopped, abruptly, he almost staggered. Catching himself, he cleared his throat, feeling a fool. Further cackling ensued.

"Thank you for the offer of... of *magic* potion, Alice——"

"*Insane* Alice."

"Sorry. Thank you, Insane Alice——"

"It's a branding thing. You understand."

"Of course. However, I think I must refuse your kind offer of any potions. Perhaps another time."

They walked back through the forest in silence for a while. Eventually, Harry felt compelled to speak. "Was she completely batty, or was it an act? I mean, sometimes she seemed normal and then..." He looked back over his shoulder nervously before continuing in hushed tones, "Well, let's just say, you could almost smell the bonfire being stoked in readiness."

"Harry, really! Alice is alright."

"Shh!" He grabbed her arm. "What was that?"

"What was what?" she whispered back.

"I heard something in the trees – ahead."

They peered into the inky blackness. It was almost dark. The nearer foliage still glowed with myriad deep greens in the dying daylight, now all joined up with patches of purest pitch in the middle distance. "Erm, do you often walk through here in the dark?" Harry asked, becoming more hushed with every breath.

"I have to," Matty replied in kind. "Insane Alice chooses her office hours to fit with her image."

He nodded absent-mindedly, fear clouding his thoughts as all his remaining perception was shunted towards hearing. Hardly daring to breathe, Harry listened intently for any further cracks or rustles of movement out in the darkness before them. *Crack.* Make that, *around* them. "Oh, no," he muttered hopelessly, hairs rising on the back of his neck. They were being circled.

"A squirrel?" Matty suggested, optimistically.

CRACK.

"I'm thinking not," Harry was forced to note the increase in magnitude. "Not unless mama squirrel got frisky with a destrier."

Matty laughed, covering her mouth immediately. She felt rather than saw Harry's pained expression. His general features were still visible, but all subtleties were now lost in darkness.

Harry swallowed with difficulty, his mouth suddenly parched. "Erm, is this forest perhaps... *haunted?*"

"Don't be such a big girl's chemise. I brought you here to look after *me*."

"I am. I mean, I will."

"So why am *I* holding *you* protectively?"

Harry coughed awkwardly, releasing his death grip on her arm. "Well, you know, you're more used to the night than I am, being a 'lady of the'."

"I'm not a wood nymph, you fool."

Another crack sounded, that of a heavy twig being snapped in the darkness to their left. It was immediately followed by a similar sound from their right. Harry covered his eyes and began to mumble.

"What are you doing now?" Matty hissed.

"Praying. What else?"

"With your eyes shut?" she asked waspishly, from the corner of her mouth. "It's hard enough to see in here as it is!"

"I don't *want* to see!"

A light moved through the trees across their path. Had they understanding of the concept, they might have said it drifted from one o'clock, on their right, across to ten o'clock on their left. It was a piercing bright white.

Matty tensed, hackles raised.

Harry froze, hoping it would go away. He made a strange, almost strangled susurration.

"How are those prayers going?" Matty asked, a quaver in her own voice now.

"Had to stop. Started swearing. Didn't think it would go over well."

"Well, try again. Perhaps God swears himself?"

"You think?"

"Well, if I'd created the world and all its wonders, I'd stop to say '*Damn, I'm good*', wouldn't you?"

"True." The light vanished in a wink and reappeared closer to them, and just behind, in a zone that would one day be referred to as eight o'clock. "*Matty,*" Harry whimpered between chattering teeth. Voices from the darkness made them grab each other instinctively.

"Reid?" A woman.

"Yes, ma'am." The response that of a man.

"Where are you?"

"Over here, ma'am."

Another light sparked into existence on Matty and Harry's right, causing Harry to release a squeak of fear. When a strangely dressed young woman stepped onto the narrow passage between the trees – Insane Alice valued her privacy, so it hardly qualified as a path – they both jumped.

She held a light in her hand that seared their eyes like the ice white of a winter sun, though it gave off no smoke. She blocked their way as the man, who held a similar magical daylight engine, stepped out of the trees behind them. The woman was blond and, to Harry's befuddled mind, could only have been an angel. He had never seen such beauty.

Matty felt him stiffen[1] and could tell what he was thinking. She stared catlike at the newcomer, looking for blemishes and imperfections she could besmirch later – she came up empty, and so had no choice but to despise her on sight.

"Are y-you an angel?" Harry asked, stupidly.

The woman of the light held something else in her other hand – a small, metallic device. She pointed it at him. "Answer my questions or I will certainly introduce you to the angel of death."

Her accent and syntax were hard for Harry to follow, but he got the gist. *And I thought Chaucer was impenetrable,* his mind sidestepped for a moment.

---

1. In the interests of clarity, and for those with dirty minds (you know who you are), Harry's whole body stiffened with surprise. No jokes, please. This is a medieval comedy; it's not meant to be funny.

When Harry and Matty failed to answer, the blonde assumed they understood and continued, "What year is this?"

Again, they looked at her dumbly.

"The date?" she demanded, angrily, pointing the metallic object at them.

Harry, ever curious about new devices and learning, bent forward to look down the hole in the end of it. "Is that a hammer for pressing dimples into plate?" he enquired, innocently.

The woman sighed, looking around them to her counterpart. "Clearly a demonstration will be necessary."

"Ma'am, perhaps we shouldn't——" *BANG*. "*Heidi!* Others may have heard that!"

"Ouch." Harry belatedly covered his ears. They were whistling. The bang was the loudest thing he had ever heard. He turned, surprised to see the man behind them getting up. He had thrown himself to the ground for some reason.

The woman, apparently called Heidi, shoved the metal device towards his face. "The year?"

Harry still had no understanding of what the thing might be, but he was not a fool. It was obviously extremely dangerous, as proven by the reaction of the man she had called Reid, standing once more, right behind them.

"Why, 'tis the year of our Lord 1399." Matty spoke for the first time since the strangers' arrival.

Heidi's eyes narrowed, not at Matty but at Reid. "Imbecile! What good is this? These people still think the world is flat!"

Harry was not sure, but that sounded like an insult, and yet... what else would the world be? A pyramid? Everyone would slide off, surely? Although that might explain why there were so many people at the bottom. Returning to the moment, he began to suspect the beautiful blonde might just be madder than Insane Alice. Too much angelic grace, perhaps?

Heidi holstered her weapon and grabbed Harry-the-Cough roughly by the neck of his garment. "You haven't seen us. Yes?"

He could only stare, completely baffled now.

Heidi sighed. "Do not tell anyone you have seen us. Do you understand?" She spoke slowly, as if he were simple.

He nodded and she let him go. "Reid, we must get back to the ship.

Come."

As she turned north-west, Harry could not help himself. "Ahem, excuse me, miss. The sea is that way." He pointed east. "If you're looking for a way back to your ship, I mean."

Heidi rolled her eyes and stalked off into the now completely blackened forest, torchlight flashing wildly as she negotiated the rough going. Reid made to follow, stumbled and fell, picked himself up and tried again. They heard Heidi snap, "Fool!" and they were gone[2].

Harry and Matty stood in shocked silence for long minutes. Eventually, Harry muttered, mostly to himself, "They must have been aliens."

"What are aliens?"

"People we don't know."

"Strangers, then."

"I thought strangers were just people we no longer spoke to? Never mind, let's just please get out of here."

"Right," Matty agreed. "Follow the track. It's not difficult, I've done it many times."

Harry looked at her with new respect – at least he looked where he thought she was. He could no longer see a thing. "You're so brave, Matty. This forest at night doesn't frighten you at all, does it?"

"Does a bit. I'm only a *woman,* after all," she added sarcastically.

Harry shared an uncomfortably introspective moment with himself, not enjoying the stiff dressing-down he gave him. He changed the subject to hide his embarrassment. "So this track, where is it again?"

Before Matty could answer, the ground shook with a terrific rumble and roar. Even through the trees, they could see impossibly bright flames lifting into the night sky before vanishing, almost instantly, leaving a boom behind that rolled across the darkened landscape.

In the sudden silence that crashed in on its wake, Harry's breathing was deafening in his ears. "Matty?"

---

2. For readers wondering what just happened, answers may be found within the New World Series of time travel novels. Some of them may even be the correct answers – though no promises are made.

She was invisible in the darkness, but her voice also gave away the unmistakable quake of fear. "Was that an omen? A portent of doom?"

"I don't know, but can we go home now? I think I've had a wee."

Chapter 5
Every Dog

Matty awoke early, refreshed. All the better for having the night to herself. She would need to be well rested before going to work at the castle. She went through her morning ablutions and was about to throw everything she no longer required out of her first-floor window, when it occurred to her to look down first. Sure enough, there was Harry, putting out his sign.

Bless him, she thought kindly. *He works so hard, and I nearly started his day with another early bath, too.* She chuckled, making him look up.

"Morning, Matty."

"Morning, Harry. I looked before I chucked this time, see?" She held out the chamber pot as proof.

He grinned up at her. "Thanks. I can't tell you how much that means to me. Being dumped on first thing really sets you up badly for the day. See you later." He gave a cheery little wave and stepped indoors.

Matty swung, aiming for the open channel running down the middle of Scrubber Alley. Just as the contents left the pot, Harry reappeared. "Oh, by the way, Matty, I forgot to as—— Urgh!"

Matty put her hand to her mouth, holding the pot's handle in the other. "Oh, no. Sorry, Harry, I thought you'd gone in."

Harry stepped back further into the alley, wiping his face. "No problem," he called miserably. "My fault this time. I just wanted to ask you——"

Splosh.

"Morning, Harry. Ew... Sorry, dear."

Harry did not even bother to turn around. "Morning, Mrs Pigden."

"You have a lovely day, now," his neighbour called, disappearing back inside.

Matty tried to cover her laughter, while Harry stood round-shouldered and dejected in the alley.

"Make way there, lad!"

His moment of self-pity was forcibly interrupted by a powerful shove. Tripping over his own A-framed sign, Harry fell back inside as Neil the pony trotted by, snorting happily as he pulled his small but solidly built wooden cart down the narrow way, practically filling it.

Old Mr Tanner, the tanner, was a local menace. Hogging the road, he always drove with total disregard for pedestrians or property. "One of these days you'll have an accident, my boy!"

Neil managed to trample Harry's sign and Mr Tanner's solid wooden cartwheel rolled straight over it immediately after, ruining it, but in a very specific way.

Collecting the broken pieces, Harry noted that where it used to say 'Harry-the-Cough', with 'Apothecary to thee Nobility' painted diligently and diagonally beneath, there was now a mucky wheel track and an unfortunate crack in the boards. One of Neil's uncannily placed horseshoes had also smashed a hole right through 'Nobility', so that the sign now read, 'Harry-the-Cough' 'A----------- -- --- Nob-----'.

Harry stooped dejectedly to pick up the last remnants, when he slipped on something else Neil had left him, only to fall onto his back in the open channel that ran down the middle of the way. As foul water sloshed through his hair and clothing, he looked up into a beautiful, wide, hopeful, blue winter's sky and had a little cry.

Matty tried to apologise but it only came out as another guffaw. Eventually, she stepped into her shoes and ran down the back staircase, through Harry's workshop, and out into the alley, to offer what moral support she could. Physical support was out of the question; he was disgusting. "Shall I heat some water?" she asked, trying not to laugh.

"Yes, please," he replied weakly from the open sewer. "Just bring it to the boil and throw me in, would you?"

Harry began to shiver. True to her word, Matty had warmed some water for the tub in the back yard that all Scrubber Alley residents shared. No one would have denied him use of it that morning. However, the problem was that it *was* outside – outside in early February, not to put too fine a point on it. It had been such a relief to wash the filth from his hair and body in the luxurious warmth of the tub, but now his filthy clothes seemed to accuse him from where Matty had draped them, neatly, over an old fence.

Harry did not own any other clothes, and he certainly could not put those back on in the state they were in. The water was cooling quickly. He whimpered. This was going to be miserable in the extreme, but he must wash his clothes in the water before it lost all its beneficent heat. The fact that he must do so stark naked and freezing wet, and in front of a mirthful audience, was not lost on him.

He mulled over his fortunes of late, as he savoured the last of the heat. Aside from his current misfortune, his business was in ruins, and he would soon be evicted from his hovel. It was difficult to see how life could get any worse – although, he fully accepted that might simply be a lack of imagination on his part.

Bracing himself, he grabbed the sides of the tub and stood. The water cascading off him turned shockingly cold, instantly, making his teeth rattle.

Old ladies, already with mid-morning tankards of ale in their hands, laughed and made lewd comments as he rushed around trying to clean his clothes one-handed, while hiding his shame with the other. In that regard, the freezing conditions helped.

A group of little boys threw small stones at his naked rump, making Harry cry out, the sting magnified tenfold by his frigid flesh. The stains on his tattered clothing were stubborn, but the speed with which he dealt with the problem was an inspiration to bachelors everywhere. Matty had gone back indoors. She never invaded his privacy in such matters – not that there was any. Knowing only too well how she earned her meagre living, Harry could only assume it was her way of compartmentalising the elements within her life; a system for keeping the personal and the professional separate. He was grateful for that. It was bad enough being a target for naughty boys and bored old ladies without awkwardness between himself and probably the only true friend he had in the world.

Mission accomplished, he dashed back indoors, only to find that Matty had brought him some kindling and already got a fire going in his hearth. He smiled as he hung the sodden clothing over the back of his chair and warmed his nether regions. He could not help thinking that Matty deserved better than her current lot. If he ever did get himself out of Scrubber Alley, he would have to see about that.

His clothes steamed. He steamed. Once dry, he wrapped himself in his shabby old blanket as a knock came on his back door.

"Come in."

Matty entered with a small bundle wrapped in a clean piece of white linen. "Thought you could probably do with this." Without explaining, she unfurled the cloth to reveal half a loaf of bread, some butter and some cheese. She grabbed Harry's workaday knife from the block on his bench and began cutting the bread. As she hung slices from a hook over the flames, the aroma of toasting made Harry's stomach growl. The morning's events may have pushed his hunger aside, but the sight and smell of food made him suddenly ravenous.

"Matty, why are you so good to me?"

She grinned. "What can I say? I like puppies and hopeless cases."

"Can't argue with you there," Harry replied miserably. "I mean the hopeless, not the puppies..." He tailed off. She was still giggling.

"Oh, Harry. You're just so entertaining. I couldn't imagine Scrubber Alley without you." She reached out and stroked the back of her hand affectionately down his stubbled cheek. As he looked down into her eyes, he noted a sudden change there; a coldness that did not quite belong. "I've got to go to work once we've eaten this." She turned away.

"I'm sorry." It was all he could think to say. *Dolt!* he remonstrated with himself. Matty hated sympathy where her work was concerned. "I'm sorry," he repeated, and winced again. "I mean for being sorry... I'll shut up."

She laughed. "See what I mean? What would I do without you to cheer me up? Let me spread some butter and I'll have a go at melting the cheese on this hot plate."

The smell of melted cheese completely distracted Harry from all else. He took the proffered slice from her hands, greedily, scoffing it down in three bites. "Is there enough for another?" he managed from around a mouthful of toast.

The rest of the morning went quickly for Harry. Once dressed, and as clean as medieval life allowed, he felt ready to face the next task – opening his shop for business. His sign was ruined, but he salvaged half the A-frame. It now leaned against the wall outside. It would no longer attract attention from higher up the alley, but he decided it was best to end all reference to 'Harry-the-Cough – a nob' before it rooted within the local consciousness. The broken half of his sign now crackled and popped as it warmed his hands on the fire.

He sold a tub of Inside and Out to a wealthy merchant's wife, wisely chaperoned along Scrubber Alley by two surly male servants, and cleaned up a child's skinned knee. The youthful laughter he heard from outside, as the urchin ran away, made him suspect he had just helped one of the boys who had so recently barraged his backside.

Never mind. It all goes towards securing my place in Heaven. He looked up, hoping for a sign. He shrugged. Worth a try.

He was almost out of raw material for his ointments and potions, but a sixth sense told him to make up what he did have in preparation for something momentous. The castle was filling up with soldiers, after all, and despite Felix L'Éternuement's drive to take every piece of business away from him, they would surely require his services sooner or later. He looked up again. When a second heavenly sign also failed to arrive, he packed his wares into the large bag he wore over his shoulder. Whatever happened next, at least he was ready. Or so he believed.

It was much too cold to sit with the door open, so the gloom was lit only by his small fire. He gazed into the smouldering ashes, mildly irritated that he had lacked the foresight to salvage an O, P, E and an N from the ruins of his sign before offering it in sacrifice. When Matty burst into his hovel, he jumped to his feet in surprise. "What's happened?"

"Harry," she fought for breath after her run, "you have to get away. Now! Out the back – go!"

"Wha——?"

She bustled him outside, barely allowing him to grab his bag of belongings on the way through. They ran across the back yard and scrambled through a hole in the fence that led into the rear burgages of New Row, the next street over. Its name may have lacked foresight thirty years on, but the houses were better built and a distinct step up from those of Scrubber Alley, despite being outside the town walls. Until Warmstirrup's current problems, and excepting the Battle of Otterburn to the south, all the major troubles had been further north or in France, for decades, leading to a false sense of security in The Sprawl. The back yard Matty and Harry charged through was easily large enough to support the family who lived there. It was also home to a vicious squadron of attack chickens.

Harry cried out as they wove and banked around his shins, pecking his calves. He may have hopped about like a coop insurgent, but they were neither fooled, nor impressed.

"Come *on*, Harry," Matty called.

Harry glared down furiously at a particularly evil-looking, one-eyed cockerel its owners, with astonishing prescience, had named the Red Baron. "I'll be back to square with you. You just wait——"

"Harry?"

Matty's call distracted him, creating an opportunity for the Baron to lead his wing in a second ambush, out of the watery noonday sun.

"Aaargh! There's a pie in your future, I'm gonna—— Aaargh! Pluck you, you little——"

"*Harry!*"

"Alright, I'm coming – ow, ow, *ouch*. I have flocking injuries, here!"

Extricating himself, he ran to catch up, the Red Baron chasing him, maintaining withering pecks until he caught up with Matty. Faced with two giants, the Baron peeled off, heading back to the coop.

Harry kicked snow at him. "This isn't over! You hear me?"

"*Everyone* can hear you," Matty scolded, waspishly. "Shut up!"

Together, they made for a narrow passageway between the buildings. Thoroughly disgruntled, Harry pressed Matty for an explanation, but she merely grabbed his hand again and redoubled her efforts to escape.

Emerging onto New Row itself, Matty checked left and right before crossing to another alley almost opposite. They hared along it, feet slapping through the slushy February mud, to eventually arrive in Dark Lane. Dark Lane ran alongside a small copse near the outer edge of The Sprawl. Matty led them right, around the northern edge of the copse, and they were soon back within the town environs. Their home in The Sprawl, well outside the protection of the town walls, suited Matty's purposes perfectly that day. She turned left and cut through into another narrow alley known locally and colloquially as Cutthroat's Way, its original name having passed from living memory, if it had one at all.

"This is a charming part of town," Harry commented acidly as they leaned against a wall to catch their breath. "As a denizen of Scrubber Alley, are you trying to make me feel lucky?"

Matty gave him a look that spoke of heartbreak. "Oh, *Harry*."

"What? What is it?"

"There's been a murder."

He straightened, his expression growing more serious. "Who?"

"Lott. L'Éternuement's boy, or helper, or whatever he was. He was found with his throat cut, and… and that's not the half of it."

"So that's why you brought me to Cutthroat's Way?"

"This isn't funny!"

"No. Of course not. Sorry. But what has it to do with me?"

"Harry, his was a brutal killing. The soldiers up at the castle are saying that he died from a slash across the throat, but after that, a second blow removed the head. The rest was fed to L'Éternuement's pigs."

"So you're saying L'Éternuement did it?" Harry asked, dubiously. He knew his nemesis to be a conman, but doubted he had the stomach for anything like that.

"No!" Matty hissed, showing her frustration with him at last. "L'Éternuement was with Lord Henry long after you left – milking his fee, I expect. He was at the castle when this terrible act took place. Harry, he's blaming *you* for the murder."

Harry sat on a wobbly stool in the corner. Temporarily ensconced within a hovel belonging to one of Matty's friends, a woman known as Dora, Matty told them what she knew. "Lott came to your workshop yesterday, while you were up at the castle. He *said* he was hoping to find you there, but I caught him trying to rob you."

"You're telling me this now?"

"I'm sorry. I stopped him from taking anything and you were already so upset about L'Éternuement getting you ejected from Lord Henry's presence, I just thought you'd had enough. Then we took our terrifying walk through the woods and... well, I forgot about it. It seemed to me that, with you out, he'd seen an opportunity to help himself to your superior products." Her attempts at flattery were wasted. Harry was simply too frantic with worry to notice. "You know how sly he is—— was," she corrected, guiltily. "But now this has happened, I'm wondering if he may not have been telling the truth."

"Did he give any clue about what he wanted?"

"No. He clammed up – said he would only tell you. Now, the earl has soldiers out everywhere, looking for you. I was there when he gave the order. They're telling people you're being sought for questioning, but we all know how that ends with Lord Henry."

"When he bothers to question at all," Dora chipped in, bitterly.

Matty smiled sympathetically at her. "I almost forgot. I have something for you." She took a few coppers from her purse and gave them to her friend.

Dora took them regretfully. "I'll pay you back for all this," she promised, earnestly.

Matty smiled and nodded. Whether she expected to see a return or not, Harry could not tell, but his curiosity was piqued. He gave her a searching look, but she merely shook her head, subtly, while Dora secreted the pennies away.

"I can't stay here," Harry decided suddenly. "I'm putting you both in danger."

"Yes, but you mustn't go yet," Matty implored. "We have to wait for dark."

He studied her. This would hurt. "There is no 'we', Matty. I must go alone. You've done enough, both of you – more than enough. I should go and find out what exactly is going on and what L'Éternuement is up to. If Henry suspected you of hiding me, the Lord knows what he'd do to the two of you."

Matty made to stand. "I'll come with you———"

"No," Harry cut her off. He smiled to soften the harshness of his reproach. "I'll be fine. Every dog has his day, right?"

Before Matty could respond, Dora retched and ran from the room.

"What's wrong with her?" Harry asked quietly.

"She… she's not well at the moment."

"Why didn't you fetch me to her – before this, I mean?"

"She has no money. Can't earn, you see? And I knew you wouldn't accept money from me, but you can't afford to work for free, Harry. The landlord will be after your blood soon enough as it is."

"He'll have to wait in line now, won't he? Now, what's wrong with Dora?"

"Occupational hazard."

"Could you be less vague?"

"Dora works… erm."

"In the same line as yourself?" Harry suggested.

"Yes."

"And?"

"And she's picked up some sort of sweating sickness from a client. She can't work. She's too weak, too ill and... well, with the way she is at the moment, who would?"

Harry could not argue the point. "And you're giving her money while she's on her back, as it were?"

"More, while she's not." Matty grinned, mischievously.

He gave her a disapproving look. "You surely can't afford to do that."

"She's starving, Harry. Getting weaker by the day. She'll never get well if she's not able to feed herself and keep warm. She was good to me when I first came here."

Harry nodded slowly, his sour expression dissolving into exasperation and chagrin. "You'll starve yourself, if you keep helping poor souls like her, and losers like me."

Dora returned, looking ashen.

"Let me look at you," Harry offered kindly.

The sick woman glanced cautiously at Matty, who nodded assent before turning to make up the fire.

Harry felt the woman's brow. "You're feverish. Hot, then cold, and then hot again?"

Dora nodded weakly. "And what little I have, I can barely keep down."

Harry reached into his bag and brought forth a paste he made from the crab apples that grew wild in the woods nearby. Through trial and error – and from being too impoverished to throw anything away, even when it was past its best – he had found its efficacy increased as the fruit rotted. He suspected it was something to do with the mould that grew on the apples' surface but had no way to prove it. In one case, the paste had induced food poisoning in the patient – not his best day – but more generally, the effects were positive.

Taking the knife from his belt, he took a scoop of the paste and scraped it off on the rim of a wooden cup. He filled the cup with a little ale from the jug on the table, placed his hand over the top and shook it well.

Dora's hands were trembling from illness and fatigue, so he helped steady her, delivering the medicinal drink to her mouth. She took two swallows and began to cough. He replaced the drink on the table and felt her neck for swellings. The humours were certainly out of balance within this poor woman. He took the paste back out of his bag, deciding to leave it with her.

"Make sure you drink every bit of that, Dora. Add a scrape of this to your small ale, three times a day until it's gone. By then you should be starting to feel much better." Dora began to protest, but he gently pushed her back down onto her sleeping pallet. "Easy now. You've already paid by giving me a safe place to hide out for a few hours. I can't thank you enough for that. If Henry's men had caught up with me…"

Matty took his arm. "Thank you for helping her. You're a good soul, Harry Bones."

"I should get moving. It's already growing dark outside. There's black cloud moving in."

"Where will you go?"

"I need to get close to the castle. There will be rumours, at least. Hopefully, I'll be able to piece it together."

"No. Don't do that."

He looked at her questioningly.

"Let me go to the castle. I've some unfinished business with the officers anyway."

"I can't let you do that. If they get wind you're helping me——"

"They still owe me!" she cut him off, bombastically. "So, I'm going, and you may as well benefit from it." Harry tried to argue, but she cut him off again. "Don't worry. I know how to take care of myself. I'm always selective with soldiers – I know what to look out for."

His brows knitted with concern. He did not doubt Matty's ability to survive in a rough and tumble environment, but dangers were not always on the surface. Some of the men in the castle would be there because they had no choice, others because killing was all they were fit for. Then there were the other dangers – dangers his profession taught him were always there, even when, *especially* when, you could not see them. The creeping deaths that invaded a man's flesh without leaving a mark – at least, not at first. He wanted to stop her, but knew he could not, nor did he have the right.

A doting smile spread across Matty's face, picking out dimples in her cheeks. She reached up, moving a stray lock out of his eyes. "Every dog, indeed."

Chapter 6
Fox on the Run

"I don't trust him," Matty commented, making it sound like a thought had escaped, but her purpose was deliberate.

Lord Henry looked quizzically down his nose at her. They were alone in his chambers.

She curtsied. "Forgive me, lord. I didn't mean to speak out of turn."

Henry knew much of the town gossip was deliberately concealed from him, so he indulged her. "Explain."

She curtsied again. "He talks about every noble he's helped, but the names he drops are just second-hand." Matty glanced up, cautiously. "At least, that's what people say, my lord."

"Who speaks thus?"

"Just townsfolk, my lord. He's a *southern*, after all. Folk don't trust him."

As a travelled man of the world, Henry knew people were the same everywhere. "His thriving business suggests otherwise."

"He was rich before he came to our town, lord."

Again, he studied her. "You have some personal grievance with L'Éternuement?"

"No, lord."

The earl glowered, eyes hard and searching. Matty became afraid. Lord Henry was well known for being as tenacious as his precious hounds when he caught the scent of someone breaking the law – *his* law. His jaw jutted belligerently. "My men tell me you whore out of a hovel above that Harry-the-Cough fellow," he declared imperiously.

Matty's heart skipped. How did he know that? "My lord?"

"Yes," he answered, stroking his beard thoughtfully. "I always make it my business to know where the women come from. Helps me avoid the poxed houses. Know him well, do you?"

"My lord?"

"The apothecary, girl! Tell me what you know of his disappearance."

"N-nothing, lord. I just see him around occasionally. He's not one of mine."

He looked at her askance, distrustful. He doubted that. "You know he's murdered a chap? Can't have that. Dear me, no. Can't have the peasants going around killing one another, can we? There'd be no scum left to pack out my pikemen, or clean the privies!" He gave a sudden bark of laughter.

"I-I thought L'Éternuement may have killed the lad himself, lord." Matty was suddenly desperate to deflect his questions about Harry.

"Why the devil would he do that?"

"I heard he was not kind with his servants, lord."

"There seems to be no end to what you've heard, young mistress. Now hear this – L'Éternuement was with me when the hue and cry went out." He grabbed her roughly by the arm. "You know more about this than you're letting on. I can always spot liars. It's a gift. I... I..." Confusion gripped the earl. His grasp on her arm relaxed.

"It's about time," Matty exhaled with relief. Having visited Lord Henry before, she knew he always dismissed his chamberlain – many lords did not bother – and he was no lover of music, either, so the castle's minstrel was never invited. She had him alone.

"Here, my lord, finish this." She handed him the pewter flagon from which he had been drinking. He downed the beverage dumbly and without question. "Right. Now let's go and sit down on the bed over here and you can tell me what *you* know."

The shout came from behind him. Harry did not bother to look round; he simply bolted, and the law bolted terrier-like after him. They figured, as they always did, that anyone running must either be running after a criminal or running away from a crime. As *they* were the law, they usually assumed the latter. Imagination was not highly prized among Lord Henry's guards. He trained them like he trained his hounds – anything or anyone moving suspiciously was to be hunted down and caught, or killed, whichever happened first.

Harry was well known around town and amongst the guards. Before Felix L'Éternuement arrived with his ridiculous fish, he had been Bodges' go-to man for the ingredients he used to create 'cures' for the soldiers, and for Lord Henry himself. He knew that being poor made him automatically guilty, so he darted for places where even the guards only went in force, hoping the pair of castle-liveried thugs behind him would have just enough nous to realise their danger and leave him alone.

He set out from Dora's hovel, earlier, with the intention of getting as far away from her as possible, to keep her and Matty safe, but the guards had changed his mind and he found himself inevitably drawn back into Cutthroat's Way. The shouts from behind had changed in tone from bellows of mindless aggression to something equating to a 'please don't go down there' before they stopped altogether. That was good news for Harry. The bad news for Harry was that he was in Cutthroat's Way, alone, and it was now fully dark.

He slowed to a sidle, sticking to the one wall, willing himself invisible. The sound of a bucket being kicked over made him jump and turn. His heart banged against his ribs until a cat squawked and hissed. He put his hand to his chest and breathed a sigh of relief, smiling nervously. That was when the knife appeared at his throat.

Felix L'Éternuement sat in his large armchair within the comparative comfort and safety of his new stone house. He had no idea whether Harry-the-Cough had murdered his henchman; he had simply been happy to accuse him. One of his urchins had told him a tale of Lott's visit to Harry that afternoon, though he knew they had not spoken – Harry had been at the castle with him at that time. He allowed himself a smile as he recalled the guards manhandling the insolent peasant, and would-be gentleman healer, from their lord's presence. Who did Cough think he was? An educated serf; whatever would be next, a commoner running England? Or a woman, perhaps? He snorted at the very thought.

A knock at the door made him start. It was late. He walked from his living room into a small antechamber with four doors, one in each wall. It separated his living quarters from the kitchen and scullery, and doubled as a reception area for guests. The third internal door, opposite the main entrance to the property, led to a staircase and the upper storey. A torch burned in a sconce on the wall. It was wasteful, but L'Éternuement hated the dark. Being new to Warmstirrup, he was especially nervous on these long winter nights – longer still in the north.

"Who is it?" He spoke gruffly, to belie his fear, suddenly regretting his decision to send the servants home early that evening. L'Éternuement may have hated the long nights, but he disliked the idea of sharing his roof with servants even more, seeing them as thieves in waiting. Who knew what they might get up to while he slept? He had toyed with the idea of keeping a young scullion named Agnes – a pretty girl – but her father was the local blacksmith, Tommy Bullock. Well named, the man had arms the size of a bull's leg, and should he be tempted one night, he could all too easily imagine them around his neck, twisting his head off.

"Hello?" he tried again when no answer came.

A crash at the back of the house made him jump round. He could hear voices, male, and carrying a timbre that was distinctly unfriendly.

"They're breaking in through the scullery," L'Éternuement commented for the sake of his own nerves. Immediately, he began drawing the bars that secured his front door. The second was just free when armed men burst into the antechamber from the kitchen. He yanked the front door open and ran – straight into a waiting grin.

Looking up from the freezing mud where he had been knocked down, he coughed, winded. "Sergeant-at-arms? What is the meaning of this?"

The grin stretched even further up a scarred face. "You're to come with us."

"For what reason?"

The sergeant-at-arms leaned down with a mocking friendliness. "You're under arrest for murder, my lad."

Already frozen to his core, L'Éternuement blanched still further. "Murder? What murder? Whose?"

"Your servant. Lott, I believe his name was." The sergeant-at-arms tutted. "Very naughty. Even if he was just a servant."

"B-but Harry the C-Cough did that. Your men are chasing him as we speak!"

Had he been privy to the events happening just outside the castle, in one of the better parts of town, Harry-the-Cough would doubtless have taken some comfort. A case of the left hand not knowing what the right was doing, so to speak. However, the fact that the guards pursuing him were also to receive the news, along with revised orders, was of little consequence right now. Either to him, or to the man with the knife at his throat in Cutthroat's Way.

"Your money. And you die." The rasping voice made the man sound like his own throat had been cut at one time.

Harry wondered peripherally if it had, or perhaps it was just a ruse to disguise his true voice? That was before a more urgent question shunted itself into his forebrain. "*And* I die?"

"'S right."

"Erm, so there's not much advantage in helping you find my money, then – wouldn't you agree?"

"Depends."

"On what?"

"On *how* you want to die."

"This sounds like an argument neither of us can win, friend."

"I wouldn't say that." The man nicked Harry's throat.

Harry took his life in his very hands and swallowed. "What? You wouldn't say we're at an impasse, or that we're friends?" He felt a hand reach under his coat and pull the small purse from his belt. "I see you found my money, what little there is of it. Well done."

The arm around his throat tensed, ready to strike. "Any last requests?"

"Requests? *Plural?* I can have more than one?"

"Why not?"

The voice at Harry's ear sounded less than sincere, but every second he delayed death was another second of life, and he would take it. "I request that you don't rob me and don't kill me."

The man sighed, his arm relaxing slightly.

"Something wrong?" asked Harry, tremulously.

"Would you believe that no one has ever asked for those before?"

Harry's eyes swivelled, trying to catch a glimpse of this suddenly talkative cutthroat. "Erm... they haven't?"

"No. Not a single one. You're the first to take the offer seriously. They usually just scream."

"So what do you propose we do?" Harry asked, curiosity shouldering its way past his fear.

"Well, if I don't honour it, word will get around."

"Not from me." Harry winced. *Imbecile!* he screamed within his own mind.

"Huh. Good point."

Harry saw no choice but to go for broke. "You're not actually very good at this, are you?"

"Wouldn't say that."

"Wouldn't you? So, these other people——"

"The ones who just screamed?"

"Aye, them. What did you do to them?"

"Had to let them go, didn't I? They were making a hell of a racket."

Harry's face contorted as he tried to work through the logic of that. "So, if I *don't* scream, you'll honour my requests? Both of them?"

"No need. If you keep quiet, I can just kill you and make my getaway. No problem."

"I'm sorry, I'm struggling with the rationale behind this."

"I'm sure you are. It's not easy being a murderous outlaw, you know."

"A bit cutthroat, is it?"

"You've no idea."

"I feel your pain. *Ouch,* and mine. Please be careful with that knife. Yes, sadly, it's the same for small businessmen everywhere – increasing overheads, people forever undercutting you all the time…"

"I find that cutting *under* heads usually does the trick."

"That's good. Funny, even."

"I take pride in my work."

They both turned as they heard sounds of marching feet and the clink of chainmail. Harry winced, nicking his neck again.

"Sorry," his attacker apologised.

"Not at all. My fault."

"Those are soldiers," the man stated the obvious.

"Looking for me," Harry stated the inevitable.

"I should really drop you here and have it away on my toes," the man stated regretfully.

"Can I state…"

"Yes?"

"That I'm against that plan."

"You have another?"

"Sorry, too scared to think. You?"

Harry sloshed a jug of ale down on the table and sat, handing a mug to his assailant. "Good idea to go to the pub instead," he was forced to admit. "These will be on you, I assume?"

"Saving your life not enough, then?" the man retorted, irritably.

"And by saving, you mean not *taking* my life, presumably?" Harry raised his hands to forestall further argument. "Anyway, that's not what I meant. You have my money, remember?"

The man sat back, crossing his arms. "So after all the work I've done, I now have to buy you a drink as well?"

Harry frowned. "You're a very strange cutthroat. Haven't I seen you before somewhere?"

The man shrugged.

Harry continued, "Who are you? Surely, I should know the name of the man who didn't not save me."

Confusion crossed the man's face for a moment. Eventually, he simply replied, "Dick."

Harry sat back himself, affronted. "There was no need for——"

"It's short for Richard."

"What?"

"I said, it's short for——"

"*Dick?*"

"No. Richard."

"I see. You look very familiar now I can see your face, erm, Dick Richard."

"No. It's just Dick *or* Richard. You're getting confused. Mind you, that does have a ring to it. If I ever go back to minstrelsy, I might use that professionally."

Harry studied his one-time murderer. "You used to be a minstrel?"

The question went unanswered as Harry's drinking partner was clearly in a world of his own. "Dick Richard. Yeees, got a ring of gold to it, that has. If I ever get back with the Scarecrows…"

"The scarecrows?"

"It's what we called ourselves – my troupe. We had to split up. Egos, you know. Dick Richard and the Scarecrows," he tried it out again.

"And now you lurk in the shadows——"

"The *Shadows!* I like that! Dick Richard in the Shadows."

"*And.* Surely you mean *and,* not *in* the shadows. Is that a blind spot with you?"

"What d'you mean?"

"Well, you said earlier, your money *and* you die. Clearly you meant *or* you die."

"*Or* the Shadows," Dick spoke thoughtfully. "I'm not sure that tracks, but I'll consider it. Thanks." He smiled and clunked his beaker to Harry's, spilling the drink all over him.

Harry grimaced, wiping frothy ale from his groin. "You're welcome. Look, we probably shouldn't stay here too long."

"Got somewhere to be?"

"No, it's just that the watch are after me for a crime I didn't commit, and now you've tried to murder me, they'll probably be after you for a crime *you* didn't commit, either."

"You think so?"

"Well, I mean you're a... well, whatever you are."

"A singer?"

"The other thing."

"A singer named Dick Richard?"

"More a *cutthroat* named Dick."

"But I didn't cut your throat."

"Actually, you nicked me twice, but I take your point. Anyway, you still robbed me! Look, are you *sure* we haven't met before, Dick? You seem very familiar. Throughout your *illustrious* career, have you ever gone by any other names?"

Dick looked shifty. "Well, in my younger days," he leaned forward conspiratorially, "I was known for a time as Bobby."

"Bobby?"

"It's short for Robert."

"I know what it's short for..." Harry trailed off, shock registering on his face. In the low light from the tavern's fire, Dick seemed not to have noticed. "Where are you from, Bob——— Dick?"

"It's Dick."

Harry laughed, an involuntary, nervous sound as the pennies began to drop. Memories surfaced, out of context, but there was definitely something about Dick he recognised. "If we formed a troupe, we could call ourselves Bob, Dick and Harry," he deflected.

"There are only two of us."

"True. Can you play *and* sing?"

Dick leaned forward, a flash of anger in his eyes. "Look here, there is no Bob, Harry. Not any more. Do you have trouble keeping up?"

They both turned as the tavern door opened, letting all the heat out as a blast of freezing cold air stormed in. "*Shut the door,*" came a general cry from the customers, sheltering from the frigid February evening.

"I'll shut your faces in a minute!" bellowed the sergeant-at-arms.

Harry turned his collar up. "Let's go," he hissed.

"Those aren't the ones that were chasing you," Dick explained.

"Like that matters?" Harry could hardly believe his ears; had this criminal no street sense? "They all saw two men running, and they're after me already. Even those morons will make *that* connection. Aren't they after you anyway?"

"Me? Why?"

"You're a cutthroat. You know, an outlaw. Aren't you known to them?"

"Well, I've not been in the game that long."

"The game?"

"I'm more sort of what you'd call a..."

"A what?"

"A singer," Dick replied in a small voice.

"You had a knife at my throat!"

"I was a hungry singer."

Harry leaned forward furiously. He was furious at the world, and he was furious at himself, for being stupid enough to get mugged by this fool and drawn out into a public place – the very thing he had spent most of the day trying to avoid. "You'll bloody well sing when they show you the thumbscrews! Now, may I suggest we——"

He stopped berating Dick as a shadow fell across them. "Hello, boys."

Chapter 7
Dave

H is cart had two wheels. They were not of a size, which gave it a tendency to wander to the right, causing a menace for fellow travellers on a busy street. Oncoming traffic rarely guessed where it would end up and were frequently hit. This often led to bruising, crushed toes and much cursing. Dave liked it that way.

The way he saw it, these were *his* streets. After all, he was only the one who ever cleaned them. Though, clean is of course a highly subjective term. What Dave actually did, was pick up rubbish left behind that *he* considered useful. No one would be silly enough to actually *clean* the streets, not even an aging street waif like Dave. At least, everyone in Warmstirrup assumed he was aging. So caked in years of filth was he, as to make scrutiny impossible – not that anyone wanted to scrutinise Dave. People parted to make way for him. That is to say, the ones fortunate enough to guess where his cart was headed made way – the rest made for the nearest stream to bathe, for Dave was surrounded by an invisible bubble of disease. The fact that he suffered virtually everything going had a nulling effect on all his ailments, as they cancelled one another out.

With his apothecary's hat on, Harry often suspected that if he cured any one of Dave's problems, the imbalance would probably kill him. Just now, he had his fugitive's hat on. A figurative term because, in truth, he would have given everything he no longer had for *any* kind of hat that evening. When he burst out into the back alley, it was freezing. For the second time in as many days he had been forcibly ejected from a tavern – this time, exiting backwards through the wall. He was extremely lucky that it was only made of wattle and daub. Dick followed him through the hole at a dive. No sounds of merriment drifted out after them this time, only the sounds of anger, frustration and violent intent.

"Run!" Dick grabbed Harry by the scruff and together they scarpered for their lives. Sounds of pursuit were on their heels within seconds, when they turned a corner right into Dave's cart.

"Aargh!" Harry cried in agony as his ribs crashed against its sides.

"Come on!" Dick reached for him again, but the soldiers arrived and grabbed Harry first.

One of the men cried out, doubling up. Dick renewed his efforts to drag Harry away and they ran again, this time followed by a hue and cry. Even Dave was shouting, unintelligibly, but he was certainly giving his all.

"What did you do?" Harry's voice was a rasp.

"What did *I* do? What did *you* do? Never mind. Run!"

"It's murder, my lord," the sergeant-at-arms reported with relish. "My man died within minutes of being pricked by that knife Harry-the-Cough was carrying."

The earl acted as though he were lost within a daze or a fugue.

"My lord?"

Matty could not believe her ears either. "Harry? Stabbed a guard? Impossible!"

"Who are you? Hang on, I know you. You're that little strump——"

"That little *advisor* to Lord Henry," Matty retorted coldly, cutting him off. When entertaining from the lower orders, the earl believed in levelling up – if ever so briefly – so Matty wore one of the expensive dresses he kept for such occasions. She looked every inch the lady of the castle.

The sergeant-at-arms made to move, but two of the earl's private guard crossed their halberds[1] in front of him. Matty crossed her arms indolently as she raised an eyebrow and smiled. "Tell him, Henry."

The earl nodded, though he was certainly not himself – docile, even. The sergeant-at-arms was immediately suspicious of witchcraft. He dared not speak out, what with the weapons pointed at his lower regions, so he merely nodded.

Matty took a step closer. "Now tell me what happened."

"My men caught up with The Cough and he stuck one of 'em."

"Stuck one of 'em, *what?*"

His face contorted, like he had been forced to eat the contents of Dave's cart. "Stuck one of 'em... my lady."

"That's better. However, you're lying. Harry-the-Cough would never kill anyone. What really happened, Sergeant-at-arms? Don't make these gentlemen get impolite."

"It's the truth!" He looked scandalised.

Matty's frown darkened.

"*My lady,*" he added quickly. "It's the truth, I swear. We all saw it happen."

"We?" Matty made the point of looking around the man to the empty hall behind him.

"My men are still out looking for him."

---

1. A battle axe and pike mounted on a shaft about six feet (1.8 metres) long. Used through the 13th, 14th, 15th and 16th centuries. They also commonly had an 'up and under spike' for reaching the places a common spear would not, so the sergeant-at-arms kept very still.

She coughed.

"Out looking, *my lady*. They all saw it. Dave, too."

"Dave? Mad Old Dave with the cart, Dave?"

He nodded.

"*Right*. Well, that clears everything up. You'll forgive me if I don't have him brought here for questioning."

The sergeant-at-arms swallowed. He looked hopelessly to the earl. "What are your orders, my lord?"

"Lord Henry has a new task for you," Matty continued speaking for their master. "One I'm sure you will be good at, Sergeant-at-arms. I wish – that is, our *lord* wishes – Felix L'Éternuement interrogated. After you brought him in, we made him safe. In the castle dungeons. He's there now. Crying. Understand, we don't want him tortured, but feel free to show him some of the devices they have down there." She patted the man companionably on the arm. "You'll enjoy that."

He nodded and bowed his way out of the chamber, but rather than head straight for the dungeons, the sergeant-at-arms first made for the small room Bodges kept. He banged on the door with all the weight of his authority.

Bodges opened it a crack. "Erm, yes?" he enquired, sheepishly.

"Bodges, what's wrong with..." He stopped shouting and looked around, furtively, continuing in a low voice – a struggle for him. "What's wrong with the earl?"

Dave wheeled his ungainly cart through the night. It began to snow. Not the sort of evening for leaving the comparative shelter of town for the pitch-black forest, but he had a delivery to make. It was already late.

Late.

Something still alive within him enjoyed that little joke.

"Who goes there?" The challenge came from the guard at the town's main gate, but it was half-hearted – his mate, keeping their small brazier from getting lonely, never even left the guard room.

Dave replied with a rambling, grunting rant.

"Oh, it's you, Dave. Carry on. I mean, pass, friend."

Dave grumbled some more as he passed out into the night.

Insane Alice stoked her small fire. Something was afoot – she could feel it. Something that should not be there, something *wrong*. She sniffed here and there, for effect. It was a silly thing to do, and she began coughing immediately as smoke from the fire went up her nose. She liked to keep her 'mad old crone' moves polished, but there was such a thing as overdoing it. She was, after all, alone – or was she?

She turned to the door. "I know you're there, dear. You'd better come in."

The door creaked open, slowly. Painfully slowly. Then began to close again, as if on its own. "Invisible?" she asked out. "Hardly sporting, dear."

The door creaked open again. "No, dear." The reply, real or faked, was that of another old crone. "I just wanted to hear that door again. Marvellous effect. You really must tell me where you don't buy your oil."

Insane Alice nodded as one professional to another, accepting the compliment. "Perhaps you should close it, dear. I may not be as decrepit as I pretend, but I must confess to feeling the chill more than I used to."

The other crone of indeterminate age stepped fully inside, closing the door courteously behind her. "Hello, Insane Alice. I am——

"I know who you are, dear."

The visitor nodded respectfully. "I congratulate you, dear."

"And I thank you, but though I know who you are, I know not why you're here."

The crone smiled, showing all gaps. "Oh, but I think you do, Alice. I think you've been expecting me for some time. You have, after all, been hiding him from me, have you not?"

Insane Alice smiled, the firelight completely failing to sparkle off her remaining brown stumps. "Why don't you take some mulled wine? Just the thing for keeping out the cold on nights like these."

"Thank you, Alice, but I think not. You understand."

"Of course, dear." Insane Alice slid the phial of poison back up her sleeve. "Well, will you not at least take a seat with me?"

"Aye, that I can do."

It was Alice's turn to smile again. "It's good to talk. Now," she sat with an exaggerated grunt and sigh, "who's this I'm meant to be hiding here?"

"Oh, no, dear. Not here. I never said you were hiding him here."

"Him?"

The visitor leaned forward into the firelight, locking eyes and showing the full disingenuousness of her sincerity. "I'd just like to shake your hand, Alice. I've heard so much about you."

Insane Alice pulled her hands away. "Perhaps not. You understand," she returned the barb.

"Of course, dear. I'll be sure to do the same for you one day."

They smiled, together, not showing their teeth – they hardly had any left.

"I know he lives in Warmstirrup," the stranger began.

"Do you?"

"Oh, yes. It took a long time to find him. I was in a bad way for a while, you see – occupational hazard. He has something of mine, and I'd like it back now."

"This man stole from you, dear? How careless of you."

The visitor's gaze hardened. "Hardly. I gave it to him, shall we say, for safekeeping – knowing that I would be going away."

"Going away," Alice repeated, the twinkle of a smile reaching her eyes at last. "Yes. I heard about that. How awful for you, dear. Now, what makes you think that I know anything about this man?"

"I hear things. Little birdies speak to me now and again, you know how it is."

"Blackbirds?"

"Crows."

"Nice."

"Thanks. But when I cast my mind's eye across Warmstirrup, somehow, he vanishes. Yet I have it on the very best authority that he's there. Now, why would that be, dear?"

Alice spread her hands, a disarming gesture that made her visitor tense for an attack. "Without knowing who you seek, I'm afraid I cannot help you, dear. As for *casting* your eye, that sounds like witchcraft – you should be careful."

Without leaving their seats, they were nevertheless circling each other like cats.

"Should I? But, I ask myself, should the earl's men storm in here, who would be more exposed – the traveller in the night, who comes and goes, or the woman who lives here?"

Alice stiffened. "I don't enjoy being threatened in my own home, dear."

"Of course you don't, dear, who would? It must be *almost* as annoying as being blocked from fulfilling one's righteous quest."

"*Righteous?* Oh, you should have said. If it's righteousness you seek, I understand the brothers always offer a warm welcome."

"Would that be the brothers of Aynlton Priory?"

"I believe they pronounce it *Ant'n*," Alice elucidated.

"But I've seen it written in the manor records as——"

"Yes, I know how it's spelt, thank you, dear. The 'Aynl' is contracted."

"Wouldn't that depend on what they've eaten?"

Alice ignored her. "Look, it's a very old name for an earlier Saxon settlement that's now gone – comes from the old English, if you must know. So can we leave it at that, dear? Right, as I was saying——"

"What's *old* English?"

"No idea. Now, as I was *saying*, if it's righteousness you seek, they always offer a warm——"

The visitor startled to cackle. It was a really *good* cackle, too. Insane Alice's annoyance at being interrupted, yet again, fell headfirst into envy. Fortunately, she used the same expression for both, so nothing was given away.

"I'm sure the brothers would offer a *very* warm welcome for the likes of you and me, Alice, hmm?" She looked around as she spoke, taking everything in. "Where is it, dear?"

"Where's what, dear?"

"The other half of the charm. I know you're hiding him, Alice. I've been very patient, out of respect for your reputation – I've learned of your origins – but my patience has limits, and stuff me, if we haven't just reached them."

"More threats?"

"You know how much power a dead body can grant to a spell. The residue of a soul, even an animal soul, is the most potent force in the world."

Alice looked guiltily at the fresh raven corpse hanging from the ceiling. "I find animal souls are the cleanest."

Her visitor nodded. "Perhaps, but have you ever felt the power of a *human* soul?"

Alice's guilt turned to shock and horror. "You wouldn't..."

A creaking noise sounded from outside. The howl of freezing wind through the trees failed to mask it entirely. "Ah, that would be the final ingredient arriving. Don't get up, dear, *I'll* get the door." The visiting crone stood and opened it, just as a man was about to knock. At least, Alice assumed it was a man; in the darkness and under the rags and filth, it was difficult to be sure. "Dave?" she hazarded, for the creature was something of a celebrity throughout the borough.

Dave dropped another disgusting creature onto the floor, halfway across the threshold. He stepped over the body to drag it further in and Alice saw him clearly for the first time.

"How dare you bring that poor creature into my home!"

It was unclear who Alice was talking about, or even to, but the other crone turned assumptively, eyes alight with a merciless triumph. "You *invited* me in, dear. Remember?"

The deliveryman was dressed and made up to closely resemble the fresh corpse on the floor – alright, *fresh* might be stretching the definition – but Alice saw through the ruse, nonetheless, recognising him. Shock and disbelief froze her in place for crucial seconds, while her visitor removed a bowl and pestle, secreted about her person. She emptied a small phial into it before stooping quickly, without any sign of creakiness or infirmity, to pluck an eyeball from the corpse so casually discarded. Pounding it to pulp with the pestle, she mixed it into the other contents, cackling and shrieking in an ancient Brittonic tongue as she worked.

"No!" Alice screamed, launching for the other woman, but the stranger expected the attack and threw the contents of the bowl across the room with unerring accuracy straight into the fireplace. Both women dove for the door as the hovel simply detonated.

A creaking alerted the guards at the town gate. This time it was the other man's turn to offer a challenge. He could hear a muttering and cursing. Peering into the darkness, he relaxed. "Ah, it's you, Dave. Pass, friend." The watchman jumped out of the way as the cart lurched towards him, the smaller of its two wheels leaving a track that cut straight through his boot prints in the snow. "You'll have someone's foot off with that cart one of these days, Dave! Dave?" He shook his head in annoyance.

The shambling figure muttered something incoherent mixed with what sounded like rasping, laboured breathing, but could have been mocking laughter.

Crossing into town, 'Not Dave' penetrated the invisible veil between darkness and the world of men, his beggars' rags rendering him invisible on either side.

Chapter 8
One Mistress Too Many

Felix L'Éternuement screamed and hid in the corner, behind the cell's rough sleeping pallet. The sergeant-at-arms stopped in his tracks, barely taking a step inside. Bewilderment quickly turned to a scowl of disdain. The apothecary was quaking before he had even issued any threats. He had been working on some really good ones, too. He shook his head, both disappointed and disgusted – this was going to be no fun at all. "Come," he ordered gruffly. "I want to show you something."

"Show me what?" L'Éternuement whimpered. "I don't want to see anything."

"No, you'll like this. I promise."

L'Éternuement's natural tendency towards greed made him lower his arms from above his head and look up. "Really? What is it?"

"Our suite of torture devices, but don't worry, I'm only going to…"

L'Éternuement fainted. The grisly veteran spat with disgust and bellowed for a couple of guards to help him carry the prisoner to the torture room.

L'Éternuement came round to find himself in a chair; not a comfortable chair, on account of the iron clasps fitted to the arms, but things could have been worse. After all, he was free for the moment, and as yet there were no rusty iron spikes sticking up into his gluteus maximus. He gave a shuddering cry of disgust, pulling his arms in close to his chest. "What do you want from me?"

The sergeant-at-arms interrupted an inspection of a thumbscrew to accord his prisoner the merest withering glance. "Your servant was murdered. Lord Henry wants me to find out what you know about it."

"Nothing. Honestly."

The sergeant-at-arms gave him a Norman look – in Chaucer's Middle Ages, this was considered old-fashioned. "As you can see, Felix – do you mind if I call you Felix? – I have all sorts of little toys and devices for discerning the truth." He clapped a pair of tongs together noisily. They had small cups on the ends, cut into teeth around the rims. "Now, what do you think these are for, hmm? Removing eyes? No? Lower down, perhaps?"

L'Éternuement swooned. The sergeant-at-arms dropped the tongs with a clatter and slapped him harshly about the face. "Wake up, Felix, you lucky lad!" he called out jovially. "You'll miss all the fun. Now, tell me everything, for as sure as my name's Sweet Walter, I'll have it out of you!"

"I don't know anything about Lott's death. I was with Lord Henry when it happened. Ask him! *Please...*"

The sergeant-at-arms turned to the other guard in the room. "Stoke the brazier, Alf. Better heat the pokers."

"Nooo!" L'Éternuement was beside himself, struggling to get out of the chair, but the sergeant-at-arms knocked him back down, securing the clasps about his forearms. Desperate for any kind of a stall, the prisoner asked, "Why do they call you Sweet Walter?"

The guards grinned at each other. "Because of his sweet disposition," the other man explained.

Sergeant-at-arms Walter Sweet guffawed. "You know, while we're waiting for the fire, let's have a look at those fingernails." He flipped a knife, casually, bringing it to bear under the tip of L'Éternuement's left index finger, exerting just the merest pressure. "What beautifully clean nails you have. Hey, Alf. Have you seen these nails? And I thought apothecaries were all about grubbing for herbs and roots to make their cures and stinking concoctions. These hands haven't done much of that."

L'Éternuement just about had the decency to look shamefaced. "I had the lad Lott to do all that. *Someone* took him away from me – remember?"

Walter Sweet considered. "Well, perhaps you can answer another question for me. What could make a man lose his will, to defer completely to another? You must know which herbs could do that."

"I make cures. That sounds more like witchcraft."

"I agree, but you must know the poisons that grow beside the cures in the forest, eh? Let's not be coy, Felix. You're here to answer questions about a murder. This isn't a witch hunt."

"Not yet."

"You believe this, Alf? Cut me to the heart, he has. Why d'you think he doesn't trust us, eh?"

"Dunno, Sarge. Maybe he needs proof of our sincerity?"

"Alf, I think you've hit the nail right on the head there, sunbeam. How are those pokers coming?"

"No. Please!" L'Éternuement cried out in alarm. "I'll tell you anything. *Anything!*"

"Right. Tell me about a potion that can take away a man's will."

"Really, Mr Sweet——"

"I spent twenty years hurting people to be called Sergeant-at-arms. Need a memory jogger, do you?"

"Sorry, Sergeant-at-arms Sweet. I really don't know. May I please see Lord Henry? He will soon tell you that…" He tailed off when Sweet crossed his arms, shaking his head sadly.

Leaning in close enough for the stench of sour ale on his breath to curl L'Éternuement's hair, he spoke in hushed tones. "It's Lord Henry that's gripped by a fugue. So I'll ask again. What can do that to a man? If you really were with the earl when the murder happened, then we need to bring him back to us, to vouch for you, don't we?"

"B-Bodges was there too."

"I wouldn't trust Bodges to know what day of the week it was. Try again."

L'Éternuement whimpered. "I really don't know. Look, I'm not very good at this sort of thing."

Sweet stood back in genuine surprise. "Your flash building and giant fish must have come from somewhere."

L'Éternuement groaned despairingly. "Always the damned fish. Look, I... help myself to other apothecaries' cures. Then I get *another* apothecary to work out how they're made for a share in the product's worth, then I move on. It's how I've amassed my modest fortune."

The guards stared at each other in disbelief. Alf burst out laughing.

"So, just to be clear," Sweet continued, "you've no skill as an apothecary whatsoever – it's all just a sham?"

The prisoner shrugged as best he could with his arms now manacled to the chair. "It's good money, and then there's the women."

Sweet's eyebrows rose another notch up his shallow brow. "Women? I wasn't aware that apothecaries were sought out by the ladies. I mean, look at you. Not exactly champion jouster material, are you?"

Alf chuckled again.

L'Éternuement looked shifty. "You don't understand. Have you any idea what some women will *pay* for a miracle cure, when they have a sick loved one? And, of course, when they run out of money..." He grinned lasciviously.

The guards burst out laughing. As already noted, Lord Henry did not select them for imagination – integrity was low on the list, too.

"So, just to recap. You can't help us with information about the murder, and you can't help us to get Lord Henry back in his senses."

"Sorry." L'Éternuement shrugged again.

"Looks like there's no point in keeping you here, then."

"You'll let me go?" The hope in the merchant's eyes was pathetic.

"Certainly."

"Thank you, sirs. You're both very honourable men."

"We'll let you go... to the next world."

L'Éternuement fainted.

Harry shivered. The woodshed where he and Dick had taken refuge from the watch seemed to funnel draughts through the cracks in its wooden walls, increasing the pressure and making it even colder than it was outside. The north wind cut through the gaps in the rough boarding like a knife. "We can't stay here all night. It'll kill us."

Dick's teeth chattered. "S-so w-what do you suggest?"

Harry thought desperately. He could hardly go back to his shop, and he did not want to bring trouble back to Dora – she had risked enough to help him, without even knowing him, bless her. That left just one place he knew of, where he might find shelter and knew the owner was out, but it was risky. He gave his new companion an appraising look. No. He would have to find out a good deal more about this familiar man before he took him to Matty's empty lodgings. It would be dangerous enough, being directly above his own hovel. Lord Henry was bound to have a watch on the place, but they really would die if they stayed out here.

Mulling their limited options, Harry asked, "Why did you stab that guard?"

"W-what?" Dick looked genuinely surprised.

"When the watch grabbed me. You came back for me – for which I'm grateful, by the way – but did you have to stab him? Surely a kick in the jewels would have done the job. If he dies, they'll be after me for another murder I didn't commit."

Dick was shaking his head. "I've no idea what you're talking about. I grabbed your collar and pulled. There *was* no knife. Look." He passed him the small blade that had so recently been at Harry's own throat. There was no trace of blood on it, but Dick may simply have wiped it. Though Harry had to admit, he had not witnessed him doing so.

"So what did happen then? I saw the flash of a blade in the mêlée and that man fell."

"I didn't see. I was just trying to pull you away. Could the tramp have done it?"

"Dave? Not a chance. He's a pillar of the community."

"Seriously?"

"Enough people have stood on him. Dave's never shown any tendency towards violence, he's just a bit... *different*."

"One of the other soldiers, perhaps?" Dick suggested. "A vendetta hidden in plain sight, that sort of thing?"

"Well, aren't you the devious one? Oh, I don't know," Harry admitted tiredly. "Why do I get the feeling that it's not just Lord Henry who's after me? He, at least, will be honest about it. He thinks I murdered that boy and will hang me – no questions asked. Literally, no questions asked. As long as there's a body on each side of the transaction, he won't care. This is all Fishy Felix's fault. Damn him!"

"Felix?"

"That faker who calls himself an apothecary, up in the new-builds by the castle. You must have seen that damned fish!"

"Why would an apothecary want you out of the way?"

"To steal my business, of course!"

"You're an apothecary?"

Harry looked at his hide-and-seek partner as though he were an idiot. "Who did you think I was?"

"Erm, Harry?"

"Harry-*the-Cough*," Harry elucidated.

"Been ill, have you?"

"Dick."

"Yes?"

"What?"

"You said my name."

"Not that time," Harry explained. "That was just an insult."

They sat in silence.

"Sorry," Dick ventured, after a while.

"For which particular offence?"

He scratched his ear. "Not sure. You just seem to be generally annoyed with me."

Harry sighed. "Look, Bobby..." He froze.

Dick stared back at him, his own brows knitting in thought. "Why did you call me that? No one's called me that since…"

"You were a kid," Harry finished for him, and it all came flooding back – all of it. Memories of childhood summers watching over sheep in the hills and keeping lookout for Scottish raiders. The small wooden toy horse they both loved. Swimming in the village pool. Winters by the fire, listening to elders tell stories of the old days. Pranks aplenty. Now not so skinny, and with a wispy blond beard, but still definitely Bobby.

"Harry?" Dick was clearly having an epiphany of his own. "Hugh and Maud's lad?"

Harry nodded, no longer trusting himself to speak.

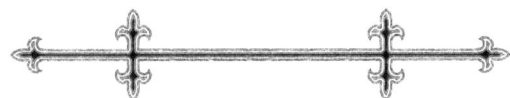

Matty escorted Lord Henry back to his chambers. His condition was beginning to draw attention, while the effects of her potion would soon wear off. She had kept it from Harry, secretly accepting Insane Alice's offer of a 'magic potion to bend any man to your will'. There was enough left for a second dose. More than that and Henry might die, poisoned. She would have a hard time wriggling out from under that, even without damning evidence, but if they found the flask, she would stand no chance at all. One more day, maximum, and she would lose control of her puppet lord. Then she, too, would have to go into hiding. The earl was not a forgiving man at the best of times; once tales abounded that he had been caught under a magic spell, her life would be worth very little. After all, he had not even received what he had paid her for. No. She would have to run for her life, but that would be tomorrow.

She yawned. Right now, she needed sleep. She mixed a little potion with some ale, just enough to keep him under control for the night, and made Henry drink. She would give him the main dose at first light, to get the most from the day. That brute of a sergeant-at-arms would have the information she needed by then.

She was about to lie down when a thought struck her. Was the earl capable of *any* free thought? Surely, parts of his mind were still free to take care of his bodily needs – or perhaps not? She ushered him towards his private garderobe and pointed towards the hole in the wooden seat.

Henry loosened the straps of his trousers and sighed with relief.

Matty covered her mouth to prevent a snigger. She would have to watch out for that tomorrow. It would not do for the earl to embarrass himself in public. That would certainly draw attention to her little enterprise. For that matter, had he eaten anything today? Oops. Never mind, too late now. Besides, with his wealth, there would always be breakfast.

She led him back to the bed and gestured for him to lie down, fully clothed, while she buried herself under the nobleman's warm blankets. It seemed witchcraft had its perks.

Lord Henry was already snoring and Matty smiled. Were he always like that, he would be adorable. Pity the devil awoke inside him each morning.

She unfolded a tatty piece of parchment from inside her chemise. Insane Alice had pressed it into her hand the night before, during her visit to the crone's hovel in the forest. The old woman was insistent that, in order for the magic to work without dangerous and unpredictable side effects, something must be given back to the victim in return. It was all to do with the balancing of powers – Matty did not really understand. Nor could she read. She held the small note up to the candle, but its letters were just squiggles and meaningless to her. She would have asked Harry to read it, but that would have given her plan away, and she knew he would never have let her go through with it. He was much too honourable, and him a peasant, too. She pondered. It was almost as though 'quality' had nothing to do with wealth or lack thereof. Worth was simply not a product of cost.

She folded the scrap of parchment back up and tucked it into Lord Henry's tunic before pinching out the candle. "I pray this brings thee good fortune," she spoke the phrase Insane Alice had given her, quietly. "But not at the expense of me or my friends," she added a caveat of her own.

Yawning again, she pulled at the blankets, pinned down by Henry's weight, and snuggled down, quickly falling asleep.

Insane Alice would get no sleep this night. For one thing, her bed was on fire. In fact, very little remained of her hovel. Years of love and repair, all vanishing heavenwards right before her eyes – and that did not even *begin* to cover her stock. She was furious, but at least she was not cold. Tomorrow night would be a different story.

She screamed a shrill curse. The explosion in her hearth had destroyed the dwelling almost instantly. The two crones had barely cleared the threshold when the roof went up, both rolling in opposite directions away from the flames. The visiting witch had been knocked unconscious instantly upon hitting the ground. Alice had forced her hand, causing her to act so precipitously, but now she had her, and could easily dispatch her while the other was out cold. Yet, it was an offence against the gods for one witch to use her powers against another while their back was turned, or they were incapacitated.

Rage and righteous indignation kept her upright for another minute before Alice, too, succumbed to shock and was forced to sit. She had no idea what had happened to the cartman, but she did know the witch who destroyed her home was Mad Mab, and that Dave was dead. Poor, grumbling, scavenging old Dave who – aside from some questionable driving – had never hurt a soul in his life, but who now lay one-eyed and mutilated, and in all likelihood, burned to cinders on what remained of her hovel's floor.

That led to the realisation that there was likely a near-invisible killer loose in Warmstirrup. Someone so base they were completely below everyone's notice and therefore able to move about with impunity. With that last discomforting thought, Insane Alice passed out, too.

When she awoke, the fire had banked slightly, but was still far too hot to approach. About the only positive to be taken from their altercation was that Mad Mab had also abided by the rule of the gods. She was nowhere to be seen, but having clearly regained her senses first, she could have killed

Alice while she was still unconscious. She had chosen not to.

Insane Alice stared balefully into the flames that swallowed her home, as the roof's centre truss collapsed among a swirling galaxy of sparks.

Mad Mab's integrity was merely fear of the gods, of course. It made her no less Alice's enemy. She pulled her shawl about her shoulders. Her face burned, while her back was icy cold. Her initial fury also cooled, and she began to notice other things – the cramp in her left hand, for example. She unclasped the fingers. In her palm were several strands of black-grey hair. She smiled grimly, tucking them safely into her scrip. "Thought you could be mistress in my territory, did you? In my very home. Well, I have you now, Mab. Name and body, I have you." She would have cackled, but no longer had the heart.

Chapter 9
Bitching Hour

"Stop complaining! And stop snoring!"

"Move your damned foot, then! And *you* stop snoring. I haven't had a wink."

Dick opened a bleary eye. "What time is it?"

"How should I know?"

"Shh. Listen. I can hear a bell."

Harry listened. In the dead of night, Warmstirrup usually fell silent, but for the occasional scream. In the distance they could indeed hear the broken *clank* of the chapel bell at Aynlton Priory. "Matins?" he suggested.

"When's that?"

"Third hour."

Dick huffed and pulled his coat tighter around him for warmth. "Those monks are off their heads."

"I'm sure they're fond of you. Now, for the last time, will you please get your foot out of my ear!"

"It's not my fault. This bed's too narrow. You'd think your friend would have a larger one, considering her job."

Harry-the-Cough coughed, already slightly embarrassed to be using Matty's bed. "I, er... don't think her *guests* tend to stay over. This isn't a boarding house."

"I thought it was?"

"I said *boarding*."

"Oh, right. Harry?"

"Yes?"

"Can I go back to sleep now?"

Sigh. "Bobby."

"It's Dick."

"Ho *ho,* right, sorry – *Dick.*" Harry laughed sarcastically. "We haven't seen each other in over ten years."

"I know, it's been quite an exhausting evening. G'night."

"You don't want to talk about it?"

"I need to think it all through first, Harry."

"Really?"

Snore.

Sigh.

Harry awoke as the first rays of diluted sunshine squelched through the gaps in Matty's shutters. He sat up to rub sleep from his eyes. Pulling his shoulder bag from within the folds of his greatcoat, he placed it on the bed and stood. It may have provided a little extra overnight insulation, but more importantly, the bag also contained everything he still had in the world, and he had no intention of letting it out of his sight.

He looked around the floor and then under the bed. "Ah." Reaching for Matty's pot, he took some small pleasure in putting something into it, rather than being on the receiving end for a change. Sighing with relief, he wondered at the dopamine rush received from the simple act of passing water. The process was beyond his understanding, but he always noted the effect, and at that moment, was happy to take anything that made him feel a little better. Once finished, he got to wondering where Dick might have gone. He had not heard him leave. Harry entertained a vague hope that the man from his past – the man with all his money, he suddenly remembered – might have gone to fetch them some breakfast.

Something had woken him in the night, something other than his general discomfort. He remembered the Matins bell from the priory, and vainly trying to engage his companion in conversation, but perhaps Dick had been right. They were both in need of sleep. Yet something still nagged at him.

The door opened with a clatter that would have been most thoughtless had Harry still been asleep. "Come in," he said, drily.

"You're awake. Good. I'm starving. What's for breakfast?"

Harry rolled his eyes. This man played the cheeky chappy to great effect, but he was still not sure he trusted him. It had been the same when they were children together, in their village. Bobby had been likeable then, too. Though Harry often suspected him of stealing. Of course, when the Scots raided, Bobby had been among the taken. Slavery was rife across the Anglo-Scottish border in those days – and still was, he reflected, if you lived beyond the protection of the large population centres. Harry's father had been cut down in that attack, his mother taken, though as far as he knew, she never even lived long enough to cross the border. Men from Harry's village found her. They spared him the details, young as he was, simply telling him she had been killed trying to escape. Though they did bring back a blue headscarf she wore. He had it still.

He had always assumed Bobby died, too, years ago. Either in that terrible event or from the hardships that must have followed. Slaves rarely lived long, especially through the deadly northern winters, and now here he was, back.

"Where've you been?"

Harry caught a furtiveness to his childhood friend's eye. Only for a moment, but he definitely saw it.

Dick sucked a new cut on his knuckle and grinned. "Needed to go, you know. As in *go* go. Didn't want to stink the place out for you."

That sounded fair enough, even though he showed little thought generally for other people's comfort. Somehow, Harry did not quite believe him. Dick *had* propelled Harry through the tavern wall, enabling them to escape. He had also come back for him, when the watch caught them. That was something, but was it enough to cement a trust? Harry had no doubt his childhood friend had become used to thinking on his feet *and* making it away on his toes. He could even believe Dick had led a hard life – though how he became a travelling singer, the Lord only knew. If that part was even true.

"Wassup?"

Dick broke into Harry's thoughts, and he realised he was frowning with suspicion. "Oh, nothing. We can't stay here. I don't want to drag Matty any further into this."

"So what's your plan?"

"I need to find out who killed Lott."

"Who?"

Again, Harry thought Dick answered just a little too quickly. "The boy who was murdered. The one they're trying to pinch me for."

"And how do you propose we do that?"

"Well, I think the first thing we need to find out is *why* he was killed." A shadow crossed Harry's face.

Dick saw it. "What's wrong?"

"Nothing. Just remembering. I've said some pretty hard words about that boy over the last few months. Now he's been killed, horribly, and I can't help feeling guilty for them. And thanks for the *we*, by the way."

"I suppose that's only natural when someone is killed because of you," Dick replied, oblivious to Harry's gratitude.

Anger flushed Harry's face. "What do you mean, *because* of me?" Again, that dishonest look flickered in Dick's eyes, if only for a second.

"Nothing. I mean, I just assumed, if you're feeling guilty about it. So you really had nothing to do with it, then?"

"Of course not!" Harry fired up, though he suspected Dick's comment had been a mere deflection to cover his mistake. He knew, or at least suspected, something. "What do *you* know about all this?"

"Me? Nothing. Haven't been here long."

"No, you haven't, have you? Just how long *have* you been here?"

"Few days, maybe. Why are you asking all these questions? I feel like I'm being trepanned!"

"Alright, alright. Come on. We're not going to discover anything here. Shut the door properly behind us, will you? I don't want anyone else availing themselves of Matty's place." He made his way past Dick and down the back steps, all the while checking around him for prying eyes. Opening his own back door, as quietly as he could, he stopped just inside the threshold. Blinking into the gloom, his jaw fell open. He never had much by way of possessions or furniture, but now he seemed to have nothing at all. Every stick of it had been smashed. He could only assume Lord Henry's soldiers had been through the place looking for clues to where he may have gone.

Harry sighed, completely dispirited, and was about to leave when he noticed marks on what remained of his upturned workbench. He strode across the hovel's single room and knelt to look closely. Spatter. More precisely, blood spatter, and next to it a small sigil scribbled in charcoal. He wiped his finger through the blood. Still wet.

"Looks like the soldiers had a smashing time," Dick said from the door behind him, echoing Harry's own first impressions. He noted again that Dick was sucking his knuckle.

"What have you done to your hand?"

"Oh, nothing. Just caught it on a fence when I hopped over to… you know." He gave the two-tone whistle often used by the English to denote defecation like it was somehow a musical event. Harry shoved all thoughts of panpipes aside, focusing his mind on the puzzle before him. Dick could not possibly have smashed his place up without waking him in the room above – the damage was too complete – but Harry still believed he had been in there. After all, the blood on his bench was still fresh – who else could it belong to? It had barely begun to coagulate – or in Harry's parlance, thicken and dry. *I wonder if there's a way to identify blood from individuals,* he pondered, distractedly. However, the more immediate question was, what had Dick been looking for amongst the wreckage?

Matty had also been awoken at three in the morning, the calamity having roused everyone in the keep – all shouting, arguing and accusing one another. Lord Henry had arisen a little foggy, but showed signs of coming back to himself, so Matty had acted quickly; her hopes for another whole day to move around the castle dashed when she was forced to give him the last of Insane Alice's potion four hours early. On the other hand, her quick action probably saved her life.

There had been no returning to sleep after that, and now, several hours later, with the dawn light gaining strength through the great hall's high windows, Matty stood behind Henry's chair on a raised dais at the head of the chamber. Lord Henry himself sat glassy-eyed but present as Sergeant-at-arms Walter Sweet explained his findings.

"My lord, our guards at the gate were found this morning with their throats cut, the gates left wide open until the change in the watch at the third hour. We know we have it right, because the Matins bell was heard from the priory." He glared long and hard at Matty, making her even more uncomfortable.

"Continue, Walter," she encouraged, trying to shake off his stare.

He nodded slowly, narrowing his eyes. "That was also when that... that *atrocity* was found outside my lord's chambers. The entrails of an animal of some kind. It's witchcraft!" He raised his voice, causing a low murmur to gust through the hall, from the lowest serving-wench to the most senior knight. A twinkle came to Sweet's eye; it was the exact response he had been hoping for. "Witchcraft, I say!" He made sure all the same.

Matty was terrified, though she dared not show it. Would the sergeant-at-arms be bold enough to draw attention to his lord's *lack* of attention? If he did, and Henry's knights supported his appraisal, she was dead. Her mind worked frantically. She had to take control and hope her bluster was enough to keep everyone in line. The one thing she had going for her was that the knights present were unknown to her, biblically or otherwise. No one else would dare speak. Not until Lord Ralph of Warmstirrup, Henry's brother, arrived from Parkworth Castle, just a few miles south. Until then, she was obviously high in Henry's favour – or so it appeared. She could use that.

"My lords, gentlemen, my lord Henry would have this murderer found

– and swiftly."

"Certainly, my *lady*." Sweet bowed, mockingly. "And we all know who the villain is, don't we? Your friend Harry-the-Cough is good with a knife, isn't he?" He turned to the knights seated at the highest table just below Henry's. "My lords, another of my men was stabbed and done to death while trying to apprehend the rogue apothecary last eve."

The nobles shared uneasy glances. One of them spoke, a young Scot of the mighty Douglas clan who ruled much of the land just north of the border. Technically a prisoner held for ransom, he hunted, hawked and whored with the rest of the local nobility, as was the way of things in medieval high society. A particularly superstitious young man, he crossed himself before speaking. "Ye ken this apothecary's a witch, Sergeant-at-arms?"

"They have hidden knowledge, my Lord of Douglas – some might say, *forbidden* knowledge."

The young Scot nodded agreement.

Matty was frantic. This was the very last thing she wanted. Sweet was loving it, too. In fact, she would not have put it past him to have left those entrails outside Henry's chambers to be found – strictly to implicate her in what would soon be a witch hunt, she felt sure. Even more worrying were the dead soldiers. Surely, even Sweet would not have gone that far to stir up trouble, but if not he, then who?

Things were turning nasty indeed. Having given the order to arrest Felix L'Éternuement in Henry's name, she had hoped to deflect their attention from her friend, hopefully clearing him altogether. Now matters were worse, for Harry and for her, and it was all because of that devil, Sweet. Her eyes narrowed. "Sergeant-at-arms, Lord Henry wishes you to send soldiers into the town to search for those men's killer, or killers. This can't possibly have been the work of Harry-the-Cough, so don't send them haring off in the wrong direction," she added, pointedly, although she doubted it would do any good. "Once you have dispatched your men, call upon our lord in his private chambers. He has awoken with a griping of the bowel this morning, and tires of this."

Sweet opened his mouth to speak, changing his mind at the last moment. He nodded, turned and left.

Matty made Henry's excuses and led him back to his chambers, though she could not help but spot the quizzical look on young Douglas' face as she led the earl away. His eyes followed her all the way out, full of suspicion. She affected not to notice, but it rattled her nerves still further. Douglas may have seen an opening for his own escape, if Henry was incapacitated in some way; though he was just as likely to move against Matty, having far more in common with his enemy than a peasant girl, who would be lady of the house. Matty moved with all sorts in her work, and could affect the role of consort, but the masquerade would not last long. She *had* to get out of this viper's nest.

Closing the door to Henry's chamber behind them, she served him some wine. *I hope Harry has found a good hiding place and stays well away from home,* she thought frantically.

"Do you think we should still be here?" asked Dick, looking around Harry's back yard nervously. "Only, the daylight's brightening by the minute and anyone watching——"

He stopped as a scream from the top of Scrubber Alley shattered the morning silence.

"Run!" hissed Harry.

Dick hardly needed telling twice. Things were truly desperate for them now, so desperate in fact, that Harry was seriously entertaining a crazy idea that had been forming in the back of his mind for most of the night. "This way."

He led them through the hole in the fence, grabbing a broken plank on the way through. As he expected, the Red Baron was waiting for him. Done with his morning crow, the little devil was looking forward to a little pecking and ordering before breakfast. Harry hurled the broken plank in a flat spin towards the Baron's head. He hated to do it. After all, times were hard and timber was hardly chicken feed. Nevertheless, he aimed straight for the beak. The cockerel leapt into the air in a burst of agitation and plumage, immediately summoning his wingwomen for a counter-attack.

Harry ran by, jabbing a finger at him. "Next time, you little git!"

Dick slowed in amazement, baffled by his associate's sudden and seemingly gratuitous attack. Harry's murder most fowl seemed to fail – though he almost got one of them – but with no time for questions, Dick simply followed him through into New Row.

This time, Harry checked left and right, as Matty had the day before. The way clear, he crossed the road and disappeared down the alley almost opposite. Before following, Dick turned to see a highly agitated group of chickens fluttering and squawking, literally hopping mad, at the boundary of their territory. Dick blew out his cheeks and ran after Harry, eventually arriving in Dark Lane.

Harry steered them well clear of Cutthroat's Way, instead heading straight into the wooded copse that ran adjacent to Dark Lane's south side. The foliage thickened towards the centre, so he hid as best he could and took a moment to look around, listening intently. Whatever, or whoever, had caused that scream back in Scrubber Alley did not seem to be following them. At least, not yet.

"I've got an idea," he whispered.

Dick did not speak, simply nodding for him to explain.

"We need to get through here to Traitor's Lane——"

"Why do all the streets in your town have such awful names?" Dick interrupted.

"It's where they used to hang criminals in a cage from a gibbet for the crows——"

"And you want *us* to go there?"

"It was all built over years ago. The town never stops spreading. I dare say we'll run out of countryside one day. All the towns will just meet up in one great mess of..." He stopped himself with a shudder. "Look, never mind all that. Traitor's Lane leads into the forest to join the main south road. I know a cut-through that leads somewhere known only to a very select few. Somewhere we might be able to hide out for a while – maybe pay for our keep."

"I don't have much money left," Dick replied, doubtfully.

"*You* don't have any." Harry snatched the purse, *his* purse, still tied at Dick's belt. "Mine. You're not a cutthroat, remember? Besides, I don't think the person we're going to ask for help has much use for pennies."

"So how shall we pay him?"

"Her. We'll have to work it off."

Dick paled. "Can't we hide somewhere else?"

"You fancy taking your chances in the town with half an army looking for us? Come on."

Matty jumped at the knock on Henry's door. She moved to open it, just a crack. Outside were two of Henry's personal guards and the hated Walter Sweet, Sergeant-at-arms. She soured. "You'd better come in. Leave your sword out here. You two, come in with us."

Once his weapon was unbuckled and leaned against the wall, she opened the door and moved back to Henry's side as the three men followed her in.

Sweet bowed, grinning indolently. "My men are out with instructions to kill Harry-the-Cough on sight, and now I return as ordered, my *lady*."

Muscles bunched in Matty's jaw. How she hated that loathsome bully, but she shoved it aside. There was one last thing she could do for Harry before they would all have to leave town. Once Lord Henry came to his senses, he would hunt them ruthlessly. *We'll be lucky to find safety in a cave, halfway up a mountain in Cumberland after this,* she thought hopelessly.

She straightened to her full, if diminutive, height. "Tell me everything you learned from the apothecary, L'Éternuement." Low born or not, Matty had the bearing of a lady and wore the dress of a noblewoman. Henry's guards bowed as they were programmed to do. Sweet, odious grin still painted in place, made a second *disingenuflection*.

"The only thing we found of note, my *lady*, was that he's no apothecary."

Matty's surprise distracted her completely from his insolence. "Explain," she demanded.

"He steals all his tricks and remedies from others. He's a total fraud!" He was laughing now. "Uses other apothecaries to crack one another's secrets and profits by the knowledge of a whole profession. Man's a genius. Have you seen his house? Knocks the few grubby pennies we earn sick, doesn't it? Me from killing men, and street rubbish like you, from humping them."

Matty was used to this kind of talk, and far worse, but then it struck her like a lightning rod from the heavens. She no longer had to take it. At least, not *that* morning. The Lord knew there would be a price to pay for what she had done here, so why not wield power one last time before she was stripped of it forever. Her eyes narrowed. "Sergeant-at-arms, hand me the knife at your belt."

Sweet was perturbed by the request, but with two heavily armed men right behind him, each unswervingly loyal to Lord Henry – who sat useless in a cushioned chair, staring at Matty like a puppy fighting sleep – he had little choice but to acquiesce.

His knife in her hand, Matty ordered, "Guards, take this man to the dungeons and throw him in the pit."

Even the usually emotionless guards struggled to hide their surprise. "The oubliette, lady?"

"Why not? The earl tires of this man's insolence, don't you, my lord?"

Henry nodded dully and that was enough. Sweet vanished from the room in a whirl of fists and feet to disappear noisily down the stone spiral stairs.

Allowing herself a smile, Matty closed the door quite deliberately behind him and returned to the earl. She bent and gave him a kiss on the cheek. "Thank you, my lord. If only I could keep you. What a life I could carve for myself and those I care about." She sighed with genuine regret. "Ah, the bittersweet of something good coming to an end." Her smile turned to a smirk. "Sweet will certainly be good and bitter about his end, anyway."

A thought struck her and she bent once more to place a hand over Henry's heart, if he had such a thing. "I don't know if this will work, but I trust..." She stopped herself from mentioning Insane Alice, just in case. "When you awaken, call off any pursuit of myself and Harry-the-Cough." It was worth a try; who knew what magic Alice had concocted to influence the man, or how strong it might be. There was just the chance her words might be remembered – heeded, even.

Her hand grew suddenly hot. She pulled back with a sharp intake of breath. Not understanding what had just happened, it frightened her. She strode across the chamber to Henry's money chest. It was locked. To her surprise, she turned to find Henry taking the key from around his neck. He held it, and the silver chain upon which it hung, out to her.

She took it and quickly unlocked the chest, gawking at the wealth in gold, jewels and plate within. If there was ever a moment in her life when she was tempted, that was surely it. However, she knew the ramifications would be spread around the whole town and Henry's manors all over England. Should she clean him out, thousands would pay to refill the coffer before her. Many would starve. She slipped a small bag of silver coins into her chemise and relocked the chest with a sigh. The silver was more wealth than she had ever seen – it was time to be content. She and Harry would certainly need it if they were to escape.

Hanging the key back around Henry's neck, she tucked it into his jacket. As she unfastened the top buttons, she caught sight of Insane Alice's tattered parchment. It was singed at the edges. Hands shaking, she rebuttoned his jacket and ordered him to lie on the bed and fall asleep.

He fell into heavy slumber immediately.

"Wish I could do that," she thought aloud.

It was still early. The kitchens would be bringing food into the great hall, where most of the garrison would break their fast. This would be her best chance to leave the castle unnoticed.

Felix L'Éternuement had lived through the worst night of his life. Even worse than that night in Lichfield, where he had pronounced a woman's husband dead, only for him to come very much back to life, while he was collecting his fee from the widow. That had been quite an evening, yet he remained unabashed and unashamed. Indeed, L'Éternuement was a man who shunned shame. Guided by avarice and motivated by fear, he was usually someone else's problem. The way he saw it, that was the natural order of things, but a night in the castle dungeons had shown him the 'other man's perspective'. He was not an enthusiast.

Some may have spent the night in penitence, praying for a chance to mend their ways, but the only mending L'Éternuement prayed for was a way to *fix* Harry-the-Cough – a man he saw as far too lucky for his own or anyone else's good. Having personally done everything in his power to engineer Harry's downfall, it was a perspective only such a man as Felix L'Éternuement could nurture, and he grew it by the bagful.

He heard a door scrape open at the top of the stone steps that led down to the dungeons. Getting up from the filthy, lice-infested sleeping pallet in the corner of his cell, he looked out of the small, barred window in the door.

A cackling came from the next cell; some mad old crone Lord Henry had obviously long ago forgotten about. Whenever the door opened it set her off. She had kept him awake half the night casting 'spells' on him. He shook his head in disgust. "Shut your mouth, you rancid old dragon!"

When the shouting began, it was as though a choir of angels visited unto L'Éternuement. The loudest voice, he instantly recognised as Walter Sweet. Bursting into view, the sergeant-at-arms rode a wave of violence down steps slick with groundwater and slime, to arrive in a dishevelled heap at the bottom – but the good news did not end there. Once the guards caught up, Sweet was dragged, struggling and swearing, straight past the cells and down towards the hole.

L'Éternuement grinned broadly. He was never a man so down on his luck that he failed to take pleasure in someone else's misfortune. "Hey, Sweet Walter, don't forget to write!"

On the way back from dropping off their cargo into a deep, yet very small hole in the ground, the guards stopped outside L'Éternuement's door. "Step back," the one known as Alf ordered – and Creation just kept giving...

Alf had a ballooning eye, already deep blue, and a bleeding mouth, but more importantly, he managed to grunt a few words around his also swelling lips. Beautiful words. "You're free to go. Get out!"

L'Éternuement almost danced up the treacherous stairway. At the top, they exited through a thick oak door into a guard chamber within one of the towers. The outer door to the courtyard was before him and already open. He shielded his eyes against the relative glare, though it was a glorious sight. He had had more than his fill of dungeons and mad old dragons. Threatening skies or no, he stepped out into that frosty February morning with an April spring in his stride.

He almost capered past the guards at the gate. A lesser man in his jubilant state might have offered them a free ticket for a jar of guaranteed, high-performance enhancement, but always thrifty, L'Éternuement was never that man. However, the notion was not wasted on him. In a flash of inspiration, the entire concept of vouchers began unpacking within his mind – including, but not limited to, the *gift* voucher. Bought from an apothecary, it would be like a form of insurance against ill health. Now there was a thought...

He kicked his heels together and laughed as he strolled out into a brave new world, and towards his luxury home at the very top of Line Street, where it became Dispensary Road. Despite his outrageous good fortune, he was still determined to get justice for his hardships endured. What was it to him if it was Her day off?

Not Dave watched him go. No one ever noticed Dave when he was alive, except when his cart veered in their direction. *Not* Dave had chosen the perfect cover.

Instructions carried out to the letter, he waited as ordered, to monitor Lord Henry's response. So far, his brutal night attack had failed to yield any. The trying – and especially the burning – of witches was a huge crowd-pleaser. Had castle staff apprehended one, they would have made sure half the town knew about it by now. A good burning showed diligence on behalf of the authorities and made the people feel safer – it also put a few pennies in the pockets of all the street vendors, thanks to the 'great family day out' a burning always encouraged – but there had been no word from the castle at all, suggesting the girl had *not* been arrested.

Until he had further orders, Not Dave would simply watch and wait. He would doubtless be summoned as soon as another plan was hatched for drawing Harry-the-Cough from his hiding place.

Chapter 10

Death, Death or Death

"I've got to say, at the moment, I'm not loving our options," Harry complained, bitterly. A deciduous copse in mid-winter was not proving the best of hiding places. There were practically no leaves overhead, but the sky compensated by depositing snow all over them. Dick sneezed.

Harry groaned. "Turn away, man. Honestly."

"Sorry."

"Have you never heard the saying 'coughs and sneezes spread diseases', hmm?"

"No. What's that mean, then?"

"It means... it means... Look, just don't cough or sneeze over me, understand?"

"Always so bad-tempered. You're not the only one freezing to death out here, you know."

"Yes, well, there's every chance I *will* freeze to death, or be caught by

Lord Henry's more murderously enthusiastic employees. I don't need you sneezing your... your corruption all over me, as well."

Dick looked genuinely taken aback. "You know, a priest once told me that when you cough or sneeze," he continued, conversationally, "you let out the little demon that was working on your innards. So how bad can that be?"

"Really? That's lovely. Thanks for sharing."

"The story or the demon?"

"Both!"

"Honestly, there's no talking with you at the moment, Harry. When do you plan on leaving here to find our paradise in the woods?"

Harry scratched his stubble. "I don't know. I was hoping for more cover, but you're right. We can't stay here."

"I am?" Dick brightened.

"Don't let it go to your head." Harry looked around nervously. "I can almost hear the sharpening of a scythe."

"What's that?"

"Oh, nothing. Come on. Try to stay low, and please be *quiet*."

Matty dared not go home, so she went to Dora's hovel. Dora answered the door looking tired, but managed to greet Matty with a smile; her first in a while.

Matty shot past, closing the door quickly behind her. "You look better. A lot better!" She hugged her friend.

"I slept right through last night," Dora agreed. "I'm still exhausted, but I think the fever has left me. Your friend Harry's a clever lad. Send him my way if you're not interested."

Matty grinned. "You *are* feeling better. And who said I wasn't interested?"

"Sorry." Dora smiled again. "I thought my time was up. What can I do for you?"

"I need somewhere to stay for a little while – I can pay you."

"No you won't, Matty. I owe you so much already. Why can't you go home? Has that Harry got you into trouble?"

"Not exactly. Well, sort of. It was my own doing. Haven't seen him, have you?"

"No, but I've heard lots of soldiers tramping up and down Cutthroat's Way. The watch doesn't normally come down here – it's bad for their health. What's going on?"

"Trust me, the less you know, the better. I'm going to have to leave Warmstirrup for a while."

Dora looked bereft. "When?"

"Soon. Very soon, but only for a while," Matty placated. She turned away. "I wish I knew where Harry was holed up."

"I could go out and ask around," Dora suggested.

"Not in your condition. You'll catch your death – again."

Dora looked worried. "The soldiers are after you as well, aren't they? You can stay here as long as you need to, you know that."

Matty embraced her again. "Thanks, but I must find Harry. He's in far worse trouble than I am. When Lord Henry wakes up…"

"Wakes up?" Dora grinned. "It's getting on for noon. What did you do to him?"

Matty shrugged ruefully. "Not what *you* think. I just hope he doesn't remember too much about it. I'm fairly sure the castle staff will try to stay out of it. He's an ogre!"

A knock at the door made them both jump. They held onto each other instinctively. "Who is it?" Dora called out weakly.

"Jack."

Matty flashed a questioning look.

"It's alright," Dora whispered. "He's sort of a friend."

"Sort of?"

"It'll be alright, trust me."

Matty had misgivings, but little choice, as Dora opened the door to let the young man in.

He embraced Dora in a friendly manner, hissing in pain when she threw her arms around his back. He missed his step when he noticed Matty in the shadows, and still in her fine dress from the castle. "My lady?"

Dora burst out laughing. It was infectious, and soon Matty was laughing, too. Confused, Jack nevertheless joined in the mirth good-naturedly. Dora introduced him as Lord Henry's master-of-hounds, from Warmstirrup Castle.

Matty introduced herself and enquired about the pain in his back.

He shrugged his shoulders gingerly, adjusting his jacket. "One of the hounds bit the earl's leg."

"What's that got to do with your back?" the girls asked together.

Shamefaced, Jack admitted that his lord had whipped him, shredding his flesh for losing control of the dogs. "Harry-the-Cough fixed me right up, though. He's a good 'un, that Harry."

"Have you seen him?" Matty asked, urgently.

"Not since, but the sergeant-at-arms put every man he had on the streets looking for him. Apparently, he's a murderer. Didn't seem the type to me."

"He's not. It's all lies started by that snake, L'Éternuement, and kept going by that vile Walter Sweet."

Jack grinned. "Well, at least *he's* in the hole now."

"I know. I sent him there."

Both Dora and Jack gawped at Matty in astonishment.

"It's a long story," she admitted, weakly. "Jack, can you help me find Harry? Please? I can't go out about town at the moment."

"Of course, but what should I tell him, if I find him?"

"What should I tell him, when I find him?" the woman in green leggings and matching jacket asked as she took the small flask of herbal remedy.

"Nothing," the crone answered. "Take this for your friend's illness. Tell her it's nothing serious. When you find him, just bring him to me. I'll be with Old Tom."

The young woman, dressed as a man, studied her. Old Tom was the local name for a great oak that lay deep in the forest. Country folk visited Old Tom in times of need or strife, to pray and request help from the ancient woodland gods. For more than ten centuries, Christianity had stalked the meadows, forests, mountains and shores of Britain, spilling from the towns along every road to every village and farmstead. Yet the old superstitions and religions still clung to being, on the periphery. Both women knew that the further one went from a town, the stronger those beliefs became – even in the shadow of the great monastic houses. Old Tom's roots were planted less than a mile from Aynlton Priory, but they went far deeper. Even the cynical prior knew better than to interfere with visitors to the shrine – for shrine it was. A patriarch among oaks, Old Tom was huge and ancient. Some said he was planted by a fellow named Artorius, the last Roman in Britain a millennium ago, and everyone knew *they* were giants. The local serfs draped Old Tom in chains of flowers in the spring and summer, and carved little wooden figures to protect him through the winter months.

"You'd go that close to the priory?" asked the young woman in forest green, surprise evident in her voice.

The crone grinned toothlessly. "I go wherever I choose. The monks' zeal may have driven them mad, but they're just the followers. Prior Augustus knows better than to interfere with my comings and goings. You know I saved his life once? Yes, he had been bitten twice by adders, a most unlucky man. He was near death when I found him. That was when his luck changed. Once I had him back on his feet, he decided I must have been about God's work all along. Now he keeps those black-clad, Benedictine beetles away from my doings."

The young woman looked impressed, nodded respectfully and they parted.

"Harry? Is that you?" Jack, master-of-hounds, who so often found himself the underdog, stooped to look under a bough. "Harry? It *is* you."

Harry-the-Cough frantically waved him down as he approached noisily through the dead winter brush. He grabbed Jack by the front of his jacket and pulled him off his feet into the trees. "Are you trying to get us killed?" he hissed, savagely.

Jack got back to his feet, wincing from his wounds and clearly unnerved. "I've been sent to find you."

"From the castle?"

"From Matty."

"Matty? You've seen her? Is she alright?"

Jack held up a hand to forestall further questions. "She's safe and well. I'm to take you to her."

"Where is she? No. Don't tell me. It's better I don't know in case they capture me. I can't go back with you, Jack. It would be too dangerous for Matty, but might you take a message?"

Jack nodded earnestly as Harry took him aside.

"I have another favour to ask, also, but I warn you, it might cause a stink in the town."

"You helped my back no end, Harry. So, if I can return the favour, I will."

"Thanks." Harry whispered into his ear.

Jack looked questioningly at Dick for a moment, before a mischievous grin spread across his young face.

As they watched the young master-of-hounds clumsily crash his way back out of the trees, Dick asked, "What did you tell him?"

"Just a private message. In case I don't see her again."

Dick gave him a knowing grin.

It was the reaction Harry had hoped for. "Come on. You saw how easily he spotted us. We must get to the forest before any soldiers come along."

They made their way awkwardly between the low boughs and twisted roots to the south-western edge of the copse. Before them lay half a mile of open fields. The dark, forbidding forest lay beyond, and within it their hopes for sanctuary. Harry shuddered. How had he come to this? Making matters worse, the snow was beginning to stick again. They would leave a beautiful set of footprints for any enterprising guardsman to follow.

An idea struck him. "Dick, follow me in single file. Try to step in my footprints, if you can."

"It'll slow us down."

"Maybe, but they're looking for two men... 'nuff said?"

Dick nodded understanding, but looked out from the trees nervously. "That's a long way out in the open."

"Maybe we could pretend to be scarecrows, if someone comes?"

"In winter? What crops are we meant to be protecting?"

Harry sought inspiration, desperately. "I read that, in Germany, the farmers make wooden witches in the hope that they draw winter into themselves to bring on the spring."

Dick scowled. "We're not in Germany. In England, we just send a gang of kids out there to chuck stones at 'em. Like we did, remember?"

"Well, you come up with something, then. We can't afford to wait 'til dark."

"Right. Follow me." Dick strode out into the fields. "Don't forget to step where I step," he called over his shoulder.

Harry sighed with exasperation, but followed – what choice did he have? As he caught up, he asked, "Are you going to tell me your plan?"

"My plan?"

"If someone sees us?"

"Ah."

"Ah? Is that it?"

"Don't worry, Harry. You'll know what do."

They had travelled perhaps a quarter of the distance when shouts came from behind. They could not quite make out the words, but that hardly mattered. Harry turned, fearfully. "Now would be a good time to tell me your plan... Dick?"

With a sinking feeling, Harry realised he was alone. He turned to see Dick's back, as he opened up a respectable distance between them. "Hey! Wait for me!" He set off at a run, and it was well that he did so.

The crossbow bolt drove deep into iron-hard soil, right where he had been standing. The modern, steel-lathed crossbows could fire a bolt well over four hundred yards which, as luck would have it, was just about the exact distance between Harry and the soldiers. At the full extent of the weapon's range, the shot that almost skewered him had been the work of a master. Lord Henry may not have put much store in his men's integrity, intelligence or imagination, but their ability to kill, he took very seriously.

Without further ado, Harry got down to work on increasing the distance between them. The *thunk* of bolts hitting the ground all around him provided just the impetus he needed.

Six soldiers followed. Only two carried crossbows, but they nevertheless managed to loose eight bolts between them before Harry was able to move outside their range. He knew number nine was said to be *it* for cats, and realising that he presented an altogether larger and far less agile target, he ran for his last life before they could reload.

Say whatever he might about Dick, the man could run. Harry had not run like this for years, though as it turned out, it was a skill one never forgot – especially when frantic barking struck up from behind to jog his memory.

Subterfuge no longer necessary, nor possible, Harry ran without worrying about following in Dick's tracks. Despite that, running through snow was especially tiring, and he was being left further and further behind. Terror alone gave him the strength to outdistance the shouting soldiers. The shouting dogs, on the other hand, were getting louder and, unless the wind had changed direction, that was bad news.

He risked a look over his shoulder. There were three of them – all off the leash. Born to it, the slavering brutes loped easily across the snow, as long of leg as they were of tooth; conditions offering no hindrance whatsoever to Nature's four-by-paws. Harry whimpered. Strength almost gone, he was still several hundred yards from the treeline, the barking growing louder with every leaden step he took. *What a week!* he thought wretchedly.

Now he could hear their snarling, too. *This is it, Harry. You may have missed out on breakfast, but you've certainly made a dog's breakfast of your life, and so it ends.*

He could see no point in running further. No man could outrun hunting dogs, so he saved what little energy he had left for his last stand and turned. The three hounds were just yards behind him. Harry held out his arms to increase his size and growled angrily with the last of his breath. It was worth a try.

The hounds leapt for him.

Chapter 11
Geese and Ganders

Lord Henry did not awaken, as such. It was more like the world came back into focus. His head banged like the day after the twelfth night of Christmas; though for the life of him, he could not remember any revels.

"BOD-ges!" Two syllables; the second spoken oh so softly. The earl's privy guards opened the door to check on their lord. "Get Bodges," Henry demanded, keeping his voice low, while applying pressure to his temples. Despite any lack of revels, the minstrels seemed determined to continue their tambouring within his head.

Bodges arrived in record time on a bow wave of nervous anxiety. "M'lord, erm...?"

"I've got a headache the size of Wales. Get me something for it, will you?"

Bodges bowed his way out of the chamber and returned quickly with a jar of Harry-the-Cough's Inside and Out, some of Harry's headache pills and a jug of small ale. Aware of the Inside and Out's mildly soporific effects, he hoped it might improve his lord's mood. He knew Harry-the-Cough believed in the healing properties of deep sleep. What he did not realise was that, after a great deal of careful observation, Harry infused his famous medicinal ointment with the milky latex sap of poppies to ease pain and encourage a restful state. On days when Bodges had to serve his lord personally, he frequently stole some for himself, to drive the demons away when sleep eluded him.

"What's all this?" Henry asked, gruffly.

"It's, erm, from the apothecary, erm, lord," Bodges deflected. He knew the earl would now assume that to mean Felix L'Éternuement. Bodges also knew that if he gave his lord any of L'Éternuement's actual remedies while in his current state, he would either be hanged from the gibbet for killing his lord, or hanged from the gibbet *by* his lord, when he recovered on his own.

"Leave me. All of you."

Bodges and the guards left the earl's chambers immediately. Henry lay back down on his bed and fell almost immediately asleep; a deep, natural sleep this time.

When he awoke, what was left of the February daylight barely lit the room through his small, but ornate, mullioned window. He sat on the side of his bed, rubbing sleep from his eyes, yet feeling refreshed. Headache completely gone, a little rest had left him in good cheer and ready to get on with some shouting. There was always someone who needed shouting at, or beating, or hanging.

Heartened, he stood and walked to the window. Down in the courtyard, his soldiers huddled around braziers, stamping their feet against the cold, while others tended horses or mended equipment. All reminders that there would soon be war. Henry's mood lifted still further[1]. He stretched and slapped his chest with gusto. On the second tap he felt something inside his jacket. Frowning, he unbuttoned the top and reached inside to find a tattered piece of parchment. Holding it up by the window, to benefit from the dying light outside, he read:

Thou shalt dye on thee fyrst and twentyeth of July yn thee year of our Lorde

1403, far from home yn a fylde bye Shrewsbury, <u>unless</u> thou hast the wyt to pardon Harry thee Cough and Matty thee harlot. Take heed, Henry of Warmstyrrup, for thou art cursedd else!

Henry's high spirits vanished immediately. He was no more superstitious than the next man, which in 1399 meant very. His mind raced. What in the world might he be doing in Shrewsbury four years from now? He was lost – but no. The missive said *unless* he pardoned the peasant apothecary and the girl.

"Sergeant-at-arms!" he bellowed, loud enough to shake the door.

A guard knocked and entered. "The sergeant-at-arms is in the hole, my lord."

"*What?*" Henry's journey to anger was ever a short one. From there it was but a step to violence. "By whose authority?"

The guard quailed. "Yours, my lord."

The earl walked right up to the man, hollering in his face, "WHAT? BRING HIM TO ME!" When dealing with underlings, Henry had

---

1. Henry's excitement in anticipation of battle was the medieval equivalent of looking forward to a match. It was not a view widely shared, because whereas modern-day sports fans like to say 'we' did this, or that, for the medieval lower classes, taking part in the event really was mandatory. Own goals were discouraged, as several mounted referees kept a watchful eye on both sides, ready to despatch anyone feigning injury or exchanging shirts. No one ever gained 'extra time', though penalties often led participants into 'borrowed time', and outflanking an enemy usually silenced anyone who might yell "Offside!" So that ruling failed to gain any traction at all for several centuries. Those unable to attend could rest assured that, whoever won or lost, both teams would certainly avail themselves fully of local hospitality en route – to and from the pitch. No one was left out. They were rarely left alive, in fact, and in that regard, at least, Lord Henry of Warmstirrup was well known for his generosity, at home and away.

developed the following equation:

$$\frac{\text{volume}}{\text{distance}} = \text{speed of reaction}$$

where volume was given in decibels that set his servants' ears ringing. Having used the formula to successfully navigate his first three and a half decades on Earth, he saw no reason to tinker with it now.

The guard vanished down the spiral stairwell like a hare from a fox.

Harry-the-Cough flew through the air like a cheap stone, set within a ring of angry dogs. Just before they hit the ground in a savage bundle, a strange, two-tone whistle sounded from the edge of town. Harry landed hard. Whatever wind he had left was driven out by a massive paw on his chest. Instinctively, he raised both hands to his face to ward off the vicious attack he knew must come, but the dog never even made eye contact. Rather, he used Harry as a springboard to change direction and lope off in pursuit of his two packmates.

Lifting his head from the snow in confusion, Harry could see the hounds in full retreat, their barking growing ever more excited as the whistle sounded again.

"Harry? Are you dead?"

The voice came from a distance, near the edge of the forest. Lacking the breath to call back, Harry simply raised a hand, making a thumbs-up gesture. Inhaling deeply, he staggered to his feet and, in the midst of a coughing fit, set off again for the treeline. Dick was a couple of hundred yards ahead now, but at least he had stopped to check. Harry hoped that counted for something.

At the edge of town, Jack hid carefully out of sight with a stinking bag of offal. Though concealed from the soldiers, his scent stood out like a tiger in church for the hunting hounds. They ran straight to him, recognising the feeding-time whistle he had taught them. It was about the only control he had over them.

When Jack took the job of master-of-hounds, he began a strict training regime, but Lord Henry complained that the dogs lacked killer instinct and destroyed the ones he had worked with. Jack loved dogs and could not go through that again, so he lived with the danger of working with a pack of killers with just enough training to recognise a food-giver. He dropped the bag of offal and sloped away into the shadows of the narrow streets. The soldiers might go after the men running across the plain or they might chase the errant dogs. Either way, he would be better off long gone from there. The dogs would find their own way home when they became hungry again. He would report back to Matty. The light was poor, but the man they brought down must have been Harry. At least he would be able to report that he had gotten back up again. It was something.

Harry ran. No breath and no strength left, he nevertheless found a hidden reserve from somewhere – the flying crossbow bolts helped. The soldiers had closed on his position after the dogs brought him down, bringing him back into their deadly range. Dick reached the edge of the forest and was now beckoning frantically, like that could make Harry run any faster.

The *whoosh* of arrows overhead confused him, but he kept his head down, not wishing to look, as he focused on putting one foot in front of the other for as long as he could. Behind him, shouts of anger became shouts of alarm, syncopated with screams of agony. Harry stumbled, falling across the treeline. Dick helped him back to his feet, but far from triumphant, he looked afraid. They were not alone.

Lord Henry was usually angry, but the state – and more importantly, the stink – of Walter Sweet when he was brought before him, sent him over the edge. Incandescent, he screamed at his men to clean the oubliette's ordure from his sergeant-at-arms and ordered them to bring Harry-the-Cough and the woman known as Matty to him immediately. "And, Sergeant-at-arms," he called, stopping the men who were half-carrying Sweet away. "I want them unmolested. You understand me?"

"My lord," the sergeant-at-arms responded miserably.

Being covered in nameless filth, left in the hole by previous inhabitants, had been a grim ordeal for Sweet. Not to mention the freezing conditions and the belief that he would die there, forgotten. Now he would be forcibly cleaned up by the soldiers at his lord's instruction. Having given similar treatment to others, unfortunate enough to have found themselves in his own dubious care, he knew what form this 'bath' would take. They would throw him in the river that ran along the eastern wall of the castle. That would not have been so bad, but on that particular day, it would mean breaking the ice first.

Sweet's teeth chattered, freezing and now dreading what was to come. One of the four men who escorted him snatched a pickaxe from the courtyard as they passed through, making for a sallyport in the eastern curtain wall. The gate opened onto a tiny wooden jetty, and he used the pick to strike down at the ice. It bounced with a *clang* as often as it bit.

The sergeant-at-arms rolled his eyes. This was going to be bad, but there was no point in arguing. He had trained these men, trained them hard and completely without mercy. He knew they would only make it worse for him, if he resisted. They smirked secretly to one another, excited by the opportunity for payback.

Before he knew it, Sweet was stripped, thrown through the new hole in the ice and ducked, several times. He scrabbled desperately at the edge of the hole's rim to stop himself from being dragged under the ice by the current. "Th-throw m-m-me a r-rope, you f-fools! Throw…" he gurgled as he was pushed under again.

"What'd he say?"

"I don't know, Ambrose. Something about 'Snow, he hopes', I think."

"Aye, reckon he's right, an' all. Sky's proper black. Though, speaking for myself, *I* hope it stays off."

"Aye."

"Aye."

"I'm d-drowning! *Heeeelp!*"

"Ooh, I nearly forgot. We haven't washed his clothes. Here…"

"I've got 'em. Oh."

"What's up?"

"I think I've lost his leggings."

Sweet bobbed back up to shout, "You b-bunch o' useless, d-docile b-bast——" *Gurgle, gurgle, gurgle.*

"What's he say, Ambrose?"

"Not sure. Something about going fast, I think."

"Aye. He's probably cold. Maybe we should have tied a rope around him?"

The guards looked at one another and then, as one man, down into the hole they had made to access the water. In a flurry, they all grappled for one last flailing hand as the sergeant-at-arms was pulled away by the current.

"There he is! Over there. Under the ice. Ha ha, look, he's waving. Hello."

"He's not waving, Ambrose. He's dying! Quick, follow him."

The men stepped cautiously out onto the ice to follow Walter Sweet as he was swept underneath with the flow to the south. After twenty yards, the river turned sharply north-east where the castle walls jutted out to the left in front of them. The water was more turbulent in the corner, the ice thinner. One of Walter Sweet's arms punched up through it.

"There he is," called Ambrose.

They skated after him. Ambrose arrived first. The fact that the sergeant-at-arms was able to punch a hole in the ice there had not occurred to him. He fell through, just as Sweet bobbed up, sucking in a huge lungful of frigid air. Ambrose resurfaced almost immediately, alongside him, also struggling for breath after the shock of his sudden plunge into such extreme cold.

Sweet brought a fist down on top of his head, sending him back under.

The other men pulled their sergeant-at-arms, naked, from the freezing river.

"Where's Ambrose?" one asked.

Sweet looked round contemptuously. "He washed out."

"Sarge."

Sweet turned again at the call of his name.

Ambrose had resurfaced and was scrambling back out of the river. "Look, Sarge, I found your trousers."

That was your whole plan? Leg it?" Harry scathed. "And I followed you! What sort of an idiot does that make me?"

Dick shrugged. That was when Harry noticed the man in forest colours standing off to their side. He squinted in the half-light. No. Make that the *woman* in forest colours – with an expensive-looking sword at her belt. She lowered her hood to reveal her face. "Who are you?" he asked, ungraciously.

Arrows were still flying from the trees near them, sending the soldiers running back towards Warmstirrup, half carrying, half dragging a wounded comrade, hit in the leg. Whoever the woman was, she had company.

"They call me Robyn," she answered.

Harry squinted at his saviour. "Who does?"

She blinked. "My... my friends, I suppose." She was vaguely aware of the initiative slipping away from her. "Harry-the-Cough, I presume? You're to come with me."

"Why?"

"What?"

"Why?" Harry repeated.

"Erm, because."

Harry and Dick shared a look. The woman was well-spoken and clearly gently born, despite her forest garb. "I don't think so, lass," Harry answered, derisively. "I mean, thanks for packing those soldiers off, but——"

"Sorry," Robyn replied. "I meant *because* I have orders to bring you before——"

"We don't care about your orders," Harry scoffed. "We'll go where we want, thank you. It's a free country."

"No, it isn't."

Dick looked Harry in the eye and shrugged again. "Well, she's right about that."

Robyn huffed, irritably. "Fine. Because we're *armed*, then. One does so hate it when one is forced to be so crass!"

That got Harry's attention. He was in a foul mood after everything that had happened, and when a man appeared as if by magic from the trees, surprising him, he spoke ahead of his thoughts. "Who's this ugly sod?"

"*That* is my husband."

"S-sorry." Suddenly abashed, Harry smiled weakly at the large man with the heavily scarred grimace. "I... I'm sure he's a lovely person."

Robyn looked down. "Not particularly. His name's Mario. They call him Mardy Mario."

"*They*, again?"

She scowled. "*We*, then. Let me introduce you to my friends. This is Joan Little. We call her Little Joan." A tiny woman, barely more than four feet tall, stepped out of the trees carrying a bow considerably taller than herself.

Harry nodded greeting. "Yes, I can see the through-line, there."

"This," Robyn continued, "is Guillaumette le Rouge – we call her Willa." A woman with a red scarf around her neck glared at them furiously. Harry unconsciously took a step back.

"And this," Robyn introduced the final member of her party, "is Sister Tick."

The last woman to step from the trees was rather plump and wore a nun's habit. She stepped right up into his personal space and crossed him. "Bless you, my son."

Harry recoiled. "Charmed, I'm sure. You're outlaws?" The question was to Robyn.

She placed a hand to the pommel of her longsword, but gave no answer.

"Four women and one man..." He tailed off as a memory surfaced. "Hang on. I know this story – sort of. Let me guess, you rob from the rich and give to the poor?"

Robyn released the sword, placing her hands on hips. "That *is* a good story, but we tend more towards robbing the rich and, erm... No. Actually, that's pretty much it. In fact, you don't even need to be rich. What have you in that interesting-looking bag of yours?"

"What?" Harry was outraged. "I thought you had orders?"

"We have, but they were mum with regards to robbing you."

"Look, we have no money——"

"You had your purse back..." Dick instantly regretted his outburst, realising what he had just done.

Harry turned to him in impotent fury. "Oh, what merry company I've fallen in with!"

"Your purse *and* the bag," Robyn amended.

"And, oh, how very *1199* of you! Nottingham's about two hundred miles south, and it's that way," Harry spat, jabbing a thumb over his shoulder. Mardy Mario pulled a long knife from his belt and crossed his arms. Muscles bulged under sackcloth sleeves. He smiled. It was worse than the grimace. A bow string creaked as Little Joan nocked an arrow. Harry swallowed and handed over his small purse and bag of treatments, all the while glaring at Dick.

Chapter 12
Dead Men, Tall Tales

Sergeant-at-arms Walter Sweet sat on a stool by the hearth, in the castle's great hall. Wrapped in a rough blanket, he waited while his clothes hissed by the fire. Lord Henry had given him permission to dry them before joining the search for Harry-the-Cough, although his generosity was probably just practicality. They had lost the daylight, after all.

Sweet stared into the flames, his thoughts curling and vanishing like the hot tongues that warmed him, and every bit as deadly. Lord Henry may have wanted the peasant and his whore back in one piece, but Sweet had a score to settle.

A commotion at the door made him turn.

Six guards returned – one of them wounded in the leg.

Sweet pulled the blanket close about him to lock in the fire's heat and got to his feet. He heard the call go out for Lord Henry's physician as he approached them. "What happened?" he asked.

"We caught up with the fugitive, Sarge. Aye, and his accomplice. But they started loosing arrows at us from the forest."

"Harry-the-Cough had a bow with him? I didn't know he could shoot. He doesn't look strong enough."

"Don't know, but someone was shooting at us. They were good shots, too. We were still at range. Did I hear right, Sarge, that Lord Henry has changed his mind and wants them back alive now?"

Sweet looked around furtively. "That's what the earl has asked for, lad. But things can easily go wrong in the field." He slapped the young guardsman's cheek conspiratorially. "You know that."

The soldier smiled knowingly. He looked down at his mate, and the thirty-one inches of ash that pierced his leg. He had a score to settle, too.

Do you know where you're going?" Harry felt compelled to ask. They had been walking for hours and he was starving. The forest was a warren of narrow animal tracks. Were it not for the reduced winter foliage and the covering of snow on the branches reflecting the moonlight, they would have been completely blind. "Oi! Boss woman," he tried again.

Robyn stopped and waited for him to catch up while her husband took the lead. "I could find my way through these woods blindfolded," she assured him.

"Really?" he asked sceptically. "I only ask because we've passed this tree three times now."

She peered through the gloom to see a tree trunk canted over so far that snow had settled along it. A mark in the snow glowed accusingly in the moonlight. "What's that?"

"It's an aitch," Harry explained. "As in, aitch for Harry? With your posh accent, surely you can read?"

"Oh." She looked around furtively before hissing, "I don't draw attention to it!"

Harry leaned heavily against the gnarly trunk and sighed. "Well, isn't this great?"

The small group trundled to a stop. As noted, they were not all men, but cold and hungry themselves, Harry would not have described any of them as merry.

"So, what now?" asked Dick. He, too, was starving and his usual *joie de vivre* was also slipping.

The crack of a twig made them start. In the centre of the narrow trail stood a young hart; a beautiful creature, his hot breath pluming high into the frigid air, flanks steaming. He had been running.

Mardy Mario removed a sling from his belt and took a smooth, river-washed pebble from a pouch. "Looks like dinner has arrived."

Harry was appalled. He peered through the gloom and blinked. "Er... I wouldn't do that if I were you."

With his head lowered, the hart stared up at them so regally, and with such noble bearing, that it almost felt he was looking down on them.

"In case the earl finds out we've knocked off one of his deer?" Mario mocked.

Harry shook his head. "No, it's not that."

Mario carefully placed the stone at the centre of the sling. "What then? Squeamish?"

"No. Well, a bit, but it's not that either."

"What's the matter?" asked Dick.

Harry turned to him. "I'm fairly certain the deer just winked at me."

Where the hell is Bodges?" demanded Sweet.

The guard sent to fetch him returned shaking his head. "Couldn't wake him, Sarge. I don't *think* he's dead, but he's dead to the world."

Sweet rolled his eyes. "It'll be the real thing when I get my hands on him. I suppose you'll have to fetch that damned fool L'Éternuement. Go!"

The man returned within a few minutes, dragging a reluctant apothecary behind him. L'Éternuement held a beautifully crafted leather satchel protectively to his chest as he stumbled into the great hall.

Extracting an arm from the warmth of his blanket, Sweet pointed to the man lying on the bench with an arrow sticking out of his leg. He doubted any further explanation would be necessary, even for a fraudulent medical man.

L'Éternuement looked beseechingly at Sweet. He may as well have begged the Devil for clemency. Arm still free, the sergeant-at-arms flung him to the rush-strewn flagstones and once again pointed imperiously at the man's injured limb.

The apothecary studied the injury and quailed. "Arrow wounds aren't really my specialty. I'm a purveyor of medicines. I..."

"Is that a fact?" Sweet bit back, acidly. "Well, you're the closest thing we have to a physician at the moment, so get to it. Oh, and, Felix," Sweet leaned down to place a friendly hand on the other man's shoulder, "get it right." He squeezed, making L'Éternuement wince.

"Erm, maybe we should..." The apothecary trailed off, afraid to continue.

"Should what?"

"Perhaps we should get Harry-the-Cough." His admission, spat through gritted teeth, cost him dearly – more than the loss of any fee. "He's more suited to the... the *messy* end of medicine," he mitigated his pain.

Sweet feigned confusion. "But wasn't it you who convinced Lord Henry that Harry-the-Cough was a murderer? Your assistant, wasn't he? The dead boy, I mean. Didn't you also say Cough wasn't fit to serve the thoroughbred fighting force under his lordship's command? I'm sure it was something like that."

L'Éternuement squirmed visibly now. "Perhaps I was a little... hasty."

The sergeant-at-arms let out a bark of laughter, and without warning, shoved L'Éternuement out of the way, snapped the bloody tip off the arrow and pulled the shaft back through before the wounded man even had chance to scream. He made up for it in the seconds that followed and bawled the place down, but the arrow was out.

Sweet grabbed L'Éternuement by the scruff of the neck, still one-handed.

"Now you know how it's done. Well?"

L'Éternuement almost swooned as blood pooled between the injured man's fingers. "Erm, thank you?" he probed nervously, unsure what Sweet was asking.

Sweet slapped him around the ear, knocking him to the floor again. "Idiot! Clean the wound or apply something, or whatever it is you allegedly do!"

L'Éternuement picked himself back up. "Of course. Of course." He took a small jar from his bag and removed the leather cloth tied around its lid. The salve stank and when he dabbed it liberally on the wound, the man screamed.

The sergeant-at-arms nodded contentedly. "That's how you know it's working, lad."

The man who was *not* Dave the tramp, but had taken on his persona, waited in darkness just outside Warmstirrup, north of the sprawl that grew each year to encircle the town walls. He was completely alone, the darkness fitting, for his was a dark business. He *was* meeting a witch, after all. He jerked around suddenly, a blade appearing in his hand.

Mad Mab smiled up at him. "Almost caught you off-guard, that time."

Not Dave put the knife away. He felt neither surprise nor embarrassment from failing to notice her until the last second. She was a very powerful witch. Besides, he never felt anything, not any more. He was dead. Had been for several years. It was better that way. No regrets, no remorse, no pain, no dreadful daily drudgery. Since the time of his death, he had been having the time of his life, and though never very good at living, since his demise, it turned out he was extremely good at killing. Enjoyment was the wrong word. Suffice to say that his job entailed bringing peace to others, and that in turn brought peace to Not Dave. He may no longer have experienced happiness, but he was not *not* happy with his circumstances.

Mad Mab took a moment to admire her creature. "You did well to follow the boy, unseen, but he has since fallen under the power of another, and I can no longer see him. We can't have that, can we? He still has something of mine. So I have a new task for you." She never used Not Dave's real name. It had no meaning when the soul was gone. In the interests of fairness, part of her hoped his soul was in a better place; it was just the rest of her that did not care.

The incantation began with low, guttural tones, in the same ancient Brittonic tongue she had used to destroy Insane Alice's house. To avoid being disturbed, she suppressed the crescendo to a frenetic hiss as she touched Not Dave's brow with a twisted twig. A spark made the flesh golem jolt.

Mad Mab completed her spell with a simple instruction. "Go."

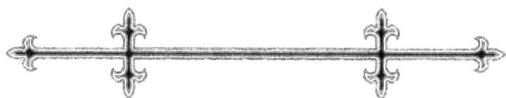

Harry touched Mardy Mario's arm. "I really don't think you should slingshot that hart."

Mario looked at him as though he were mad. "You've been bellyaching about being hungry for hours, and now we have a meal right in front of us, you want me to let it go."

"Even if you could bring it down with a single stone, there's something strange about that deer. Trust me. Can't you just knock down a couple of rabbits for us, or something?"

A frantic rustle in the bushes on the forest floor caught their attention. They were just in time to see a fluffy white tail vanish into the underbrush.

Dick clamped a hand on Harry's shoulder. "I think you may have made a bad impression there."

Harry stared in disbelief. "Why do I get the feeling we've left the real world behind and walked right into a faerie tale?"

"Snap out of it, people," Robyn chastised them. "We need to find our way back. Enough of this 'communing with animals' nonsense. There are no such things as faerie tales… what?"

Harry was pointing at the hart, his jaw hanging open.

They all watched as the young deer scratched something through the light dusting of fresh snow on the forest floor. Once complete, he stepped back, eyeing them warily. Unconsciously, the not at all merry, not all men, moved forward to see what he had left for them.

"What is it?" asked Robyn.

Harry blanched. "It's an aitch."

"As in, aitch for Harry?"

He nodded dumbly.

"You think he wants us to follow him?" asked Dick.

"I don't know. Maybe he just stopped by to write my initials in the snow?"

"It's only an aitch," Dick mumbled, moodily.

"You're right, of course. Perfectly normal behaviour for a young deer. What was I thinking? Perhaps by the time he's learned his twelve-*tines*-table, he'll be able to expand on his work!"

"That another one of your intellectual japes, is it?"

"Will you two shut up!" Robyn cuffed them both.

"I want to go home," Harry grumbled. "I really want to go home now."

Bodges was never at home. He fidgeted and cried out in his sleep. Even when drugged, the demons never strayed far from his side. Being of a nervous disposition and working for Lord Henry would do that to a soul. His dream body ran through a dark forest, followed by whoops of delight from the armed men chasing him. He never found out why they chased him; it was enough that he spent his rest hours running for his life. Nature was cruel that way. She waited until her victim was wracked with fever or pain, or distraught with mental anguish, and then deprived them of the one thing they truly needed – sleep.

He approached the ravine. He would slide down the near side in terror and then spend the rest of the night trying to scale the other side, never able to gain any purchase. It was the same every time he closed his eyes, but this time, something new happened. The stream cutting the bottom of the ravine always dragged at his legs, pitching him forward to grab the slick, muddy far side. From there, he would begin his Sisyphean climb with spears and arrows falling all around him, but this time the stream was not water. It was foul and stank like urine – horse urine, unless he was mistaken. It was disgusting, and the overpowering reek of ammonia took his breath away. No matter how he moved or turned his head he could find no relief, until...

He sat bolt upright on his sleeping pallet. At first, he thought the stench had followed him out of his dream, but then he saw the figure in black, and screamed.

Robyn stomped through the dark forest in a brooding silence. She felt quite ridiculous following a wild animal. She, the 'all new and improved Robyn i' the Hood' – at least, that was how she saw herself – was lost, and in the forest, too. She may as well have had her hood on backwards. Then there was the hart himself, and not even a royal, either. A mere ten-tined youngster. It was embarrassing. What made it worse was the way he skipped and danced joyfully.

When a small bird – a robin, no less – landed on his antler, Robyn expected them to break into a duet. It was absurd. However, the tiny redbreast merely imparted a course correction and flew away again. It was the only explanation, because the hart veered immediately and sharply right.

Robyn shook her head, vowing that this would be the last time she worked for a witch. It was just too weird.

"What was that?" She stopped dead, causing Mardy Mario to crash into her.

"What?" he asked, mardily.

Crammed into a single-file track, Harry tried to bob his head over Mario's shoulder. Lacking the height, he tried bobbing around, but lacked the room. In the end he settled for lifting the large man's heavy arm and tucking his head underneath. "What's going on?"

Robyn shushed them. "I can hear singing. Listen..."

"Christos est natus..."

She grabbed Harry, pulling him under her husband's arm and to the fore. "This is your fault, Harry-the-Cough!"

"Ex Maria virginae, gaudete..."

"What is?" Harry was both unnerved and baffled.

Robyn grabbed him by the scruff of the neck. "The bloody deer is *singing!*" she hissed.

Harry grabbed the hand to prevent her from throttling him. "Don't be ridiculous. If that's the case, who's singing the harmonies? Singing deer, indeed..."

"It's probably best, at this point, that you don't look down." Dick spoke from somewhere further back, obscured by man-mountain Mario.

Harry closed his eyes. "It the rabbits, isn't it? They're singing, aren't they?"

"Now I *know* you're losing your mind, Harry."

Harry's eyes snapped open. "Oh, thank God."

"Can't you see there're several hedgehogs amongst them, as well?" Dick elucidated. "They've got quite a range, too. Let me try – *Gaudete, gaudete, Christos est natus, ex Maria virginae, gaudete——*"

"Shut up! Just shut up, all of you!" Harry bellowed, balling his fists into his eyes against the insanity. "This isn't happening."

The singing stopped abruptly with a rustle through the undergrowth.

"Look what you've done now!" Dick rounded on him.

"This isn't happening," Harry declared again, trying to make it so. "And I can prove it. It's February. *Gaudete* is a carol!"

"That's what you took from that, like that was the strangest thing?" Robyn glared at him, askance.

"Maybe they just liked the tune," Dick suggested. "My favourite, that one."

"Well, alright, the hedgehogs, then," Harry tried again, desperate to bring them all back to the real world. "They sleep through the winter months – so that puts paid to your entire baritone section, doesn't it, eh, Dick?"

"Oh, you did see them, then?" Dick replied from his safe place behind Sister Tick.

Robyn took a step back from Harry, warily. "When was the last time you slept? Oh, look. You've scared the hart away now, too. Nicely done!"

Harry looked to where the hart had been waiting for them – where it had led the choir. Just visible through the winter branches, he could make out a warm glow among the trees. A fire. He pointed. The others turned to see, and cautiously, they set off towards it. Less than a hundred yards and they stepped out into a large clearing with a huge, solitary oak at its centre. They had reached Old Tom at last.

A little way off to the right, respectfully outside the reach of the ancient tree's canopy, a campfire roared cheerfully. Around it sat what looked like an old woman, along with an assortment of forest fauna. Insane Alice cackled theatrically to herself, and her circle of woodland friends.

The scene was laughably surreal, but for one thing – the glorious smell of cooking, of food. Harry darted forward, regardless of the consequences. Dick followed, as did Robyn, and her suddenly merrier followers.

"Welcome, Harry," Insane Alice greeted without turning around.

"You knew it was me?"

"A little rabbit told me," she replied harshly.

Harry had the decency to look shamefaced, when a small stone struck the back of his head. "Ow!" He looked around, rubbing a new bruise. Standing at the outer reach of the firelight, he just caught the glint of an eye at ground level before it vanished into the trees. He had never seen a rabbit angry before; it was quite disturbing. He changed the subject. "Is that fish I can smell cooking?"

"Just a little offering from the river, courtesy of my forest pals. The fish don't move around so much when it's this cold. Makes it easier for them."

"A bunch of rabbits and deer went fishing for you?" Harry could hardly believe he was even asking.

"I couldn't reasonably entrust a task like that to Mr Foxy, could I? Or Mr Badger?"

"Reasonably? *Mister* Badger...?" Harry faltered, teetering around the edge of a breakdown. He fought to control himself. "Why, of course, so you sent the eaters of berries, nuts and leaves... *fishing?*"

She turned to him at last – cackling, naturally. "Exactly. Like so many good vegetarians, they couldn't give a stuff about fish."

Harry opened his mouth to reply, but an involuntary nervous laugh erupted instead. As the other humans approached, the remaining woodland creatures retreated to the treeline, freeing up places around the fire.

"We couldn't find our way," Robyn confessed without preamble, warming herself gratefully. "I thought I knew every leaf and twig in this place——"

"You were mazed," Alice cut her off.

"Yes, well, I can't deny, I was pretty astounded——"

"Not *amazed*, mazed. It's a spell to make a person lose their way. Someone is working against us. Someone powerful. That's why I sent Mr——" She caught Harry's eye and relented. "That's why I sent the hart to find you and bring you here."

Harry slapped Mardy Mario on the arm. "There you go! I told you to leave the deer alone."

Mario slapped him back, knocking him over in the snow. Harry got back up tetchily, rubbing his arm. "Who works against us, Insane Alice?"

The crone gave him an appraising look, clearly hiding something. "As I said, someone powerful. That's why I summoned you and why we're all here. I don't just sit about in the forest on freezing winter's nights waiting for any old Rob, Dick and Harry, you know."

Dick blinked. "She knows my name." He grabbed Harry's sleeve. "How does she know my name?"

Harry shook him off. "Never mind that. Who is it, Alice?"

"I'm not sure I should tell you."

"Why?"

"Because you're in a nervous enough state as it is."

Harry leaned forward to throw a fallen log back onto the campfire. "Oh,

I don't know. Fishing rabbits and singing hedgehogs… I think I'm holding up fairly well, all things considered. So you may as well tell me now."

The crone stared into the flames, deliberating, and then dropped the name like a slab. "It's Mad Mab."

Harry looked up from the fire, sharply. "That's impossible. She's dead."

Insane Alice cackled again. "Oh, you don't know the half of it, boy."

Bodges' eyes bulged as the hand clamped around his mouth. "Mmphemphu?"

"Eh?" enquired the intruder.

"Mmphemphu?"

"Oh, right." He released his grip. "It's me, Dr Bodges. Don't you recognise me?"

Bodges fainted.

Not Dave made his way through the forest in the same way that he did almost everything else – alone. He picked up the trail of Harry-the-Cough and those who were helping him easily enough. They moved in a party of seven, following the tracks of a smallish deer – but following slowly, not hunting. He would probably have found that strange when he was alive, but everything was so much simpler now.

He followed the tracks for some miles, even when they crossed themselves, to make sure he had the right course and order of events. In the distance he heard the peal of a single bell, although its flat, fractured *clang* made it sound more like an appeal for a new one. Aynlton Priory was a poor monastic house, barely hanging on, yet they kept the canonical hours – some might say, religiously. The bell rang for Vigil, the eighth hour of the night[1]. By the time it rang again, for Matins[2], he would have just one hour to find them. To find them, and deal with them. For Matins was also 'witching hour'. Mad Mab's commands were burned into his mind and during the darkest hour of night, they would grant him power.

The foul stink of horse urine, reduced to crystals, brought Bodges round once more with a shudder, a shudder that turned into a shake. "It can't be. Erm, you're d-d-dead!"

"I get that a lot – no pun intended," said Lott.

"But you were murdered. Erm, beheaded! The pigs ate your, erm, remains."

"They ate *someone's* remains," Lott replied, a little embarrassed.

Bodges stared at him in disbelief.

The young man shrugged. "Alright, I had to raid the churchyard, but they didn't feel a thing, I swear. That's why I hid the – that is, *my* – head, so that I, or rather *he* couldn't be identified. After that, it was just a matter of making myself scarce for a while, you see?"

Unfortunately, Bodges was beginning to. He reached out and grasped Lott's arm, not so much to restrain him as to prove he was real. "But why?" he asked quietly.

Lott smiled craftily. "I was made an offer I couldn't refuse."

"But, erm, L'Éternuement…"

"Is no apothecary," he confessed casually. "And the way he runs his business means he doesn't stay long in any one place, either. He's very

---

1. 2 a.m.

2. 3 a.m.

rich. Well, by our standards, anyway. I don't know how long he intends to continue doing what he's doing. Maybe he wants to buy himself a title – become a nob. I don't know. But whatever his plans are, he never lingers, so I have no future with him. In fact, I wouldn't be surprised if he did try to have me murdered, just for knowing how he works. I recently had my eyes opened to the likelihood of that fate."

"By, erm, whom?"

Lott smiled knowingly, but offered no answer.

"So," Bodges tried a different tack, "what, erm, are you doing here?"

"I'm here to save you."

Like Lott himself, Bodges was scrawny, pale and unhealthy-looking. When he paled further, it was almost as though he glowed. "Save me? Erm, from what?"

"More, erm, from whom, actually." Lott grinned, mocking Bodges' nervous *erming*. "When my master – that is, my *old* master – was summoned here earlier this evening——"

"Summoned here? Felix L'Éternuement was summoned to the castle?" Bodges kicked his legs over the side of his sleeping pallet, coming fully alert. "Why? Erm, who's, erm, been taken ill?"

"One of the soldiers took an arrow in the leg, I understand. Anyway, when you were summoned but didn't attend..."

Bodges' breath caught. He grabbed Lott by his jacket. "Does Lord Henry know I didn't attend? I take a draught sometimes, one of, erm, Harry-the-Cough's concoctions. It's the only, erm, way I can rest."

Lott peeled the older man's fingers off him. "Don't worry. The earl doesn't know. Not yet. That's why I'm here. My new mistress wants you kept alive. Alive, but out of the way."

"Sh-she does?" Bodges absolutely believed Lott's story. Perhaps it was because, all at once, things were looking worse for him than even he had imagined – how could it *not* be the truth? "Erm, to whom do I, erm, owe this, erm...?"

"Favour? She's a witch."

Lord Henry's physician, a tall beanpole of a man, sprang to his feet so quickly that he quivered. "Heresy," he breathed. "I c-cannot hear these, erm, tales."

"Well, if you don't, you're a dead man."

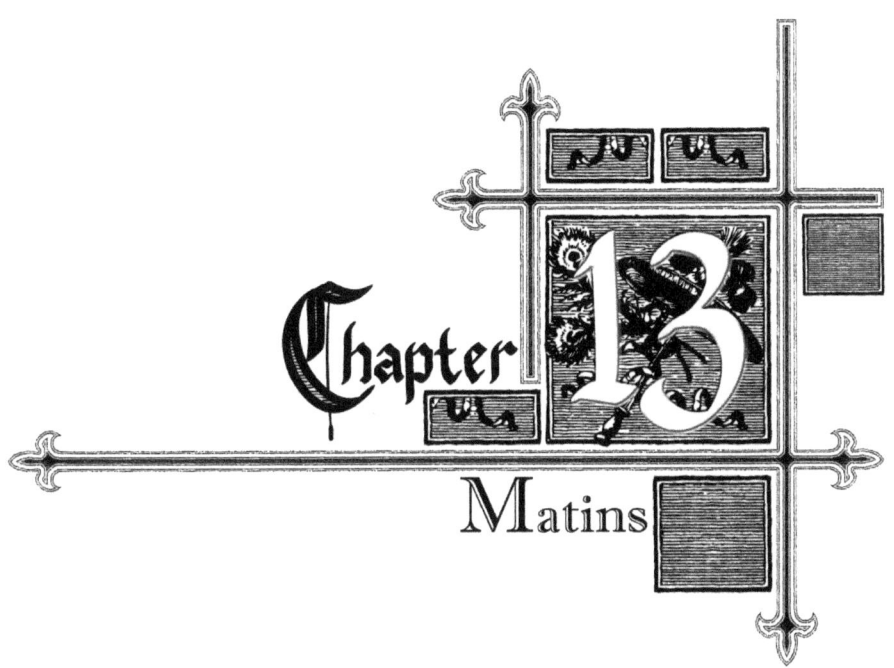

Chapter 13
Matins

Not Dave made good progress at first, but the closer he got to his quarry, the more their trail became difficult to read – even to the point of leading him awry. He suspected some form of magic was being employed against him. His mistress forewarned that it might be so. There was nothing to be done, so he did nothing – a prerogative of the dead.

Twenty minutes he waited, silently, absolutely still. Snow fell, blanketing him in white, effectively merging him with his surroundings. In the distance, he heard the toneless *clang* of the Matins bell, a mile north and east.

Unsure what to expect, it was as though the sun came out in the dead of night. Suddenly, he could see everything. Even the pathways his prey had taken were lit up with golden threads, ready to be followed. He set off, shedding snow with each step he took. Within a dozen yards, he was once again the black-ragged man; a walking 'five-a-day' for any disease-spreading parasite on the go.

Nocturnal creatures of the forest shied away as he passed. Alone, he made straight for Old Tom.

Insane Alice awoke with a start. Mardy Mario turned questioningly from his vigil as she stood and looked around. "Still first watch?" she asked.

Mario nodded. He had drawn the shortest straw this night, which only fed into his temperament.

"Has the Matins bell sounded?"

Again, he nodded.

"Don't say much, do you?"

"No one listens if I do," he complained morosely.

Insane Alice was distracted, not really listening. "Wake them. Do it now."

Mario stood and shook or kicked everyone awake with total equality.

Robyn scowled at her husband, but stood stiffly. "What's happening?"

"You must go," Insane Alice answered, without taking her eyes from the treeline. "All of you. We have a visitor, and it would be as well for you not to meet him. Harry, do you still have the book Mab gave you?"

"My recipe book?"

"If you like."

"I did have it. I was robbed."

Insane Alice turned sharply. "What?"

Harry pointed an accusing finger at the merry-not-all-men. "Don't look at me. Ask Robbing Hood, Princess of Bag-Snatchers, over there."

"You were already paid," Insane Alice stated, with enough said. "I thought you were trying to distance yourself from the antics of your father?"

Robyn rolled her eyes. "There's just no profit to be made in this country any more. Sister Tick, return the bag."

"And everything that was in it," Harry added, more confident now. "There's also the little matter of all my money, Mrs Hood."

"Don't push your luck, sunbeam. Unless you want to be known as Harry-the-Coughing-Blood?"

"Enough!" Alice silenced their bickering. "Harry, you must go to Aynlton Priory. Ask for Prior Augustus – no one else. You understand? Those idiot monks won't let you in, if they think you have women with you, but if you can get to Augustus and tell him I sent you, he will keep you safe until morning."

"But what about you?" Harry felt concern for the old crone. She was Matty's friend, after all, and she had helped him. "If this man is so dangerous?"

"I'll be alright." She smiled, secretively. "It's time for some 'how's your father'." Harry's face screwed up in disgust, which only elicited a cackle from Alice. "Besides," she continued, "he's not after me. Now go." She beckoned to the outlaws' leader. "Robyn, a word?"

Robyn knocked on the priory gates with the pommel of her sword. The chanting of the monks was eerie on the still night air. At times it rang clear, while at others it was dampened by falling snow that came and went.

"I couldn't help noticing," Harry attempted polite small talk, "that Insane Alice referred to your father…" His leading question led nowhere, so he cleared his throat and tried again. "Might I ask what she told you when we left?"

Before she could answer, a small hatch opened within the heavy gate and a face appeared. It was not a friendly face. "Well? Who are you?"

"I——" Robyn began, but before she could even give a false name, the monk took a sharp breath and shied away.

They heard hissed voices through the still-open hatch.

"*Who is it, Brother?*"

"*It's a... a... a* woman."

"*God save us!*"

They could all envisage the monks crossing themselves in the face of evil. Robyn was nonplussed.

"Let me try." Harry moved in close, looking into the courtyard. "My name is H——"

"Only devils be abroad at this hour!" a bald-pated head snapped, cutting him off. "Where's my box, Brother? I *told* Brother Carpenter not to cut the hatch so high. He never listens, that man. Anyone would think carpenters were as important as bishops, the way he carries on!"

"I, er... thought they were?" a second monastic voice asked, timorously.

"Don't let the Prince Bishop, down in Durham, hear you say that. Walter Skirlaw has ears all over Northumbria. Now, where *is* that box?"

Harry turned to Dick and smirked. "Hey, Brother, what do you call a really short monk?"

"I don't know," came the slightly muffled reply through the gate.

"What's your name?"

"Brother Luke."

"There you go."

Dick and Harry guffawed. Robyn crossed her arms and tapped her foot in annoyance. "We're meant to be seeking sanctuary."

Harry coughed and cleared his throat. "Of course. Sorry. Erm, Brother Luke——"

Dick carried on laughing, infecting Harry again. "Stop it." He waved him down, trying to regain his composure. "We're sorry to have disturbed your devotions, Brother. I realise it's a tall order at this time of night..." They fell about laughing again.

"Oh, for Chri——"

"*Blasphemy*, child!" Luke rebuked, furiously.

"——ing out loud," Robyn finished lamely. "Brother Luke, we've been sent to ask for Father Augustus. He's your prior."

"Good job you explained that," Harry commented out of the side of his mouth.

Robyn shoved him back out of the monks' view. "Please tell him we have an urgent message for him. The whole future of your house may depend upon it. Well? Scuttle off, there's a good fellow."

The hatch slammed shut with unnecessary force.

Dick nodded contentedly. "I think that went fairly well."

Robyn skewered him with her glare. "I've my eye on you, *Bobby*."

Dick grabbed Harry's sleeve. "Now *she* knows my name, my *other* name. How does she know my other name?"

Harry pulled his arm back irritably. "You're asking me? Maybe you're famous?"

"Famous? Really? What for?"

"I don't know. Perhaps for harmonising with hedgehogs, or something."

Dick let the matter drop and looked away, perturbed by Robyn's glare.

The hatch snapped open again. This time an older, more kindly face greeted them, briefly, before disappearing amid several bumps and bangs against the inner face of the gates. "Who left that box there? What a stupid place... Bloody hell!"

"Father *Prior!*" They recognised Brother Luke's scandalised tones.

"Sorry, *sorry*. Just get it shifted, will you?" The bristly bearded face reappeared. "Erm, who goes there, or some such?"

"Harry, Father. Harry-the-Cough from Warmstirrup. I've been sent to you on urgent business from..." he leaned close to whisper, "Insane Alice, sir. May we enter?"

Prior Augustus started at the mention of her name. "These are dangerous times. Do you have any proof of the truth of this, or carry any surety I can trust?"

Harry shrugged. "Only her name, Father."

Augustus knew what Alice was. He also knew that only a fool would be bold enough to use her name without permission – that or a high-and-mighty noble lord, which often amounted to the same thing. He nodded. "Very well, but just you."

"But, Father, my friends and I are all in danger."

"Then the quicker you explain your business, the quicker we can invite you *all* in."

I know you're there," Insane Alice called out to the darkness surrounding her circle of light. "Won't you approach, warm yourself, maybe? Share my fire?"

No movement answered her words, but that in itself was indicative. The forest was unnaturally still, the only movement from gently falling snowflakes.

"Perhaps you can't feel warmth. Does my light hurt you?"

The voice, when it answered, sounded like gravel sliding from a shovel. "It means nothing to me."

A flicker of sadness crossed Alice's face. "Do you remember all that was?"

"Yes."

"Does that also mean nothing to you?"

"It was. Now, it is no longer."

She took a deep, shuddering breath of freezing air, wrapping her tattered cloak close about her. "I cannot let you harm him."

"He has something my mistress desires."

"I can't let you have that, either."

"Then you are in my way."

She sighed. "I don't wish to destroy yo—— that is, what is *left* of you. Don't force my hand... please." Her voice shook, emotion causing her to shiver more than the cold.

"We are done, then." Not Dave turned to leave.

"Wait!"

He stopped, looking back over his shoulder.

"Do you understand that, wherever your soul resides, your actions here are shredding it to pieces?"

"I do not feel it."

"But surely you care?"

"I do not."

Alice took a step forward. She opened her arms, beseeching. "You can put it back together, you know. One pure act, and then move on."

He vanished into the night.

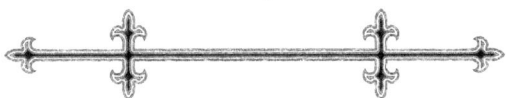

Why do you travel with outlaws, young Harry?" asked Prior Augustus, holding out a cup of mulled wine.

Ensconced within the prior's office, Harry accepted the cup, and the proffered seat by the fire, gratefully. "I didn't have much choice. They kidnapped me, Father."

Augustus looked astonished. "And you wish me to take them in?"

The younger man scratched his head, slightly embarrassed. "It's... complicated. Insane Alice didn't tell me much, but she did say that Mad Mab is back – I thought she was dead, but apparently, she isn't – and she's after me. I don't know why. Robyn Hood, and her bunch of miscreants, kidnapped me and robbed me, but they've sort of kept me safe, as well." Harry grunted as he reached into the folds of his coat. Pulling out his small purse, he shook it once. "Look, I got my money back... erm, again."

Father Augustus blinked in surprise.

Harry winced. "I know. It's hard to explain, but I feel that I owe them. Someone, or something, bad is pursuing us. Alice said the sanctuary within these walls would be our only salvation, during the witching hour——"

"*Don't* speak of such things here, I pray you," Augustus interrupted. "The hour is Matins." He crossed himself and Harry tried inexpertly to follow suit. The prior raised a wry smile. "Not a strong believer, young Harry?"

"I pray, Father," Harry explained. "Just not, you know, professionally."

The prior chuckled. "When we're alone, you may call me Gus. I have to retain a certain austerity in front of the brothers and obedientiaries, you understand."

Harry nodded. "Thank you. About my friends, Gus."

Outside the Priory gates there was much arm swinging and stamping of feet to keep the chill out. "What the hell is he playing at in there?" Dick complained, getting colder by the minute.

Sister Tick slapped him about the face. "That's for speaking of God's house in such terms."

Dick could hardly believe his ears. "You're an outlaw!"

"I still took my vows, you ruffian!"

"*Ruffian?* You're an outlaw!"

"That's quite the repartee you've got there," Robyn drawled, sarcastically.

"Quiet!" Mardy Mario hissed. "There's someone out there."

"Suits me," growled Guillaumette le Rouge, drawing her short sword. "I'll cut his privates off!"

"Willa, *really*," Sister Tick complained. "You'll never get into Heaven with that filthy mouth of yours."

"What, that's worse than all the killing?"

Tick expanded to her full rotundity, always her way when pontificating. "Killing infidels cleanses the soul."

"So, that's what? A *maybe?*"

"Will you two be quiet?" Mario hissed again. Then they saw him. The black-ragged man.

Lott pulled Bodges into a doorway to hide. "The town gates are just ahead. There're torches lit, but the gates are open. That's good news for us, but it also means they must be expecting someone, which is bad news for us."

"How, erm, so?"

"Because, if the gates are open in the middle of the night, there will be a much heavier guard than usual. I heard that Lord Henry's brother could be joining him at any time. He's been asked to come sooner because of the earl's illness – that's the soldiers' gossip, anyway. Perhaps they're expecting him."

Bodges quailed. Sir Ralph was as violent and belligerent as his brother. "Where should we go?"

"We must get out of the town. You'll be in all sorts of trouble by morning otherwise. Walter Sweet is a pig. I heard some of the castle guards talking about that, too. He told them he wants to make an example of you for not tending the wounded – or get Lord Henry to do it for him. I think he's just got it in for medical men. He'd better hope he doesn't need us."

Bodges gulped. "B-but you want us to go out of the, erm, town? Into the night?"

"You'd rather stay here?"

"Oh..." The physician swooned.

Lott caught him. "Don't do that again! I need you to get us out of here."

"*Me?*"

Lott nodded, smiling craftily. "I have a plan, *Doctor* Bodges."

Barely had the lad explained his idea than Bodges found himself propelled towards the gates, right down the middle of Line Street. They could hear rowdy voices from the guard house. Lott had been right; there were indeed many guards on duty that night. In the low, flickering torchlight within the gateway, they could make out two figures, almost completely black but for the occasional copperish twinkle of firelight on mail.

"Friend or foe?"

"Who goes *there,* Ambrose. You've got to ask them who goes there before you follow up with friend or foe. I'm sick of telling you, lad. Look, it's really not difficult. Here, watch me... Who goes there? Friend or foe? See?"

Ambrose nodded with an unnerving keenness. "Got it, Roger. Do I chop at them with my sword now?"

"*No,* Ambrose. We have to let them answer before we despatch them – it would be unchivalrous otherwise."

"Right. Got it."

"Erm, erm, erm..." Bodges was shaking so much he could barely speak.

"Why, it's Dr Bodges, isn't it?" the guard named Roger enquired, suddenly oiling his manner. "Well, I haven't seen you in a hen's age – I'm glad to say." He winked and slapped his stomach heartily. "Fit as a granary cat, I am."

"Roger, why are you glad you haven't seen him?"

Roger rolled his eyes. "You remember young Ambrose, don't you, Dr Bodges? He's still learning the trade, you understand." He winked again. "Where might you be a-going at this hour? Only, I has to ask, see? And who's that with you?"

"M-my nephew, erm, *Roger*, was it? Erm…"

"That's nice, sir. And now, why is it you're up and about, and trying to pass my gate?"

"There are certain medicinal roots that only bloom just before first light, Sir Knight," Lott cut in, before Bodges could flounder any further.

Roger chuckled, though he seemed to stand somehow taller. "You've noticed my new sword." He unsheathed it lovingly. "But I ain't no knight, young master. Just a man-at-arms. Well, on you go, then. I'll let the boys know you've gone out, Dr Bodges. Just in case you get into any trouble."

"Erm, erm…"

"Thank you, Man-at-arms Roger," Lott called over his shoulder, bustling Bodges through the gateway quickly, before the man's nerves gave out altogether and he collapsed. "We can all sleep soundly knowing you and your brave lads are watching over us so vigilantly."

"He never answered." They heard Ambrose's voice as they slipped away into the pre-dawn blackness.

"Answered what, lad?"

"Whether he was a friend or a foe."

"Because we recognised him," Roger tried to explain.

"Does that mean he couldn't be a foe?"

The last thing Lott and Bodges heard was the dull *thwack* of a leather gauntlet connecting with a loosely fitting helmet.

Standing just four feet and three inches, Little Joan knew from bitter experience that giving an opponent the benefit of the doubt was a bad idea. So, as soon as she saw, she fired. The arrow *whooshed* through the air towards the target, almost quicker than sight. It struck with a leathery, percussive sound, like a foot striking a pig's bladder. The target did not move. Not at first. So she shot him again. Little Joan had also learned lessons about letting opponents get back up, too. A second hit – dead-centre of the chest.

Dead would have been the operative word, too, had it not already been too late. Indeed, dead, and late, described Not Dave rather well, which made it all the more surprising when he came for them.

Willa cried out, "Shoot him again, Joan!"

Another arrow grouped beautifully with its fellows, the triplet of goose feathers standing out like a bizarre chest wig. Not Dave staggered from the extreme force expended by Little Joan's long*ish* bow, but continued forward, nonetheless, and was soon upon them.

Willa screamed as she ran at him, hacking, her short sword chopping into his side to stick fast. She pulled but failed to free it. Without even glancing in her direction, Not Dave batted her aside. He was unarmed, but that hardly seemed to matter as Willa flew twenty feet to land, headfirst, legs kicking out of a lucky snowdrift.

Sister Tick produced an ass' jawbone from somewhere within her voluminous habit and swung for their attacker's head. When it connected, the sound was like a mouldy cabbage being hit with a bat.

Not Dave simply ignored the impact and continued forward to grab Mardy Mario by the wrist, rotating the knife out of his hand. Mario bellowed in pain as the golem twisted, a cry that died abruptly as he was struck so hard with a flat-hand to the chest that he, too, flew through the air like an empty wineskin.

Dick ran for the priory gates and began beating on their oaken boards, screaming to be let in.

Robyn was terrified, but drew her sword to stand in the monster's path. Taking a fighting stance, she prepared for the end, when a commotion from the priory gates behind them gave her hope. Sure enough, monks were drawing back the locking bars and shouting for the outlaws to be quick and enter.

She could see Mario stirring groggily to her right, and on her left, Willa was taking a second run at the dead-man-walking. Robyn knew Willa would never back down and if she gave ground to race for the gates herself, Mario would never make it, so she attacked. Her first swing took Not Dave's right arm off at the bicep. Robyn had no time to wonder about the lack of blood, she simply swung again – a backstroke – but this time, her arm juddered hard into Not Dave's raised left-handed block. It stopped her stroke dead, the shock down her arm making her cry out in pain.

Before Robyn could gather herself, Willa snatched up her leader's longsword from the ground and swung it for the creature's head, while Mario collected his wits enough to grab his wife from behind, manhandling her away towards the open gates.

Left alone with the adversary, Willa circled.

With his remaining arm, his left, Not Dave pulled Willa's short sword from his side and faced her.

Robyn's beautifully crafted longsword gave Willa the advantage in reach – or at least it would have done, were she not confronted by an opponent who could not be killed.

"Willa!" Robyn screamed as she was dragged away. "Don't be a fool – *run!*"

Willa continued to circle until her back was once more to the gates. Sensing she might bolt, Not Dave attacked. It was not a skilled attack. Whatever this golem had been in life, he was no fighter, but being indestructible made the point academic. The swords *clanged* with enough force to drive Willa back. She went for the initiative and swung low, to take him in the belly. Although unskilled, he was quick, and the short blade intercepted hers, even creating a few sparks in the night where the sharpened edges met.

Robyn was scrambling to get out of her husband's grasp, but so strong was Mario, that she may as well have been a rabbit caught in the coils of a python. "Let me go!"

By this time, even Willa's tower of rage was beginning to crumble. She waited for her foe to lunge and deflected the blow, sending him off balance. In the moment it took to regain his posture, she ran like a hare, dove through the open portal and rolled in the snow. No sooner did her feet leave the ground, than her short sword left Not Dave's hand, burying itself in the oak planks of the gate, exactly where her head had been just a split second earlier. The whole priory alert now, several monks gathered to slam them closed, while others began to slide the draw bars.

"Wait!" Willa cried. Running back, she thrust Robyn's sword back into her hand and pushed the men out of her way. Reopening one of the gates, she began prising and wriggling her own blade free of its boards. When the weapon came loose, she hollered, "Thank you!" and slammed the portal shut against the night and its creatures.

Chapter 14
In the Grey Light, Blackest Deeds

Felix L'Éternuement awoke at dawn. He usually did. The best hours for skulduggery passed at night, but business opportunities presented early, and L'Éternuement was a strong believer in the adage that an hour before noon was worth two after. He certainly had a lot to do.

Once the elation of regaining his freedom faded, he soon realised that yesterday had handed him mixed blessings. His plans for medicinal gift vouchers and health insurance were coming together splendidly – and he was sure they would catch on, too – but when Sweet summoned him back to the castle, he knew he was no longer safe.

The mere threat of torture had been enough to make L'Éternuement spill the beans about his business model to Sergeant-at-arms Walter Sweet. A vicious brute, and about as trustworthy as a wax cauldron. The very fact that Sweet was free again meant that someone knew his secret. The word was out – or could be, at any time of Sweet's choosing. Which meant L'Éternuement was suddenly at the beck and call of a very dubious character.

He had thought the situation dealt with when Sweet was thrown in the hole and like to die, forgotten. Of course, there was the other torturer, Alf, but L'Éternuement knew he could out-think and out-talk a numpty of that calibre – not to mention the fact that Lord Henry would never take the word of a serving man over gentry.

Now everything had changed. The earl *would* listen to his sergeant-at-arms. Despite differences in rank, each was cast from a mould that defied class distinction. They were brothers in violence.

L'Éternuement needed to move on, but it would take time to realise his assets, sell the house, and so on; time he doubted he had. That said, he never sat around when his own neck was on the line and had spent much of the night plotting a way to not only expedite his escape, but also to achieve his next goal into the bargain. Slicker than a goose's stool, he smiled at his own brilliance.

Consolidation and escape, yes, but first, breakfast. Taking a platter from the pantry, he sat at his kitchen table, removed the cloche, and munched on a couple of drumsticks and some cheese, left over from his so rudely interrupted dinner.

An hour later, and he was astride his grey gelding, heading south on the Parkworth road. Two miles from Warmstirrup, he spotted a large party heading north, towards him. They were led by horsemen, though the main body were on foot and escorting several carts. The road at this time of year was little more than a couple of grooves that cut through the slush and mud. Many men helped the ponies and oxen along by pushing the carts from the rear.

As he drew closer, and from his vantage point eight feet in the air, L'Éternuement could see the misery on their faces as flurries of alternating snow and sleet battered them, driving in from the coast to the east. Even the ponies' ears seemed to droop, although the oxen simply sweated stoically, snorting plumes of hot air as they huffed and puffed.

At the front of the column rode a wealthily dressed man wrapped in a vibrant red cape, clasped at the throat by a large silver brooch. If the clothes were not enough, his straight-backed manner and obvious comfort in the saddle picked him out immediately as Sir Ralph of Warmstirrup, Lord Henry's brother, en route from Parkworth Castle. The small town of Parkworth lay in a loop of the Foquet River near the coast, some six miles south-south-east, and L'Éternuement knew those men had every right to appear miserable. They must have left well before dawn to have made it this far, so early.

He shuffled his gelding off to the side as they met, bowing low over the pommel of his saddle. Once Sir Ralph had passed, he turned and fell into step with the horsemen, giddying-up his mount to draw level with the nobleman. Allowing Sir Ralph's horse to lead by a head, in due deference, he asked, "My lord, may I speak with you?"

Ralph looked down his nose at the stranger, mentally tallying the value of horse and tack. Noting a man of some means, unarmed but for a small knife at his belt, he nodded. "And you are?"

"Felix L'Éternuement, merchant of Warmstirrup and apothecary to the earl, your brother, my lord."

"L'Éternuement?" he scoffed. "And what could you possibly want from me, Master Felix the Sneeze?"

Ralph and Henry were brothers alright, they had all the same lines, but L'Éternuement resisted the impulse to roll his eyes – if he had, his head would surely have followed. "I have something *for* you, my lord. Do I guess correctly that you travel from Parkworth Castle to your brother in Warmstirrup?"

"Pork."

"Excuse me?"

Sir Ralph studied him coolly. "Locally, we pronounce it Porkworth."

"But it's spelt..." Sir Ralph's eyes flashed and L'Éternuement tailed off. *Same temper as his brother, too,* he thought hurriedly. "Of course, my lord. *Porkworth* Castle, it is. How silly of me."

"Why do you wish to know where I travel? What's it to you?"

L'Éternuement bowed obsequiously. "Only in that, should you indeed be heading for Warmstirrup Castle, then the offer I have for you is along our route, my lord."

"Explain."

"May we trot just a little way ahead, my lord, to avoid being overheard? It really would be worth your while."

The heavy banging on the door woke Matty and Dora with a start. Instinctively, the women held each other in fright as the door gave way and armed men burst into Dora's hovel like they owned the place.

"Matty the whore?" their leader enquired brusquely.

Matty let Dora go, gently pushing her friend away and behind. "I am Matilda."

He looked her up and down, taking in the expensive gown she had stolen from the earl. "You will come with us. Lord Henry demands your presence."

"And if I say no?"

He slapped her hard across the face, knocking her to the floor.

Dora screamed and tried to help her friend back up, but in her weakened state, only fell herself.

"You will come with *me!*" he snarled. "Don't think that fancy rig will save you, girl. I know what you are. Now get out, or the other whore will pay for your insolence. She looks like she's at death's door already."

"No!" Matty regained her feet, pulling Dora up behind. "I'll be alright," she comforted. Turning back to Henry's brute, she said, "How did you find me?"

He scoffed. "In that dress? Around this part of town? It wasn't difficult. Even Ambrose could have found you."

"Ambrose was better before he became a guard. He's a simple boy. You're turning him into a monster."

"He's simple, alright." He cuffed her again. "Now shut your face, trollop, or I'll have you whipped all the way to the castle – see how much you earn covered in scars, eh?" He leered over her, his breath stinking of sour ale.

Matty straightened. Looking him in the eye, she spoke coldly. "Lead on."

Leaving Dora with a reassuring smile, she strode out, the other guards following.

Lord Henry's throne-like chair sat upon a staged area at the end of the keep's great hall. Behind it, a large, mullioned window threw what light the morning offered into the chamber. That light streaked through it in all the blues, reds, yellows and greens available to the 14th century master glazier, the glass itself having been rescued from a local church, burnt down in a Scottish raid some years previously. Even on a cold February morning, Lord Henry was thrown into silhouette; a deliberate device, while the supplicant was fully lit for his scrutiny.

He brooded in silence, waiting for Matty to regain her feet after being thrown to the rushes before the dais. Mustering all the dignity she could under the circumstances, she stood, straightening her frock, brushing rushes and dirt from its folds. Straight-backed, she glared defiantly up at him.

Lord Henry sat with elbows on the arms of his great chair, fingers steepled in contemplation as he studied her. The seat and the leather jerkin under his plate armour creaked as he leaned forward slightly. "You wear the blue silk," he began, unusually quietly. "An aristocratic colour to which you have no right, but you wear it well, nonetheless."

Matty stared, not trusting herself to speak. Unsure whether she would rage or collapse in tears, she held herself in check and remained silent.

"Would you like to keep that dress?"

"What?" His question caught her so completely off-guard that the word just dropped out.

The chamber fell silent, everyone awaiting the earl's response. When he began to chuckle, others followed his lead and the tension lifted – but not for Matty.

"I said there might be a way for you to earn that dress – the one to which you have no rights. Interested?"

Matty's mind raced, but what choice did she have? "My lord." She curtsied, lowering her eyes. It was neither a yes nor a no, but he took it as acquiescence, as she knew he would. A peasant girl's refusal would have been unimaginable to him.

"Approach," he ordered, beckoning with a finger.

Once again, having no choice, she approached the dais to stand before the great chair, looking even further up at her lord's silhouette. It was all about power, she knew, but it worked. She was terrified. Completely at the mercy of a man whom she knew to have very little. To her surprise, he rose from his throne-like seat and sat down on the edge of the stage, feet swinging, his face only slightly above her own. She tried to hide her confusion. Was this a show of favour? If so, favour for what? She could hardly imagine him remembering her kindly – not after she had drugged and practically enslaved him for a couple of days. Perhaps it was merely a display of dexterity, to show off to his men how easily he moved, despite his full plate armour; armour that was hinged and detailed beautifully, only missing a great helm. It probably cost more than a small church.

He reached into the underside of his left gauntlet and pulled out a piece of tatty parchment, holding it out to her. "Recognise this?"

She considered lying, and he must have read it in her eyes.

"The truth now – your life may depend upon it."

Matty squinted, still unable to fully make out his features with the light behind him, while her every twitch and expression was lit for him to read with ease. "Yes." She felt more than saw him stiffen. "My lord," she added, quickly.

Henry relaxed. They were on show before his men. He could allow no lapses in deference, and Matty knew full well that should she cross the line between acting with dignity and acting with contempt, her life might be forfeit. She took the parchment and opened it. It was indeed the short script Insane Alice had given her with the potion she procured.

He surprised her by taking her chin in his hand, not ungently. "Someone has hit you."

Belatedly, Matty realised that pig of a guard must have marked her when he slapped her to the floor of Dora's hovel. Expecting little better at the hands of the earl, she decided to give neither the satisfaction. "I fell, my lord."

Giving no warning, Lord Henry clapped his gauntleted hands together with a *clop*. "Leave us," he shouted, loudly enough for all to hear.

Matty jumped in spite of herself, breathing deeply as she tried to calm her nerves and drum-rolling heart. Obviously, Henry needed to be seen as fully in control of the woman some believed to have bewitched him. That task accomplished, he wished to question her alone. Matty had no idea whether that would be a good thing, but guessed she was about to find out.

L'Éternuement and Sir Ralph entered Warmstirrup's southern gate with no great inconvenience. Both men were known to the guards, who already had orders to expect a force travelling north from Parkworth Castle. Peasants and traders attempting to go about their early chores were simply shoved off the road or out of the way by spearmen, to let the earl's brother pass unimpeded.

Sir Ralph's entourage made their way noisily and carelessly along Line Street, towards Warmstirrup Castle. L'Éternuement rode in a place of favour, just behind Sir Ralph. Many of his neighbours were preparing their business frontages for the day ahead, and he revelled in their attention, making sure he greeted his peers, one by one. Theirs were among the most fashionable addresses in the far north and he would now be the talk of the place. Even looks of outright loathing flushed warm currents beneath the wings of his ego, for he knew them to be born of envy.

Presently, they drew to a halt in front of his new house and shop, just outside the castle gates. He turned expectantly to Sir Ralph, who looked the property over with an experienced eye for calculating value, if not worth. He glanced to L'Éternuement and nodded once.

L'Éternuement smiled and bowed low over his pommel, once more. He was about to take his leave, when one of his liveried urchins splashed noisily through the slush towards him from the north gate. "Master," the boy called, breathlessly.

L'Éternuement noted the child still bore the package he had been sent to deliver. Having no wish to be embarrassed by minor problems of business before his new benefactor, he jumped down and took the parcel from him, exchanging it for his reins. "Take Caligula to his stable and brush him down, boy."

"But, master," the urchin continued, unwilling to be swayed. "I've seen a demon!"

This caused a stir all around them. L'Éternuement looked down murderously at the boy for bursting his bubble of self-regard.

"What's this tale?" demanded Sir Ralph, grandly, but with concern, nonetheless.

"It's true." The boy turned away from L'Éternuement, infuriating him further. He addressed Sir Ralph directly. "At Aynlton Priory, lord."

L'Éternuement span the child back to him. "You were to deliver this package. What happened?"

"Never mind that, L'Éternuement," Sir Ralph grunted as he dismounted. "Tell me, from the beginning, boy, what have you seen?"

Most peasants quailed in the presence of a great magnate, but the child simply blinked at him, staring brazenly, as only a small boy can. Once he had his breath back, he recounted his run to deliver a poultice to the miller, just west of the monastery. "The road along the river passes Aynlton Priory just before you reach the mill, your worship."

L'Éternuement slapped the urchin around the head. "Address Sir Ralph as *my lord,* you little scrote."

The boy gawped, only half understanding. "I often say hello to the brothers," he continued unabashed, "if any of them are out on their lands, but today only one man stood in front of the priory gates. At least, he looked like a man, m'lord. I was about to wish him a good morning – folk are less likely to take a kick at an urchin if you says 'ello, m'lord. That was when Brother Luke started shouting from the little hole in the gate." He turned to L'Éternuement. "Shouting for me to run for my life, master. He said the thing was no man, but a demon. A thing of dead flesh, he called it, m'lord. He told me to fetch soldiers. So I ran."

L'Éternuement clipped him around the ear again. "You took it upon yourself not to deliver the poultice to an injured man, risking *my* reputation!"

Sir Ralph scowled. "Enough. If the brothers really were shouting such warnings, and calling for our help, then we must take this very seriously and investigate. Of course, if this is just some trick to get out of your duties," Sir Ralph clutched the boy's shoulder and bent down to eye level, "then you'll wish you'd never been born. Understand me, boy?"

The urchin nodded, frightened, at last. "I swear, lord."

Ralph straightened. "Very well. We'll take the boy with us."

L'Éternuement looked up in surprise. "But, Sir Ralph, what about our bargain?"

"It can wait." He leapt lightly back into the saddle. "Have no fear, I'll track down that renegade apothecary that murdered your apprentice, but clearly this is something that must be dealt with quickly. If Aynlton is under attack, I'd rather nip it in the bud than suffer endless, interminable begging letters and visits from that old rogue, Prior Augustus, to repair any damage!"

Ralph barked orders for half his men and two of his knights to continue into the castle with the carts. There, they would stow their provisions and report to the earl, explaining the possible threat to the priory. He looked L'Éternuement up and down, as he stood in the slush, still holding his horse's reins. His first impulse was to force the wealthy apothecary to join them, in case this was all some trick, but then he decided the journey would be more agreeable without him. After all, he knew where he could find him, should any punishment become due later. "Sir William." He beckoned one of his knights to him.

A great bear of a man expertly slalomed his destrier between the soldiers rushing around them. "Sir Ralph?" he growled.

"Will, this boy can take us by the local paths, but I don't want him slowing us down. Lift him up with you."

"Wait!" L'Éternuement pushed the poultice back into the child's hands. "If you're going back near the mill, you can take this. And don't forget to ask John the Miller for a penny, understand?"

With that, the urchin was hefted bodily and wide-eyed to sit in front of the giant's saddle, ready to ride into battle.

"I can't read, my lord," Matty admitted, sadly.

Henry studied her. It was no surprise, of course. Virtually none of the peasantry could, yet he was still not sure whether he believed her. She was obviously as cunning as a vixen with a back door key to the henhouse. "You're telling me, you've no idea what that missive says?"

She shook her head honestly. "No, my lord. Do you wish me to know?"

He gave her a sideways look. "It prophesies my death."

Matty's sharp intake of breath went some way towards convincing him. Unaware of the note's full contents, she thought, *Oh, Alice, what have you got me into?*

Henry stepped down from the dais and moved to one of the long feasting tables that were placed at either side of the hall while not in use. A large jug of ale sat at one end, along with several wooden cups and one pewter tankard. He filled the tankard and one of the cups, handing the latter to Matty. "You look like you could do with a drink."

She smiled, in spite of herself. He was almost charming when it suited him. She drank deeply. It was best quality ale, not the small beer everyone took with meals because it was safer than drinking the water. It was strong, and he was right, she needed it.

He smiled back at her, every inch the rugged northern hero in his shining armour. Had she not seen his other side, she would have been quite enamoured – but she had seen his other side, so she drank, dreading what might come next.

"Sit." He invited her to take a seat beside him, on one of the long benches.

Again, having no choice, Matty did so. She just hoped this was going where she thought it might be going. She knew men well enough, after all. If there was something else afoot, it might be far worse for her – she knew that, too.

"Now," he began, pleasantly. She had not heard this tone from him before. She suppressed a shudder as she imagined herself a noble lady, about to be wooed by a creature of shining silver, only to find herself ensnared and then caged by a new owner, with naught to look forward to but dangerous births and brutal, drunken mood swings. "I believe you, that you can't read this," he continued, charmingly. "But there's surely something you *can* tell me."

"My lord?" Matty's nerves shook her voice, though she tried to conceal them.

"Who gave it to you?"

Oh, God, please help me, she thought.

Harry climbed the narrow spiral stair. It was of stone and located within a corner of the prior's lodgings. The building, constructed so that the prior could entertain visiting church or state dignitaries in the manner to which they were accustomed, showed signs of decay from lack of use. Augustus was a traditionalist and usually shared a dorm with his monks, as set out within the Rule of St Benedict, while also saving money the priory could ill afford. Light pooled across uneven steps at each level from slits built into the walls. Each no wider than a hand's breadth, they granted periodic glimpses over the priory walls to the river and forest beyond. As he neared the top, Harry could see all the way to Warmstirrup and its castle, two miles southeast.

Harry guessed Prior Augustus, or Gus, must have been at least sixty, and in his experience, few lived to be so old. Yet he scampered up the stairs quickly enough to embarrass a younger man – which he did.

Harry finally wheezed his way to the top and found a small oak door already open. It led out onto the roof where Gus waited, looking out with concern.

Blinking in the full morning light, Harry looked around the decorative parapet walls. Though beautiful, they, too, were in a state of some disrepair. The randomly coursed stone slates that covered the cut-raftered roof also showed gaps, some having broken in half to slide down into the lead valleys around the perimeter, where Harry and Gus now stood. Others had slipped when the wooden pegs holding them rotted and gave way. Even the lead showed damage from too many seasons of expansion and contraction. It occurred to Harry that, under the patchy snow, things might be even worse. He made light of it. "Looks like you need a few masons up here."

"Have you seen how much those characters charge? It's enough to make the angels weep." Gus spoke with equal levity, though Harry guessed the state of their roof must have been a source of great concern for the old man. If the angels did weep, they'd certainly feel their tears first, through all the holes.

"He's still there," Gus continued in more sombre tones.

Harry looked over the parapet, and sure enough, there stood the undying man, motionless in the open ground between the priory and the River Aynl[1]. Blown snow covered him all down one side. It was a strange, unnatural sight. The heat from a living body would have melted the snow as it landed. Harry squinted, craning forward unconsciously. No, that was not weirdest thing, not by a long way. The man also seemed to have *reconnected* his lopped arm.

The two men on the roof looked at each other gravely. "Have you anything, in all your learning, that might explain this, Gus?"

The old man thought for a moment. "All I can suggest is that you and your friends stay here for now. No devils or unclean things may trespass on hallowed ground. If he could, he would have taken you all in the night. Speaking as of right now, we have no way to dispatch the foul creature, but my sacrist, Brother Michael, and my librarian, Brother Barnabas, are searching our religious texts for rites of exorcism." He sighed, shaking his head. "Though, I confess, we have no idea what we're dealing with. I hate to admit it, but..."

Harry looked at him sharply. "Go on."

The old man sighed again. Whatever he had to say, it was clearly costing him. "We may find that the only person with understanding of the evil sent against us, is——"

"Insane Alice," Harry completed for him.

---

1. Warmstirrup's people remain insistent that Ann'l is the correct pronunciation.

Gus nodded, looking down at his hands. "All we can do is pray for guidance from God and for the strength of our Lord Jesus Christ. The old wi..." He tailed off mid-sentence. "That is, *Alice*, obviously knew enough to send you to me. She knew the creature would not be able to enter our walls – praise be to God. Perhaps she knows how we might dispose of this... this *monstrosity*, too."

Harry was unsure about that. If she did know, surely she would have done so already. Unless she was merely keeping him safe while she was about it, but then that begged the question, why? Indeed, she had gone to some lengths to keep him safe. Alright, he had been inadvertently robbed along the way, but that was not her doing. Why *did* she care? What was going on? Just a few days ago, his financial situation seemed grave – and was still, for that matter – but all that seemed like a minor inconvenience compared with what had happened since. He had been accused of a murder he knew nothing about and sentenced to death by his lord; attacked and robbed by a cutthroat, who turned out to be a childhood friend; hounded and shot at by soldiers; kidnapped and robbed again by outlaws; and now he was being pursued by some order of undead creature.

He cupped his head in his hands. "What the begat[2]?" he exclaimed in disbelief.

"What was that, my son?"

"Nothing, Gus. Perhaps I'm suffering from a bout of woodnesse[3] – or maybe it's the rest of the world. I don't know any more." He lowered his hands and looked to the older man. "I just can't see how things could get

---

2. Harry-the-Cough had no idea that 'what the begat' or 'wtb' would form the base root of an initialism that would pop up again six centuries later, and thousands of miles away across the Atlantic, to mean exactly the same thing.

3. Woodnesse was a word used in Middle English to describe madness. The base form, 'wod', evolved from the old high German 'wuot', which was also associated with rage. Harry found he was experiencing both at the unfairness of his situation.

any worse."

The prior's hand shot out from his robe, pointing along the riverbank to the south. "Look, armed men, coming this way."

Harry bowed his head. "I stand corrected. Why don't I just go for a bit of a jump, now?"

Gus was scandalised. "To even think that is a most terrible sin, young man."

Harry swore, ending on a double.

Not for the first time, Matty's mind raced. How could she possibly answer without getting Insane Alice into trouble, and by trouble, she meant killed. For if Lord Henry knew that a witch lived in the forest near Warmstirrup, he would deem it his Christian duty to burn her alive. The old crone may have her strange little ways, but she was the closest thing to a doctor the peasants in the countryside could hope for – and unlike the majority of doctors, most of her patients got better.

Lord Henry's expression softened once more. Matty really was seeing another side to him, false or not. "You're loath to give up a friend," he surmised. "Loyalty to friends is a fine thing," his eyes flashed, "but loyalty to your lord is a given!"

She flinched as he took her arm. "Tell me who gave you that parchment." When she failed to answer he nodded, as if to himself. "Very well. I know you used some form of magic to confound me when you slipped that note into my jacket. Therefore, I can only assume *you* are the witch. Sergeant-at-arms!" he bellowed. "Prepare a fire in the courtyard. Mount a nice tall stake at its heart, so we can watch the witch burn, slowly."

Walter Sweet appeared as if by magic, himself. Matty wondered if he had been listening all along and whether Henry knew it but did not care.

Matty screamed. "No!"

Henry shook her roughly, bruising her arm with his gauntlet and a vice-like grip born of hours spent engaging in swordplay every single day. He had no intention of killing her, or Harry, after the stark warning he had received, but he could tell from the fear in her eyes that she did not realise that – his ruse was working. "No? Then tell me what I wish to know. Otherwise, it will be the fire for you and for your friend, Harry-the-Cough, when my men find him. You may be interested to know he has taken up with outlaws in the forest, but not for long, I assure you." He grinned, nastily. "Well?"

Matty could see no choice, but just as she opened her mouth to speak, glorious inspiration struck at last. If she gave up Insane Alice's hovel, they would surely raze it to the ground and murder her, horribly. So she gave them another location to search, a place that sounded suitably 'witchy', but one she knew Alice rarely visited. It would not fool them for long, but if she could just buy some time...

"She's with Old Tom," she confessed, with all the feigned contrition she could muster.

Life is full of disastrous good intentions. Desperate to save Insane Alice and Harry from Lord Henry, Matty had no idea that Alice's hovel had already been razed to the ground by Mad Mab, forcing her to camp near the great oak known locally as Old Tom. Or that Alice was only there so that she could keep vigil over Harry-the-Cough. Despite her understanding with Prior Augustus, any closer to the priory would be to risk becoming the centrepiece at the heart of her own campfire.

By virtue of Alice's written warning to Lord Henry, Harry no longer lived under threat of execution, although no one *but* Lord Henry knew that. Harry desperately needed Alice's help to keep Mad Mab at bay – although he was yet to find out why. Meanwhile, Mab's creature awaited Harry and the rarely-merry-not-all-men, should they try to leave the hallowed grounds of their cloistered enclosure. Something Harry had no intention of doing, until he spotted Sir Ralph and his entourage bearing down on them, after making a secret deal with L'Éternuement.

The priory walls would offer Harry no protection from Sir Ralph and his troops, and Lord Henry's soldiers would be in no position to rescue him from Ralph's grasp, either, as they were on the opposite side of the river with orders to capture Insane Alice.

At such times, Lady Fortune is often accused of being fickle, but that is largely unfair. Indeed, she provides a helpful framework within which mere mortals may glimpse their future. Hence, when things are up, they are up, and when things are down – look out. She actually gets her kicks from hiding the turning points – what some might call, the switchbacks – which is why mankind so frequently crashes through the barriers.

Sir Ralph had no idea he was about to crash in on Harry's hiding place. On the seesaw of life and luck, he was all set to launch, kicking out his legs and whooping with joy, while Harry was all set to land hard at the other end, hurting his bottom.

Yet in the universal game of 'heads or tails', life by no means had it all its own way. Death, too, had its ironies in store for the unwary. Harry was about to find out about those, too.

Chapter 15
In Troubles of Plenty

Harry burst into the refectory, shouting. His companions were still at breakfast and looked up in alarm. Sub Prior Robert glared at him furiously, whereas Sister Tick stood, bowed to the sub prior and slapped Harry about the head. "That's for causing such a fracas in this holy place of con-tem-pla-tion." She slapped him again and again in time with each syllable.

"Ow-ow-ow-ow," Harry cried out in time with each blow.

The sub prior nodded his approval and continued to read from the Rule of St Benedict.

"Listen!" Harry hissed urgently. "That *thing* is still at the gates and now we have soldiers galloping along the river towards us, too. What should we do?"

Robyn got to her feet, instinctively reaching for her sword, but of course, it was safely stowed in the sub prior's office with much of their other gear.

He would never allow men – let alone women – to wander about the precinct so armed. Charged with keeping his monks' thoughts on holy matters, he felt that it was bad enough the women *had* hips, without carrying weapons at them.

Extricating himself from Sister Tick's correctional services, Harry walked quickly to Sub Prior Robert. "Father, forgive this interruption," he remembered his manners at last.

Robert stopped reading once more to glower at him. "Yes?"

"We must gather our belongings. There are soldiers coming."

"Of course there are. One of the brethren called out to a boy this morning, telling him to fetch them. Doubtless they ride from Warmstirrup Castle to our succour."

Harry visibly wilted. "Really?"

"You should rejoice, young man!"

"But…"

"But? Are you outlawed?"

"Er… it's complicated, Father. May we get our things, please?"

Sub Prior Robert hissed with annoyance. "Brother Luke! Continue the reading. You," he jabbed Harry with a long, schoolmasterly finger, "come with me. The quicker you and your *men* are outside our walls the better!"

Harry summoned his companions, overarm, and they followed the obedientiary from the chamber as Brother Luke continued reading from the Rule.

The horsemen urged their steeds to a gallop as they approached Aynlton Priory. Sir Ralph, like his brother, believed in speed and violence, with no time wasted thinking things through. It was for that very reason they had both been captured by the Scots a few years ago, and at the same time, too. Their combined ransoms paid for the building of a small castle, yet it was the Warmstirrup way to charge in where angels fear to tread, a strategy that earned them respect among allies and enemies alike – though perhaps the latter had more to do with the free castle.

Sir Ralph bellowed, just in case the opposition failed to notice their advance. Say what you like, there was nothing covert about the man.

At the same moment, Prior Augustus held his crucifix out through the small hatch in the main gate. "Be gone! In the name of the Father, the Son and the... ooh." He brightened as the unclean creature turned away and strode out into the river.

Much of the ice had melted overnight, and Not Dave crashed immediately through what was left, disappearing into the murky depths.

"Ah-ha!" Gus shouted, drunk on the power of the Lord. When Sir Ralph charged in, screaming, he looked a little put out.

"Where's the devil gone?" bellowed the knight. "Find him, damn you!"

"He walked into the river, m'lord," a child's voice pointed out.

Sir Ralph span his mount to see where the boy was pointing and could just make out what remained of a disturbance in the patchy ice floating slowly downstream. "Damn!" he spat, sheathing his sword.

"What's wrong, Sir Ralph?" Sir William boomed from behind the urchin's head.

"What's wrong? I'll tell you what's wrong, shall I? My brother's the first born, so he gets pretty much everything. Have you any idea how much I have to pay these lazy monks to sing for my soul each year? Then there's that useless hermit in his cave, just outside Parkworth. At least, he calls it a cave. Have you seen the place? He's got it looking like a mini-minster in there, replete with decoratively carved fornications – and while we're on *that* subject, I can see why he set up shop away from prying eyes——"

"Sir Ralph," someone interrupted, calmly.

Losing his thread, but unwilling to be diverted from his rant, Sir Ralph continued, "My money buys more pies than piety! Then we have the 'all-night vigils'. Ha! Parties more like! With loud campanology going all hours. It's not appealing for the people who live on the opposite bank of the Foquet, I can tell you that. And I'm paying for it all[1]! I thought this wretched demon might get me a year off, maybe two, or even ten! I mean, just how much would the killing of a demon be worth to these damned monks? Come spring, and with a down payment like that, I could have raped and pillaged my way through half of Middlesex[2] – and still marched straight into Heaven."

He roared in wordless fury.

"Ahem."

Sir Ralph turned his horse at last. "Oh, it's you, Father Augustus. Good morning."

"And good morning to you, Sir Ralph," Gus greeted, frostily. His usually kindly face contorted with disapproval, he crossed the nobleman, adding, "Bless you."

Robyn led Harry and the rest of their party out from the smaller north gate. While dear old Prior Augustus kept the soldiers talking at the south gate, they ran west for the distant treeline, over the monks' fields. During the night, the easterly wind had drifted snow against the edges of the forest, so it came as a surprise when three of their number vanished from sight with a crack, a splash, and a cry.

---

1. Some might hold out such a statement as proof that almost every working soul in the world is broke, just at a different level.

2. Middlesex (Middle Saxon) became the County of Greater London in 1965. Of course, Sir Ralph and Lord Henry had no idea that their, and others', actions in Middlesex, supporting Henry Bolingbroke (the future King Henry IV), would eventually lead to the Wars of the Roses. It's still a bit of a thorny subject in the north.

Dick leaned down to pull Harry back out – the second time he had pulled him out of trouble – as Sister Tick bent to help Robyn. Her husband was nowhere to be seen.

"R-r-roll in the s-snow," Harry called. "T-trust me." Without further ado, he set words to actions and came up looking like a snowman. Robyn was too shocked with cold to harangue anyone, so she did as he suggested and was flabbergasted to find that, rather than dying of extreme cold, she was suddenly merely unspeakably miserable.

For Mardy Mario, miserable was his default, but there was always room to slip – physically and metaphorically, as it turned out. He would have bellowed in fury, had he the breath. It took four of them to pull him from the freezing stream.

"W-what the hell?" he managed.

"It's a leat – a d-damned l-leat!" Harry explained angrily. "It carries a controllable and constant flow of water down from higher ground to run the mill. Either the first miller or the monks must have tapped the Aynl upstream when they originally built on this site, a hundred and fifty years ago. Quick, into the forest. Those men would have to be deaf to miss all this going on!"

Having discovered the leat, they leapt it easily, vanishing into the forest beyond. Another hundred yards of stumbling among roots and underbrush brought them to a stop for breath. Harry checked his belongings. Poor weather was not uncommon when visiting clients, so he had always used an oilskin bag to protect his medicaments, though he never dreamt he might be undertaking any amphibious operations. He opened the bag, dreading what he might see inside, and was greatly relieved to find its contents relatively dry, including his recipe book. His very life was written into those pages. Should he lose them...

He barely had time to mull that prospect over when a thought hit him like a fish in the face. Mad Mab's spell. "That m-must b-be it!" he hissed through chattering teeth.

Dick hunkered down next to him. "What must be?"

Harry cursed inwardly. He had never told anyone about Mab's ancient writings in the back of his apothecary recipes book. With a snap decision, he explained, "I have all my notes in a book. Everything I know. But there's also something else. Before she gave me the empty book, so that I might keep notes, Mad Mab wrote an incantation down in the back. I don't know what it is or what it means. I don't even believe she realised what she'd given me, and then she died and, well... it didn't seem to matter after that. Now it appears she didn't die, so it does matter. She's after me for something and I can't imagine what else it might be. It's not like she ever cared for me."

Harry watched closely during his explanation. Maybe he imagined it, but Dick's eyes seemed to light up, just for a second, when Harry mentioned the book and Mab's spell. It was a risk. He still felt unsure about the boy he once knew, now inhabiting the body of a man he had only just met, but rather than wait for a stab from behind, Harry thought it best to set up his new-old friend for a fall and see what happened. At least, if *he* set the trap, he might be able to control the situation.

Then there were the outlaws. He was far from sure about them, either. About the only thing they had going for them was that they worked, at least some of the time, for Insane Alice. Matty trusted the crone, and Matty, though young, was nobody's fool. Guiltily, he wondered how she fared. Thinking about her at the castle *working* hardly helped. So he returned his thoughts to the moment.

As far as he could tell, they had gotten away free. There were no sounds of pursuit, despite their untimely dip in the miller's leat, and with that came another idea – he knew John the Miller.

Insane Alice knew the soldiers were coming for her, long before they arrived. A rabbit told her. She bowed respectfully to Old Tom and headed east, towards the Priory. She knew Harry would be safe there, but could she trust him to *stay* there? She knew little of the man he had grown into, except that mentioned in passing by Matty, and one or two other clients they shared. Even if *he* were not the impetuous type, could she rely on Robyn and her full-spectrum band to stay put?

One thing was certain, she could not remain where she was, and that set her to wondering how anyone *knew* where she was. She doubted Robyn would have blabbed – besides, there had been no opportunity. So how? Matty, she felt sure, would never have given her away. Neither did she have any knowledge of Alice's visit to Old Tom. "Oh…" She stopped in her tracks, realising what must have happened.

If she was right, then Matty must also be in trouble. Alice was grateful the girl had kept secret the location of her hovel, but her timing was awful.

She stepped into the treeline, vanishing from Old Tom's clearing with nothing more than a rustle of snow from a branch. Just a few yards in, she gave a shrill, keening call, and within moments, a circle of woodland creatures occupied every available space upon the ground and lower branches around her; all waiting attentively for orders. She communicated her wishes with gestures, language and symbolism that Christian moderners of the late 14th century might well have called 'eldritch', the word 'hippy' not having been invented yet. Rabbits, badgers, robins, deer, and even Mr Foxy, scattered immediately once she had finished. Insane Alice nodded to herself and vanished further into the forest.

When Sergeant-at-arms Walter Sweet arrived with a detachment of soldiers, they found the clearing empty but for an abandoned campfire. Snow, from the night before, was criss-crossed with the tracks of every kind of woodland creature imaginable. Sweet shuddered. What the hell had they been up to? Dancing around the campfire? Ever one for a timely jest, he crossed himself.

"Where did you learn that trick about rolling in snow?" asked Robyn, also hunkering down next to Harry. She was shivering again.

"From an old shepherd. You might say, he fell into it, when he went through the ice while crossing one of the frozen pools up in the hills, after his flock. Said he got out, slipped again, and rolled down a bank. Being encased in snow warmed him up enough to get his breath back and get moving – gave him time to find his hut. He swore it was the only reason he made it back alive. I always try to remember anything people tell me about remedies and treatments, however odd. I've never tried this before, personally. Now I have, I can see the method has a flaw…"

"W-what's th-that?"

"It m-melts." Harry shivered in sympathy. "We c-can't stay here. It'll be the death of those of us who took a p-plunge."

"We can't b-be s-sure those soldiers have left," Robyn countered.

"That's alright. I know s-someone who'll take us in. F-follow me." Without their leafy cloaks, the trees offered less concealment than Harry would have liked, so he kept low at first, continuing west and south. Ducking under bare branches, they travelled no more than a quarter of a mile before they smelt woodsmoke.

The trees were thinning, eventually opening out onto a plain, and before them, they saw the mill near the river. The miller lived in a small shack, built against the side of the larger building. Harry assumed John the miller was in because his chimney belched smoke. The old mill and its welcoming fire made for a cheerful winter's scene as they set off across the open ground towards it.

Sheltered from the wind by the forest, the snow had not drifted this side. Having cut through the forest, the leat was clearly visible and crossed by a small wooden cart bridge, close to the mill itself.

"Walk in single file," Robyn instructed them as she followed in Harry's footsteps.

They crossed the water without incident to knock on John's door.

"Who is it?" The voice sounded weary, even through the timber.

"It's me, John. Harry-the-Cough."

"Oh, good."

Harry turned to Robyn and Dick, raising his eyebrows. "Sounds hopeful."

They heard the sliding of a wooden bar from inside and the door swung open. "Harry!" greeted the miller. "Come in——" His greeting died as he noticed the others. "Who are these?"

"Friends, John. May we shelter with you f-for a little while? Th-three of us took a t-tumble into your leat and we're catching our d-deaths."

The miller's expression cleared. "Yes, yes, come in. Of course. Well, bless me, Harry-the-Cough. Who told you?"

"Told me what?"

"About my accident." He rolled up a sleeve to reveal a nasty cut and some heavy bruising to his forearm.

"How'd you do that?"

The miller wore a rueful expression. "Caught it in the cogs on the main driveshaft from my wheel. Lucky I got it out, before it took my arm off."

"Lucky indeed, but why didn't you come to me, or have someone fetch me? That's a few days old."

John looked shamefaced. "Sorry, Harry. My wife wanted me to go to that *southern,* you know, the one with the stinking fish. What's his name? Lecherer?"

Harry soured. "L'Éternuement. But close enough."

"Well, you know how it is, Harry. All her friends in the town are making him out to be some sort of miracle worker and——"

"He has miraculous powers to part people from their money, I'll give him that," Harry interrupted bitterly.

"Aye." John smiled. "I just wanted a bit of peace, lad. You know, a quiet life. So I agreed in the end. When I heard your knock at the door, I thought it might be my delivery."

Harry soured some more. "Delivery?"

John nodded, innocently. "All part of the service, apparently. You should get into it."

"That's what Bavol told me."

"Bavol the sail? That old bag o' wind could fill his sails all on his own."

"Maybe, but he was right about L'Éternuement. He's burying me. Or at least, he's in the queue to finish me off." He studied John's wound, squeezing it as gently and carefully as he could. It was alarmingly swollen, and pus came from the cut. The miller was tough as old boots, but the sharp intake of breath gave away his suffering. "You're lucky I came by, John. You'll get no peace with this. In fact, if you put that idiot's filthy muck on it, I'm not even sure I could guarantee you the 'life'. It needs treating, properly, and now."

"It's that bad?"

"It's septic."

The miller noticed Harry was shaking. "Some of you are wet through, freezing. Here, come and dry yourselves by the fire."

Willa seemed fascinated by the miller's wound.

"Robyn," Harry called across the room. "Would you ask one of your men to——"

He stopped talking abruptly when Willa glared up at him with a berserk intensity.

"Erm, that is, one of your wom——"

Willa growled.

"Perhaps you could ask one of your *associates* to keep watch up the lane for those soldiers?"

Robyn nodded to Willa, who left without a word.

"What's wrong with her?" asked Harry, quietly.

Robyn shrugged. "She had a bad start."

"Doesn't say much, does she?" he continued uncertainly.

"Doesn't usually need to."

"Right. I can see why that might be the case. Man-hater, is she?"

Robyn considered the question. "No... At least, I don't think so... She doesn't usually discriminate."

Harry nodded, deciding it was best not to speculate. He took the long knife from his belt and heated it in the fire.

"W-what's that for?" the miller stuttered nervously. "Haven't you just got a, a... I don't know, an ointment or summat?"

"*You* should have called me in earlier, John. Now this, my friend," he held up the blade, now glowing gently red, "is what they call being cruel to be kind. Don't worry, there'll be all the ointment you can eat, later."

John gulped. "Maybe we should wait. You know, 'til the missus gets back, eh?"

"Oh, I don't think so." Harry smiled, his wet things hissing as he turned his back to the fire. "I'm not sure how long we'll be able to stay."

John Miller screamed.

Mad Mab watched Sir Ralph's soldiers as they milled about, searching for her creation on the opposite bank of the River Aynl. Or perhaps, she reflected, *re*creation described him best. After all, Not Dave was not *all* her own work. He had been a man once, born of woman, and into the world from a magic far older and more powerful than her own; a man with a family, and it was that family which was to fuel Mab's envy. She had once longed for a child of her own, but her local fame, as a mad crone of indeterminate age, kept her list of suitors rather short.

Never possessed of any motherly instincts to speak of, she merely felt the need to pass on what she knew. Harry, the boy from her village, orphaned after the Scotch raid, and now known as Harry-the-Cough, had shown promise, but then came the ducking. Being left for dead by the village people who had benefitted for years from her help and healing, albeit for payment, left her changed. No longer merely mad, she had been furious. More than that, she had been determined. She would never again allow herself to become so exposed.

Several years spent researching a spell, or more precisely, a lamination of spells that would protect her from the world of men, had brought her full circle. It was all that mattered. She could live for centuries with power like that, so there would be no need for a child, or to pass on her skills. When the villagers ransacked her hovel, after thinking they had murdered her in the pond, they destroyed much of her research.

Forced to reconstruct and notate every experiment into a new book, her pilgrimage for knowledge had taken her to Wales and Ireland in search of others like herself – a dangerous quest, to be sure – cajoling, bargaining, fighting and even killing for that knowledge, on occasion. Now she was close, she was so close, there being but one spell still to replicate.

Some, living in the highlands of North Wales, had heard of it, but none remembered its secrets. The irony was, she had had it all along, but while realising its worth, she failed to understand its full power. Fortunately, and understanding its value, she had left that spell with the boy for safekeeping, in the event of an attack – a wise move as it turned out – written within the only possession she knew he would never lose or leave behind. What made the plan perfect was that she also knew he was oblivious to what he had.

After years of searching, of wandering far and wide, she left Wales, finding herself drawn to what remained of the stone ring at Mitchell's Fold in the Middle Marches. While sitting cross-legged in the shadow of Corndon Hill, arms raised to the sunset in the west, Mab chanted an ancient circular prayer to the old gods – a prayer with no beginning, nor end.

Hoping for guidance, epiphany came at last, two hundred and fifty miles from where she began.

The journey home had taken weeks, via some of the worst roads imaginable, but by the winter solstice, she was back – half-dead from her trials and tribulations, but she was back.

For years she cursed the villagers, whose religion demanded her execution. However, death was part of the circle of life, and despite being on the receiving end of their attempted murder, she understood the need to appease their God. What she would never forgive was their destruction of her work.

After years of plotting her neighbours' painful demise, thoughts of revenge faltered when she returned to a village ravaged by the sweating sickness. She could not have foreseen that. The settlement was drastically reduced, and none recognised her. Any survivors who might have remembered Mad Mab believed her long dead, after all, yet she did find what she needed – hostages and soldiers. Although the hostages came later, Not Dave had proven a great asset, while her other resource was yet to be tested. Caught on the journey to Warmstirrup, it had proved quite a find, and well worth the delay caused by going back for hostages. Fate did indeed move in ever decreasing circles until a singularity was formed, and by reading the signs, Mab was able to plot the when, and the where.

All plans of smiting suddenly put to one side, she decided on a deliberately low-profile return, instead. Not Dave's first death presented exactly the opportunity she had been looking for. From there, tales quickly reached her about another witch in the area – one journeyed down from the Scottish Borders – Insane Alice.

Mab did not blame Alice. Not at first. She was just another wise woman trying to survive the world of man. The likes of Lord Henry hardly helped. A fairly typical feudal lord, born with everything a man could ever need, he lacked the experience that should have been his after thirty-five years in the world – instead having but one year's experience, thirty-five times. Then there was the church of the new religion. That was what she and her kind called it, although it was perhaps not so new any more, and it certainly showed no signs of going anywhere any time soon. Mab always avoided entanglements with the zealots in their myriad, almost identical guises. She knew from experience that there was no reasoning with 'the righteous'; they were capable of all manner of evil. Once her spell of protection was complete, she might yet have to deal with them at some point – or others just like them. One step at a time.

She had learned much on her voyage of discovery and regretted nothing, but to think that the final and most significant piece was here all along, brought a rueful smile to her lips. So close to it now, she could feel its power. It stood to reason that Alice probably felt it, too. Yet she had not taken it for herself, when it would have been easy for her to do so. Why?

Mab faded into the woods. Not Dave was already waiting for her.

"You failed."

The golem merely shrugged.

Mab sighed. Being forced to work with the uncaring and the unthinking was a lonely existence. She imagined that thought echoing through the ages, but it was too late to stop it. "Never mind. The boy has left the monastery. Has our spy gone with him?"

Not Dave nodded.

"Good. Why are the soldiers here?"

Not Dave shrugged again.

"After you?"

Another shrug.

"Hmm…" Mab often marvelled at how communicative he could be without words. "I always enjoy our little chats, but I believe it's time to take some direct action. Come."

Tears streamed down the miller's unconscious face. Harry always wished there was some safe way he could reduce the pain. Using milk of the poppy seed, in quantities significant enough to numb that level of agony, could be more dangerous than the shock of the pain itself. He so wanted to help people, but it was a fact that he sometimes had to hurt them first. While the large man was out cold, he cleaned the wound with warm water and lavender before applying some of his famous 'Inside and Out' to prevent further infection.

Robyn had quailed when he dug the hot knife deep into the miller's arm to kill the infection in his flesh. Sister Tick had taken herself off to pray, while Little Joan had busied herself boiling water and drying some of their wet things. Mardy Mario and Dick merely helped themselves to the miller's ale by the fire.

"You're cleverer than you look," Robyn admitted, begrudgingly.

"Your praise is above any reward," Harry replied, deadpan.

Robyn tried again. "You know, when this is all over, someone with your skills could be useful to our band."

"Thanks, but I think I'm too upbeat."

"What's that supposed to mean?"

"Well, if you're using Robin Hood and his Merry Men as your model, some of you are falling a little shy of the mark, wouldn't you say?"

Mario belched loudly, grumbling about the weakness of the ale he had stolen.

Dick grumbled about Mario not leaving him enough of it to tell.

Harry raised an eyebrow.

Robyn frowned. "It's because I'm a woman, isn't it?"

He laughed, bringing a smile to Robyn's face, too, as John Miller woke up.

"How are you feeling?"

"Thanks for dropping by, Harry," he answered weakly. "Always a pleasure. Here…" John took a small purse from his belt and presented Harry with a silver coin. "Thank you. My arm's numb, but it's a good kind of numb. I was in so much pain before, but I had to hide it – from the wife, see?"

Harry inspected the coin. It was shiny and obviously new. "Seriously, John. Don't ever let that fool L'Éternuement near an injury like that. It might just be the death of you. By the way, this coin… new, is it?"

The miller looked a little shifty. "Aye. What of it?"

"Don't see many like this in these parts. Not so far north of York." Harry wandered over to something that had caught his eye earlier, high on a shelf. He took one of the two small, barrel-shaped steel blocks down and studied it. One end was mushroomed from being hammered, the other bore an indented motif. He took it closer to the fire for a better look. "RICARDVS REX ANGLE, written back-to-front. Look, there's even a little king standing in a ship holding sword and shield. How nice. What's on the other one, John? A fleur-de-lis, by any chance? For minting the other side?"

Fear crossed the miller's face. "Harry, they're not mine. Don't tell anyone, will you?"

"You're involved with someone forging coins?" Harry could not believe it.

"It's a favour for a friend. I'm just hiding them for a while."

"*Hiding* them? Good job!"

"Look, Harry, if they found out…"

"Who? Your friend or Lord Henry?"

"The earl, of course."

"John, they'll hang you for this, if you're caught."

"I know, but I owed him, and…"

"And he paid you," Harry completed for him, holding up the coin. "Look, John, I'm on the run myself – even though I didn't do anything – so I can hardly preach, but what about your family?"

"The weather was terrible last year, Harry. You remember. There was a lot less grain, and less grain means less milling, and less milling means less money. I needed to make ends meet."

Everyone looked from one to another, awkwardly. With the exception of Robyn, all were born of the lower classes, each living one step ahead of starvation. How easy it was to cross the line to save oneself, and they all knew it.

"John," Harry said at last, "get these back to their owner, for your own sake. And as for those bright silver coins, I wouldn't try spending them round here. They *will* be noticed."

"I just thought, you know, a few here and there…"

Harry shook his head in disbelief. "You weren't seriously thinking about rolling down the tavern with mittful of snide farthings? And then what? Put them across the bar? Ask them for change, perhaps?"

The door crashed open, making them all jump. Willa ran in, red-faced and breathless. "Soldiers!"

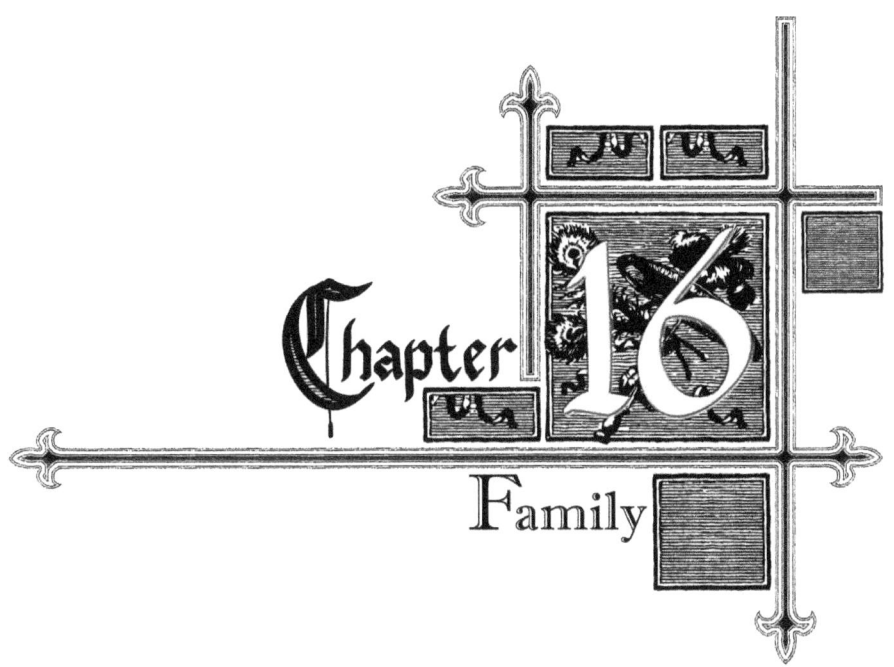

Chapter 16
Family

Insane Alice could indeed feel the power of that which that *witch* sought. Since Mad Mab had arrived near Warmstirrup, it felt like everyone and everything was converging, not so much on a fixed point as on a fixed person. She knew Harry had no clue why he should suddenly be so popular, which was probably for the best.

The river was close. She would find a place to lie low while she kept an eye out for Harry, Robyn and her tame outlaws. It was no great surprise that others already had the same idea, yet it still came as one, but then hope was like that; it often crossed over into belief.

Insane Alice placed her hands on hips. There was nothing else for it; she tutted.

Mad Mab turned, fearfully. Not Dave ignored her, keeping his vigil across the river.

"Good spot," Alice greeted, noncommittally.

"I thought so," Mab retorted. "Just room enough for two."

"Good. Move over then."

"I *meant* me and him."

Alice appraised the golem at Mab's side. "He killed poor old Dave, didn't he?"

"Poor old who?"

"Never mind. You burnt my house down, dear," Alice accused.

"You forced my hand, dear."

"By not giving up the boy?"

Mab nodded.

"So, you thought you'd burn my house down, and in the dead of winter, too?"

Mab shrugged, arms outstretched. "An unfortunate consequence born out of your reluctance to help a fellow witch."

Alice glowered. "We'll have to agree to disagree on that point." She gestured to Mab's creature, still with his back to her. "Did you have to dig him up? I mean *him*, specifically? Couldn't you have remade another?"

"Sorry, but you can't just churn them out like a place of doers and makers."

"Doers and makers?"

"A factory[1] , then. From the Latin. Hmm... yes, I like that word, I must remember it."

To Alice, 'factory' conjured the image of a place where fact and story could be reforged into something less than either, a process that sounded a lot like fabricating. "You're lying."

Mad Mab smiled scornfully. "Fair enough. I needed the connection between hunter and prey. That's how I found him in the first place."

"Ah. Of course. And now you have the three of us, all more or less in the same place, what do you propose?"

"All three of *us*, or all three of *you*?"

---

1. 'Factory' would not become a widely used term for a place of manufacture for another century and a half, but witches were renowned for having crystal ball moments like that.

"You know who I mean."

Mad Mab smiled again, triumphantly this time. "I know who you *are*. I'll admit to that. I must confess, after learning about you, and your origins, I was intrigued. I would love to hear your full account."

"Would you." Insane Alice's reply was completely toneless, not even worthy of a question mark.

"Yes."

"And if I gave you my story," Alice gestured once more to Not Dave, "would you be willing to let *him* go?"

"Let go of my staunchest ally, for a *story?*"

"What if I promised to retrieve what you seek, and give it to you? You know I could have taken it at any time."

"Yes. Why didn't you?"

"Because some things," Alice nodded again to Not Dave, "should not be."

"Really? Nothing to do with family? The ties that bind, and all that nonsense? Still, you offer an interesting proposition, dear. And while we're *theorising,* perhaps you could tell me why I shouldn't just kill you, instead?"

"Because I might kill you."

Mab's smile returned. "Sure of that, dear?"

"Are you, dear?"

Mab's head tilted to one side while she considered. "Usually speaking, only the golem's maker can – how did you put it? – 'let him go'. Perhaps, if you had my property in your hand, I might be willing to make a trade."

"And Harry-the-Cough? You'd let him go, too?"

"I would have no further use for him. You have my word on that."

Mad Mab's word was something Insane Alice would never take, especially when guilefully couched to mean whatever she wanted it to. However, there was always the chance that she *might* release the golem before damage to the soul of the man he used to be became irrevocable. She might release Harry from her machinations, too. The trouble was, if Alice gave Mab what she sought, she would become so powerful that there would be no choice but to rely on her promise. Alice's alternative was to save Harry herself and destroy Mab's prize. That would lead to confrontation – a battle she might easily lose. It was not for herself that she feared. Amongst other things, it would guarantee that the soul of the man she used to love would be destroyed. *Family!* she thought angrily, completely trapped between two extremely unpalatable alternatives.

"Well, dear?" Mab prompted. "It was, after all, your proposition."

"Yes, it was, wasn't it? Very well. I agree."

Mad Mab held out her hand, making a forked gesture to deflect a lie. It was nonsense – they both knew that – but while Mab suspected Alice of lying, Insane Alice was sure of it.

It was more comfortable than a cell in the dungeons, and it was certainly not the hole, but it was a prison, nonetheless. Matty sat on the edge of a bed in one of the castle's guest rooms, the draw bar having slid into its keep with a deliberate *thunk.* Only the aristocracy installed bolts to the outside of their guests' doors. Almost a day since she and Harry had parted, she wondered if he was alive and safe, praying for the former but doubting the latter.

Somehow, her every fibre was screaming to find him, a sixth sense warning of things coming to a head. In the two years they had known each other, Harry had been one of the few men who saw her as a person, rather than, at best, an object, at worst, rubbish. Suspecting he had feelings for her, she kept her own under tight control. If she let him in, she knew her work would break his heart. A hopeless situation because she knew he could not support her. Harry Bones could barely feed himself, despite working himself, rather poignantly, to the bone. Now, suddenly terrified she may never get the chance to tell him, she got to her feet, pacing like a caged animal – but tell him what, exactly?

Furious with herself for not insisting that she go with him, there seemed but one course of action left to her. Perhaps it was because she had never admitted her feelings before, not even to herself, but for the first time, she felt that what she must do next was a betrayal. Yet, what other course could she take? She must use the tools she had. After all, only a fool would entrust their future to the mercy of Lord Henry. So, with heavy heart, Matty summoned the guard. Perhaps he might be open to negotiation? Should that fail, there was always outright distraction. Guilt would have to wait – life came first. Hers and Harry's.

Horsemen approached. They both heard them. There was barely room for two in Mad Mab's foxhole among the rushes at the river's edge. With no alternative, Insane Alice hurled herself forward and shoved Not Dave for all she was worth. The golem fell forward into the river with a loud splash.

Mab reacted furiously, but Alice waved her down. "Be still!" she hissed. A partially broken bough hung out over the slow-moving icy waters. She uttered what sounded to Mab like a curse and the branch snapped its remaining connection and slipped soundlessly into the water close to where Not Dave had gone under.

The mounted soldiers, trotting along the opposite bank, turned at the splash. The branch, gliding gently downstream, seemed to satisfy them and they continued on, barely breaking stride.

Grasping Alice's intentions, Mab kept low and watched. "I'm surprised to see you treat him with such disdain," she whispered.

"That body is long dead, Mab. We both know that. It's his soul I want you to release. You're burning it up to power a corpse that should be at rest. Don't you ever——"

"Shh!" Mab was looking behind them, peering into the forest. "We've got horsemen this side of the river, too."

"They must have picked up my trail. Whoever leads them is good."

Mab refocused on her hidey-hole's uninvited co-tenant. "You know these men?"

"Not exactly. I *believe* they were sent from the castle to capture me."

"Why?"

Alice glanced at her. "I have suspicions. No more. I won't bore you with any more theories, dear. *Listen...*"

The two groups of armed men were calling across the river to one another. From their hiding place, the crones heard one man introduce himself as Sergeant-at-arms Walter Sweet. He addressed the leader of the horsemen on the opposite bank as Sir Ralph.

"That must be Lord Henry's brother," Mab whispered.

"Shh."

Listening hard, they heard an exchange of descriptions for the quarry each sought. Insane Alice was not flattered. Sir Ralph admitted to pursuing a demon, an undead creature. The witches looked at each other. "Despite the snow and ice, don't you think it's getting a little warm here, dear?" Alice suggested.

Mab nodded, then her arm shot out. "Look!"

Alice turned to see a small group running from behind the mill, upstream, back towards the forest. She instantly recognised Robyn's band and Harry. "If they're spotted, they'll be run down."

"Not really my problem," Mab announced, matter-of-fact.

"No? So what do you think that puffed-up oaf in the red cape will do if he finds that spell in Harry's possession? Hmm? He'll burn it. Aye, and Harry along with it!"

"Alright. What do you suggest?"

"A distraction. If they need to chase someone, let it be your creature."

Mad Mab gave her an appraising look. "You want me to sacrifice your husband to those fools?"

"My husband is *dead!*"

"Very well." Mab's incantation caused the river to stir. Within moments, Not Dave appeared near the opposite bank, climbing up a tree root with icy water sluicing from his tattered rags. She caught Alice's sorrowful gaze, following the golem as he left the cover of the river. "Don't worry. He doesn't feel the cold."

"Neither will we, if those soldiers catch us," Alice snapped, tetchily. "We'd better make ourselves scarce."

It was quite depressing, how easily the guard allowed himself to be manipulated. Putty in Matty's hands, he was certainly promised an awful lot more than he got. Still, he did receive a *bonk* on the head, so he was in the ballpark.

Matty locked him in the room, unconscious, and tore down the empty passageway towards the spiral stair. Her foot barely on the first step, she heard men's voices, rowdy and raucous. "Great!" she growled under her breath, looking around for a place to hide.

Being the better part of the castle, there were two large tapestries draped along the hallway walls between rooms. She twitched them aside, desperately. The second covered a small sconce in the wall, just big enough to conceal her. She tucked in close as the men approached, swapping bawdy stories.

Holding her breath, she attempted to recognise them by their voices, hoping to glean some sense of the men she must evade. Lord Henry's men-at-arms were liberally salted with any number of unpleasant types. To Matty's relief, none were among this little group.

She rolled her eyes at their boasting and general enlargement of the truth. As policy, she never judged – though she knew for a fact that one of them was lying. Indeed, had Matty only realised it, she was in the presence of some fairly progressive thinkers, sharing stories and attitudes that would continue to entertain in certain quarters for the next six centuries.

Go on, she urged them by thought, *go away!*

As they reached Matty's chamber, one of them had the wit to question why it was unguarded. Her heart leapt and sank, seemingly at once. One of the soldiers began beating on the door and calling for the guard. They obviously thought he was up to no good with the prisoner, because they began hurling lewd insults through the door. Matty could only shake her head at their dismal powers of observation – had they not realised the door was locked from the outside?

Panic gripped her. Morons or not, she was impossibly overmatched physically, and with no choice but to make for the stairs, she stood every chance of being caught – and if they caught her...

She shuddered. Hardly a shrinking violet, even she did not want to consider what that might be like. *What should I do? What can I do?* Her mind raced, and then, disaster.

"Hey, look. It's bolted."

"So?"

"From the outside."

"So?"

"You're thicker than Ambrose, you are! He can't be in there if..."

Out of options, Matty bolted, missing the end of their revelation. Though she did hear them call after her, as she flew down the stone steps, three at a time.

"Back of the..." Robyn puffed breathlessly as she ran.

Equally winded, Harry failed to catch the beginning of her sentence. "What?"

Not realising, and with no air to waste, Robyn repeated only what she considered to be the important bit. "Back of the..."

"*What?*" he asked again, a little irritation creeping into his voice.

"Back of the!"

It was no good. They were well into the treeline, so he risked a brief stop to ask again. "Back of the what?"

Robyn pushed her longsword to the side and bent down, hands on knees, breathing hard. Straightening up, she glared at him. "Not the. *Thee*. As in, I'll be glad to see the back of! You've brought us some right bad luck, you have, Harry."

Harry blinked. "Me?"

"You!"

"You *kidnapped* me."

"Don't just stand there arguing," Mardy Mario snarled. "Keep moving."

Dick held up a hand to speak. "Can I just say that I second that."

"I heard him the first time," Harry snapped, tetchily[2].

"If they catch us with that dodgy coin-minting gear, we're for a hanging," Mario continued. "What the hell did you bring it for?"

"Because those soldiers will be all over the mill by now. If they found it there, Warmstirrup would be looking for a new miller. He helped us, and we brought soldiers to him. What would you have done?"

"It was his bed. I'd have let him lie in it. He didn't even come to you when he was injured. He went to that Felix-the-Fish bloke!"

Harry opened his mouth to respond but realised that Mario's last point was true. "That's not actually his name, by the way, but I like it," he admitted instead. "John Miller did take us in when we needed help, though. You stole his ale, for goodness' sakes. We owed him *something*."

"You cured him, didn't you?"

Irritated, Harry knew Mario was right again. "I don't like leaving people in trouble," he stated, quietly; not much of an argument, but it was all he had.

Mario loomed over him, intimidating. "Well, *I* suggest you learn how, if you want to live."

Angry now, Harry spat back, "Just what kind of people are you?"

"Outlaws, dummy!"

Harry stood on tiptoe, nose to nose with the giant. "Well, you picked rubbish role models then, didn't you? Maid Marian!"

Mario blinked. "Eh?"

"Robin Hood and Maid Marian? Oh, come *on!* You hadn't twigged it?"

Clunky wooden wheels and cogs turned slowly within the huge man's head. Harry fancied it was like watching John's mill go round in there, as Mario slowly put the pieces together. When his counting engine finally

---

2. Harry could be forgiven for not immediately understanding. The term 'I second that' would not be used again until AD1597, in Parliament. Who could have guessed that the first Dick to say it lived two hundred years earlier?

arrived at an answer, he stiffened. Slowly, he turned to his wife and brought forth some astonishing language.

Harry stepped back, quite embarrassed.

Robyn affected bewilderment, though the glare she threw Harry promised a reckoning to come. Eventually, Mario stormed off into the woods to attack the first thing he came across with an axe.

Harry sidled closer to Robyn. "Look, I'm sorry. I didn't expect that. I mean, how was I to know he hadn't worked it out? Your model's not exactly subtle, is it? Where did you find him, anyway? That is, how did you two...?"

"I won him in an archery contest."

"You *won* your husband in a competition?"

"Yes. It was advertised door to door. They called it 'The Serf Challenge'. As the strongest, he was the prize. Interestingly, another competitor had already struck the bullseye. So I thought, hey, that's a fine shot, but just you try and live with thi——"

Harry held up a hand, forestalling her. "You know what, I don't want to know."

"But it's a really exciting tale of skill and derring-do."

"I don't care. All I want from life at the moment is to be really, really bored. So, please, just derring-don't."

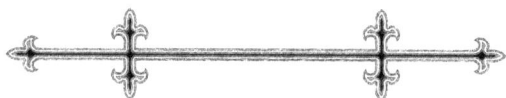

Many words could be ascribed to the experience of being stalked by the undead. Terrifying; horrifying; shocking; alarming – all those, and many others, would fit the bill adequately. Boring, on the other hand, would be unlikely to even make the lists. Again, it was just not Harry's day.

Mab had subtly modified Not Dave's orders. Sometimes her words came to him, as if on the wind, and so he followed the now decidedly fractious not-all-men through the forest, keeping his distance.

They seemed to be arguing about what to call themselves – strange behaviour given their peril. Were he not dead, he might have wondered why people facing such dangers might tear into one another over the naming of something that never mattered in the first place, especially when surrounded by so many lethal enemies, but he *was* dead, and that gave him perspective – though some might argue, fairly, that it came too late.

His bickering quarry had slowed, probably without realising it, and he could now hear shouts from behind, too, gaining on them all.

Sir Ralph dismounted to approach one of his men, who stood just inside the treeline. "The creature entered the woods here?"

"Aye, my lord. We won't be able to follow with the horses."

"Are there any paths or less dense ways we might take?"

"Not in this part of the forest, my lord. Should we follow?"

Ralph looked pained as he thought for moment. It was not the sort of exercise he favoured. "Can you tell which direction the creature is headed?"

"I've been into the forest about a hundred yards, my lord. It seems to be heading north, following a small band."

"Harry-the-Cough has help?"

"So it seems, my lord. At least half a dozen, mostly women, unless I miss my guess."

Ralph grinned fiercely. "Then we shall have sport before we hang the apothecary."

The soldier returned his grin.

Ralph gave him a comradely slap about the shoulder. "Leave a detail to watch the horses. We march from here!"

Matty exited the staircase at the great hall and ran for the main doors. A few men looked up disinterestedly from their midday meals to watch her go. Glad to be in from the cold, the last thing they wanted was to be called to action. When three guards flew out of the stairway, shouting and skidding into one another, and crashing into one of the benches, the diners called out, laughing and slamming their ale cups on the tables. Some even threw their cups at the interlopers for disturbing their lunch.

In her fine blue dress, blond hair unbound and flying, after the fashion of an unmarried woman, Matty cut a striking figure as she streaked past the long tables.

Collecting themselves, her three pursuers set off again, shouting for their comrades to stop the girl. Unfortunately, the soldiers, seated in small groups, took their pleasure from taunting and tripping the men instead. Bored and misunderstanding the situation, they were enjoying this spot of unexpected lunchtime entertainment. By the time they reached the huge oak doors blocking the end of the chamber, the three men were beer-soaked and covered with ignominy – and gruel. Slipping and sliding through the doors, they ran to the keep's main gateway.

Entrance to the keep was via a drawbridge. Two storeys above the ground, it provided a final defence should the castle's inner ward be compromised. Matty was already through the gates and running down the ramp to the bailey below. Desperate, she knew she would never make it to the second set of gates that led to the outer ward, and after those there was still the castle's main gatehouse and drawbridge to negotiate before she finally reached the street. Thinking quickly, she changed course, darting right and straight for the main kitchens.

Always the most likely place to catch fire, castles usually housed their kitchens within external buildings somewhere in the courtyard or against the inner face of the curtain walls, and Warmstirrup was no exception.

She shot through the door, slamming it shut behind her, chest heaving, heart hammering. The beautiful dress that had served her so well, while Lord Henry had been under the control of Alice's potion, now made her stand out like a clean face in the market. How she wished for her make-do-and-mends. The women working the kitchens, as one, turned to stare, as though Matty had descended from a cloud.

One of the older ladies curtsied. "M'lady." Straightening up, she peered short-sightedly, then her expression cleared. "Oh, it's young Matty – it's just Matty, girls. And I thought we'd got somebody important. You're not meant to be in here, pet. The, erm," she coughed with embarrassment, "*entertainment* girls are all up in the keep, if you're looking for——"

"No," Matty interrupted. "Some soldiers are after me."

"Well, isn't that why you're here, lass?"

"Not..." Matty floundered, "*exactly*. At least, not on this occasion. Can you hide me? Please?"

Mere seconds later, the door crashed open and three men burst in, causing the women to scream and dash for hiding places. All but the head cook, who stood in their path slapping a rolling pin into her hand, dangerously.

"Have you seen a young woman?" the lead guard asked.

Cook looked around ironically. "One or two. Seen 'em just now, as it happens."

Some of the other women guffawed, coming out of hiding to rally around their lynchpin.

"You really are thicker than a cheeseboard," the second man in line muttered to the first, eyeing the rolling pin warily.

"She was wearing a blue dress," the third man tried. "The dress of a lady."

"Doesn't sound like one of ours, eh, girls?" Cook was playing to the audience now.

The first guard grew angry. "We're going to search these kitchens. Get out of the way, old woman."

He pushed past Cook, who fetched him a resounding *clunk* across the back of his helmet. He pitched forward, eliciting a further burst of laughter from the women, making him angrier still.

Cook swung for the other men. "If I call the sergeant, you'll be for it! None of you soldiers are allowed into the kitchens by order of the earl himself. Thieving beggars, the lot of you!"

"We're chasing an escaped prisoner – a criminal!" the second guard protested as he fended off Cook's rolling pin with the shaft of his spear.

"The only thing criminal in here is how little we get paid. Get out!"

A cacophony outside distracted them all. Shouts of men were quickly joined by the barking of several large dogs. There was a loud *clank, thud* and *rattle,* the distinct sounds of something heavy going over and spilling its contents everywhere. Further shouting erupted as the inner ward was thrown into chaos.

The second guard ducked under the rolling pin again as he tried to look out through the still-open door. "What the f——"

"Don't you *dare!*" Cook bellowed, connecting the solid wooden baton with the top of his head.

The man collapsed – all sounds and voices suddenly muffled around him.

"*You've knocked him out!*"

"*You want to follow him, lad? Do you? Well? Do you? Do you want some?*"

"*Stop. Stop. Ouch. Stop it!*"

"*Get out then.*"

"*He needs to see the physician.*"

"*Not in* my *kitchen, he doesn't.*"

"*Bodges has gone missing, too.*"

"*What?*"

"*What?*"

"*'S what I heard.*"

"*We'll have to get that fancy Frenchman in then, L'Éternuement.*"

"*He's not a Frenchie, he's a southern.*"

"*I don't care if he's St Peter's next-door neighbour, he's not coming in my kitchen spreading his pig's doings!*"

"*He's here!*"

"*What?*"

"*The apothecary. He's here.*"

The semi-conscious man heard a storm of laughter, and then something about a giant fish being carried into the inner ward and torn apart by Lord Henry's hounds.

Matty slipped out of the kitchen's side door and hid behind a large barrel used for catching rainwater. Out in the middle of the courtyard, Felix L'Éternuement was indeed there, chasing after several hounds in a desperate and completely unsuccessful attempt to save the last remnants of *Thee Piscator Fortuna's* formerly famous mascot. She covered her mouth to hide a snort of laughter. It appeared Jack had kept his word – and Harry had been right, it certainly had caused a stink. Matty only hoped he had been wrong about the second, more secret, part of his message. *I have to get to him,* she thought anxiously, although she was powerless to stop the giggles caused by the scene before her. She would have loved to watch all day, but knew that if she was ever going to get a chance to escape, this was it.

Keeping low, she made her way past some packaging boxes and barrels to duck behind the next building over. Fortunately, the granary was built away from the castle walls and mounted atop two dozen mushroom-shaped staddle stones – both measures for keeping the castle's grain supply beyond the reach of rats and other pests. The timber building had the appearance of being on stilts, which did present Matty with another problem, as she was again reminded that her bright blue dress might give her away. Added to that, she was freezing cold and had no coat or cloak. Thinking quickly, she hitched up her skirts, so that when she walked around the back of the granary, anyone who saw her would only make out a pair of legs. Hopefully, any observers would be too far away and too distracted to notice they were female.

She was discovering something about L'Éternuement – he knew how to swear, when roused. While some soldiers tried to control the hounds or stay out of their way, most were in fits of helpless hysterics at the apothecary's forlorn antics. "Just keep it up a little longer, there's a good boy," Matty muttered to herself as she made her way around the side of the granary. She was close to the gateway now. Dare she make a dash for it?

With the best will in the world, she just could not see a way to cover thirty or forty feet of open compound in a bright blue dress without being seen. It seemed her luck was waning when a roar from the keep confirmed her worst fears. Hiding behind another barrel, she could see Lord Henry on the keep's drawbridge, still in his armour with hands on hips, hollering furiously at the men below in the inner ward.

Matty shrugged resignedly. Her luck may have run out, but she doubted L'Éternuement would be getting an invite to the spring banquet after this, either. The earl's face was purple. She had never heard such cursing, Henry's language even trumping L'Éternuement's.

With failure looming, her thoughts strayed back to Harry. *If only I could see you, to tell you...* She could not even bring herself to finish that thought. Both orphans and without family, it seemed they had no time left to find each other, and time wasted was the bitterest of all regrets.

A chuckle, and a chesty, winter's cough close by, made her jump and shrink back. A guard stepped around the corner and proceeded to loosen his hose to take a pee. Matty held her breath. Terrified, she cursed silently.

Forcing herself to breathe again, an idea struck, but with just seconds to act it would require all her courage. Fortunately, the man seemed to have single-handedly drunk an entire barrel of ale, because he was still going, like one of Henry's destriers. She looked around for inspiration and found it.

Work was taking place on the battlements, high above. Though the building season was still months away, last season's timber scaffolding remained against the inner curtain wall in places. Matty felt bound to take back her cursing, because she just happened to be in one of them, and leaning against a cross-brace was exactly what she needed – a four-foot length of three-by-two oak.

Sodden from a winter spent outside, it felt heavy and ungainly, not to mention slippery in her small hands. Nevertheless, determined, she turned the corner once more. "Hello, soldier."

"Ooh!" Startled, the young man tried to cover himself up before he had finished – never a wise move for a gentleman. Matty actually felt rather sorry for the poor lad, but that did not save him.

Thunk! Thump.

She hit him around the head. He hit the ground at her feet. She winced, more than a little appalled by what she had just done to a completely defenceless fellow, merely answering the call. "Sorry," she told him, genuinely, as she turned him over to steal his large grey-brown cloak. "Perfect."

Wrapping it about herself, she bent again to steal the man's cap, too. Tucking her hair up into it, she tugged it down onto her head. About to leave, she had one last scruple. Turning the man over again, this time onto his back, she delicately tucked him back in. "Don't want you getting frostbite, do we, soldier boy?" She tapped his cheek affectionately and turned for the gates to the outer ward. Her new cloak was warm, though it now bore the rather unfortunate smell of urine, but she was a big girl now; she would survive it.

Chapter 17
There's a Storm Coming

Robyn was confused. "Of course it's a real one." Another shout made them crouch lower still. "What did you mean by that?" she hissed. They were pinned down, unable to move. Mario, on Robyn's right, was still ignoring everyone. Harry, on her left, replied, "It's just that, often, when someone says that, they're being metaphorical."

"Metaphorical?"

"I thought you were educated. You being noble, and all?"

Robyn soured. "I am, to a degree, but my teacher thought a little girl's mind would overheat if overtaxed by anything worth knowing. I asked my father if I might read the same subjects as the boys, but Teacher got there first. He warned Father that, should his teachings lead to female hysteria, he might have to admit me to the Bethlehem Hospital[1], and that might prove expensive. Naturally, Father left it for him to decide after that – I was only a daughter, after all."

"So much bitterness in one so young."

"You trying to be funny?"

"No, no, I wouldn't dare. Besides, I was taught by a woman – even my letters."

"Really?" Robyn was genuinely surprised. "I take it *her* mind didn't melt, then?" she added caustically. "Who was she?"

"Er…" Harry smiled ruefully. "Mad Mab."

Silence, but for the breeze through the trees.

"Bad example," they said together.

"*Well,*" Robyn drawled, "what do you expect? Of course I was bitter. While the boys were reading history, philosophy, theology and earth sciences, I had to make do with lightweight religious texts and a few romantic tragedies."

"Really? Greek?"

"No. I meant they were rubbish."

"Oh."

"I got some poetry, too."

"Oh."

"Hmm, I know."

"Sorry," Harry commiserated, when a sudden gust of wind shook snow from the boughs above them. It fell unerringly down the back of his neck, but before he could cry out, Robyn's hand clamped across his mouth.

---

1. Some sources suggest the Bethlehem Hospital, or Bedlam, as it later became known, transformed from a medieval hospital – that is, a place of hospitality and alms – into the world's first asylum between AD1377 and 1460. The early dates are difficult to verify, and little is known about how medieval society treated insanity. Evidence of shackles and chains suggests some methods may have been dark indeed – although they were perhaps reserved only for the violent. Nevertheless, it would be hard to imagine anyone entering by choice.

"Told you."

"Mmph?"

She rolled her eyes, letting him go. "There's a *storm* coming. And, yes – it's a real one. You get to sense such things when you live in the forest."

The afternoon sky had darkened with thick, almost black, snow clouds. That first gust merely heralded the beginning. The trees around them erupted into movement. There would be no softly falling snow this day. Almost at once, it was as though the clouds were firing at them. Instantly soaked and freezing cold, Harry stated the obvious. "We can't stay here. We need better cover."

Willa moved silently through the trees to kneel beside them. "Two dozen soldiers on foot, beating their way through the woods from the south."

"Will they find us?" asked Robyn.

"Definitely. It's only a matter of time."

Harry sighed. "Any good news?"

Willa glared at him. "They don't have dogs."

"Oh, good."

"Yet."

"Great." Harry turned up his collar against the wind. "So now what? If we go back out into the open, they'll cut us down for sure."

"This was a stupid idea," Mario growled, sullenly. "We should have left the apothecary in the main forest with the witch. We'll need a miracle now."

As if on cue, a figure stepped out of the trees right in front of them.

Harry looked up. "Oh, no."

Sergeant-at-arms Walter Sweet had been searching for hours. Ever since Sir Ralph's men galloped away in pursuit of Harry-the-Cough – and some creature the earl's brother seemed determined to catch – leaving him a free hand. Yet, he was confused. After searching all along the west bank and through much of the forest in that area, his men returned empty-handed. He had tracked the witch to the riverbank, he was sure of it – his best tracker had confirmed it – but where had she gone from there?

Although Lord Henry had repealed the death sentence for their missing apothecary, Sweet made sure he waited until the optimum moment to broach the subject with Sir Ralph. He also made sure several of his men heard him *begin* to explain the matter. Of course, he knew by that point the nobleman would not listen. Having sighted his quarry, he was off.

He smiled to himself. No doubt about it, it was a job well done. He would have his vengeance on Matty, by allowing her friend – if that was all he was – to be cut down *accidentally* by Ralph, while Sweet carried out his current orders, which were to bring a witch before the earl for a spot of summary execution. A footnote alluding to a trial might end up on a scroll somewhere, but he never concerned himself with that type of nonsense.

Yes, all that, and better than even odds of war, too. A spring and summer of running around the country raping and pillaging with his master. With so much to look forward to, Sergeant-at-arms Walter Sweet was truly a man who enjoyed his work. Even the approaching storm hardly dampened his mood. It was a little frustrating that the crone had temporarily given him the slip, but she would not be able to hide forever.

All was silence. It was restful – at first. By the time Sweet really noticed, his world was filled with it. A freezing fog drifted out from the forest and across the river. He thought that odd – it would normally have been the other way around, when a moving river was warmer than the air above. There was something else, too. As an outdoorsman, Sweet recognised the winter stillness – this was not it. The sense of eeriness only increased as he realised his men were nowhere to be seen, nor heard.

His mare snorted and stepped sideways, nervously. "Steady, girl." He patted her neck soothingly. A horse was an immensely strong animal; a great comfort to a man suddenly alone in the forest surrounded by otherworldly mist. She granted him height, power and speed, but they were on lease. Sweet was not her master, merely her passenger.

"Looking for us?"

He turned sharply to see a ragged crone step out of the thickening fog behind him. The range of his sight was no more than ten or twelve feet

– she was close. He grinned, savagely. "We?" he blustered. "Lord Henry never told me I was hunting royalty. I shall have to get down on one knee to chop off your head!"

A flicker of confusion crossed the woman's face, just for an instant. "Oh, you allude to the 'royal we'."

"Ha! We'll have new royalty soon enough. My master and young Bolingbroke will see to that, at the point of a sword. And I'll be along for the ride. Who needs 'em, eh?"

"I think you misunderstood me, young man. I have no royal pretentions. I leave those to the royals, and it hardly matters to the poor which violent bully ends up on top, taking from us, does it? No, I asked, are you looking for us, because——"

"I'm here, too." Mad Mab stepped out in front of Sweet's mount, making him turn in the saddle again.

Faced with two crones and in that eerie mist, alone without his men, he paled. The mare stamped and turned nervously away from Mab only to face Alice. She snorted and stomped, pawing at the ground with her hooves. Sweet was struggling to keep her under control. He considered giving the horse her head to run the witch down, but in this fog, and in the forest, any pell-mell drive through the low boughs might be the last thing he ever did. Yet he dared not dismount. The mare was his only power. After all, what use was a single sword against sorcery?

Alice stepped forward. Of all things, she began to sing. It was a tune Sweet had never heard before, and he always listened to the travelling minstrels who visited the castle when they came round. The song sounded ancient and lilting, Celtic, maybe. He had no way of knowing. Besides, it seemed the song was not for him.

The mare calmed immediately, allowing Alice to approach and gently stroke her nose.

"That's a good trick. I'd like to learn it," Sweet admitted, in spite of himself.

Insane Alice looked up at him, smiling toothlessly in the half-light as she continued to sing.

Mad Mab giggled from behind Sweet, breaking the spell – for him, at least. Suddenly nervous again, he realised he must be missing something.

Alice's song moved smoothly to a minor key, sounding immediately darker and more menacing as her voice changed, developing deep tones he would not have thought possible from such a tiny female frame. Her final death growl caused the mare to rear sharply. Sweet held on for his life, but when his mount bucked, he flew forward, over her head, to hit the ground hard.

Panicked, his veins coursed with the terror-drug, but neither fight nor flight were available to him. He could not even move. The arch-bully looked up beseechingly, but the mare had already cancelled his lease and bolted. War horses were expensive, and as the greater threat, often targeted first by enemy soldiers on the battlefield. In answer, they were trained to attack as efficiently as the men who rode them – though perhaps without the pleasure many of their human counterparts took from killing. Expecting a flying, steel-shod hoof to seal his fate, all Sweet could do was close his eyes against the inevitable and hope for a quick end, but she leapt over him and galloped away through the forest.

"Oh, dear," Mab commented drily. "All those horses and men to hunt down one little witch – or so you thought – and now *we* outnumber *you*. How's that feel?"

Alice cackled. "I thought the mare was going to do for him then. Such a majestic creature. It would have been an end too good for him, wouldn't you agree, dear?"

"I would agree, dear. She spared him, so let's see about that reprieve." Mab gave an equally nutty cackle to disabuse Sweet of any 'good witch, bad witch' scenarios he may have conjured as a coping mechanism.

Insane Alice shoved Sweet from his awkward, twisted posture to flop onto his back. "Can't move, dear?" she mocked.

"What have you done to me?"

"Nothing, dear," Mab supplied. "Being dropped onto your head from all the way up there will do that to a man. I think he's broken his neck – wouldn't you say he's broken his neck, dear?"

"I would, dear."

They both cackled in unison.

"B-but you can heal me, right?"

They cackled louder.

"We might," Alice answered, jovially. "If you tell us all we wish to know."

"Yes. Anything. Just ask."

She looked at Mab. "Now that's what I call a healthy spirit of cooperation, wouldn't you say so, dear?"

"Yes, dear. Such a nice young man."

More cackling. Sweet whimpered, completely paralysed.

"We heard you speaking with that twerp in the red cape earlier. Who was he?" asked Alice.

"Sir Ralph? He's Lord Henry's brother."

"So it was him." She scratched her chin thoughtfully. "And what interest would he have in finding young Harry-the Cough?"

"H-he said there was a price on his head, and also the head of that, that *thing*."

Mab tutted. "So rude. That thing, as you called him, was this lady's husband. When he was alive."

Sweet gulped, eyes bulging.

Alice glowered at Mab, but let the comment pass. "You started to tell that posturing peacock something about the search for Harry, something about it being called off – admit it! Didn't you?"

He gulped again. He would have nodded but no longer possessed any feeling below his chin. "I, I tried, but he wouldn't listen——"

"I wasn't born yesterday. You want Harry dead. No. Don't deny it. Now... I would know why?"

"That whore had me thrown in the hole."

Alice's eyes narrowed. "What's this?"

Sweet explained about Lord Henry's strange malady and Matty's taking control, filling in any gaps Alice had not already guessed. "Very well, Sergeant-at-arms, and how did you find me?"

"The whore——"

"Her name is *Matty*," she corrected him, frostily.

"I mean Matty. She gave you up."

"Rubbish."

"She did, I swear."

"You're a fool, like the bullying idiots you work for. What did she actually say?"

He told her about Matty swearing to Lord Henry that Alice might be found with Old Tom, the great oak in the forest.

Alice thought for a moment. Sweet's terrified blathering confirmed her suspicions, but there were still questions. It seemed Harry had no cause even being out there any longer. Those brutes and their leader were hunting him down for their own ends. Now this Sweet, the worst brute of the bunch, had hoodwinked Sir Ralph into continuing pursuit against Lord Henry's orders, while covering his own behind – Alice knew nothing of L'Éternuement's duplicity at that point. Matty's 'betrayal' had merely been Matty sending them off on a wild goose chase, probably as a delaying tactic. She really needed to find out if the girl was still a prisoner within the castle. Matty had risked her own life to protect Alice. She may have sent Sweet to Alice's exact location, but would have had no way of knowing it – her intentions had been pure. Should her ruse come to Lord Henry's notice, she would be in greater danger yet. Henry's fear of the curse, and that Shrewsbury field, might stay his hand for a while, but when dealing with a towering arrogance like his, who really knew? On the other hand, Alice knew Matty to be clever and resourceful; she may have escaped the castle already, and if so, where might she go?

Matty was used to the forest walk to Insane Alice's hovel and easily found her way in daylight, but discovering the place burned down upset her greatly. Having no idea about Mad Mab's presence or the witches' altercation, she had mistakenly cursed Walter Sweet until her tears ran dry.

Cold, miserable hours passed, while she worked up the courage to search through the wreckage for bodies. There was some evidence, but what little was left could have just as easily been table scraps as a person's earthly remains. Confused, lost and alone, she made up a small fire to keep warm. First Harry, now Alice. What was she to do? The few friends she had were all scattered, or worse.

The winds gained in strength, bringing a storm that engulfed her campsite and put her little fire out comprehensively. With nowhere to go, she retreated into the limited cover of the naked winter trees.

Dithering and wet through, she cast about for better shelter. Matty had visited Insane Alice many times, and not always professionally. One summer, she had found the crone down by Snugly Burn, just to the south. Most importantly, she had been fishing from Hollow Ash. At some point in the past the ash had been struck by lightning near its base. The resulting fire hollowed the base of the trunk, but the tree had not died. The remaining trunk fed the rest of the tree, allowing healing and eventual recovery. Matty knew Alice loved to sit there in the summer, with her line stretching out into the burn. Her heart leapt – might she be hiding there now?

The journey was short but brutal. Fierce winds whipped the branches into a fury. Matty was scratched and her borrowed cloak torn as she made her way through.

Upon reaching Hollow Ash, her heart sank. No Alice. With a sigh, she climbed into the hollow and snuggled herself in next to Snugly Burn – which was by no means as cosy as the name suggested. The snow and melt cycle had the large stream in high fettle and it roared through the narrows between the rocks. The small pool, where Alice fished in summer, was a white-water maelstrom.

Matty shivered and allowed herself a little cry, this time for her own fears and woes. After a perfectly horrible few days, she felt close to despair, eventually drifting into a listless sleep.

Voices shocked her awake. Hairs stood up on the back of her neck as a thrill of fear shot through her. She listened intently – two men. The roar of Snugly Burn made it impossible to discern their words. She backed further into the hollow, terrified. Where could she run? Who could possibly help her, out here?

The voices drew closer, allowing her to catch snatches of conversation.

"The old wo... here sometimes... I'm telling you."

"On a day... this?... break our necks..."

"Stop complai... to find her, you saw the house. I... now."

"But... looking all day!"

Matty risked a peek around the edge of the hollow. Seeing the dead man, she almost collapsed.

Harry was lifted bodily from the ground by the man who stood before him. While his feet kicked, Mario also grabbed for him, huge arms flexing powerfully, but it made no difference. Anchored to the earth from which he had been raised from death, the flesh golem held Harry out as though he were weightless.

"What do you want from me?" he wailed. Then movement in the woods drew his eye. "Look out – over there!" He choked out the words to Robyn and Willa, pointing south before bringing his arm back immediately, to continue wrestling against the iron grip pushing his clothing up into his throat.

The categorically unhappy not-all-men formed a circle around Harry and the creature – facing outwards, as a larger circle formed around them all. "This is bad," Robyn roared above the storm.

"You think?" Harry shot back.

"Listen to me," Not Dave spoke in his gravel pit voice. "You have a powerful talisman in your possession, a spell. My mistress has foreseen that you might destroy her if you unlock its secrets. She sent me to kill you and retrieve it."

"I knew it. I bloody knew it! If she wanted it, what the hell did she give it to *me* for?"

"You'd have to ask her."

"From beyond the grave?"

"It's not so bad."

"*What?*"

Not Dave shrugged – eloquently.

"Here's a thought," Harry tried desperately. "Why don't I just give you the spell and then you leave me alone?"

"You don't understand its importance – or yours."

"Here they come!" Robyn bellowed. "Luck in battle, my merry... erm. Oh, sod it. *Get them!*"

The mêlée all around was extremely distracting for Harry. "Me? Important? How?"

"She has my soul. It burns. You are the key to setting it free."

"Well, I'm very sorry, but as you may have noticed, I have my own problems just now." He struggled, legs dangling. "I've already offered you the damned spell. I don't want it!"

"No! She must never have it."

"What? Whose side are you on?"

"If she gets that spell back from you, she will live forever, but not her life – she will live the lives of others."

"Look, don't think me rude, but I don't know *what the hell you're talking about!*" he screamed over a timely clap of exceptionally atmospheric thunder.

"Mad Mab will use the spell to take for herself the life force of others."

"And why would you help me?" Harry ducked as a crossbow bolt shot past. "Do you *mind!*"

"I have my reasons."

"Give me a couple. Quickly, before I get shot!" Not Dave turned, shielding Harry from the bowman just in time. Harry heard the bolt *thump* sickeningly into the creature's back. "Erm, thanks."

"I know she will never release my soul. Not until it's all used up and I am no longer of any use to her. Fortunately, there is another way my soul might be freed, but you must promise me you will *never* let Mad Mab have that spell."

Harry frowned. The sounds of violence and shouting all around them seemed to fade. "Who *are* you?"

"I am but Dave the barrowman."

"You're not Dave."

"So much has been established."

"Eh?"

"Never mind. What do you know of Dave?"

Harry began to struggle again. "I know *you* must have killed him."

"No. *I* am Dave."

"Rubbish!"

"Alright. My name is Ken."

"Seriously? Bloody *Ken*? That the best you could come up with?" He freed his right hand and struck out at Not Dave.

Not Dave may have sighed, but the groan sounded more like a tree being uprooted. He caught the ineffectual blows in his own vice-like grip. "Alright, you leave me no choice. My name is Hugh, and I am – that is, I was – your dad."

Harry hung suddenly motionless. Eventually, he managed, "Really?"

"Yes. Well…? What do you say to that?"

"Can I have my hand back?"

Matty would have fallen to her death amidst the angry waters of Snugly Burn had Lott not caught her. "B-but you're dead!" was all she could say.

"That's, erm, what I said," Bodges noted, conversationally.

"Where's the old woman?"

"But you're dead!"

Lott rolled his eyes. "Can we get away from this edge? I can't swim, not that I think it would help, looking down there. Come on."

On their way back to the ruins of Insane Alice's hovel, Lott explained about his faked death and the unfortunate graveyard excavation. "Had to make it look like the pigs were eating *my* corpse, so I removed the head. I left it in the grave, though – buried respectfully, like. I mean, that's the important bit, right? I once heard a priest telling people that was where the soul lived."

"Respectfully…? You fed his body to the pigs."

Lott looked abashed.

Matty pressed on. "Did that priest also mention a little thing they call judgement day?"

"Don't think so. Why?"

"Because, when the rest of us 'rise up from the grave', I reckon that poor gent's corpseless head is going to have a few choice words for you. Anyway, how do you even know Insane Alice? She doesn't trust men – they have a tendency to try and burn her alive."

"She…" Lott tailed off, suddenly embarrassed.

"Go on."

"Yes, I'd like to, erm, hear this, too," agreed Bodges. He turned to Matty. "He's had me, erm, looking for her all day. I'm drenched to the skin! And at my, erm, time of life."

"Well?" Matty prompted.

Lott sighed. "She caught me stealing. One of her increasingly rare visits to town. Lucky me."

"Alice was in town?" Matty was genuinely astonished.

Lott nodded. "It wasn't long after I began working for Felix L'Éternuement. She said she would keep my theft a secret *if* I agreed to spy for her and keep an eye on Harry-the-Cough."

Matty was suspicious. "You agreed?"

"Of course."

"And you actually kept that bargain?"

Lott sighed again. "Have you ever had your hand chopped off for stealing?"

"No," she acknowledged.

Lott wiggled his fingers. "What a coincidence. But if I went back on my promise…"

Matty understood. "So when *I* caught you stealing, from Harry's shop——"

"I told you. I wasn't stealing."

"And *I* told *you*, *I* didn't believe you."

"What can I say?" Lott held out his hands, palms up. "One of us was wrong!"

"Or lying."

Lott turned to Bodges. "I should have let her fall in the river."

"So, how can I set your soul free?" asked Harry, his voice small, barely audible above the storm and clash of swords in the growing darkness.

"It's what I can do for you. One pure act, and then move on. A wise woman told me that, once. You swear to keep the spell from Mab?"

"I swear."

The ragged man set Harry back on his feet. "Goodbye."

"Wait. Please…"

Not Dave but Hugh turned back. His rotten face lacked the equipment to smile, but he did his best. "I've yearned for the chance to say goodbye to you for ten years. Until we meet again, live well, my son."

"Dad!"

The golem turned away and smashed into Sir Ralph's soldiers, throwing them around like stick men. Harry's eyes misted over as he stood dumbly at the centre of it all. The only thing to penetrate his shock was the fact that Hugh did not kill, though neither did he pull his punches.

"Come on!" Robyn shouted, grabbing Harry by the arm and forcing him into a run.

They left the woods and ran across the fields to the west, not for any other reason than to get away. Overhead, thunder rolled, while lightning threw hard shadows across the snow.

Chapter 18
Shepherd's Warning

Sir Ralph burst into the great hall of Warmstirrup Castle like a red cape chasing a bull, yelling at the top of his lungs. "Henry! Henry, call out the guard!" Several men hobbled after him, following in his wake. Some used spears as walking staffs, others carrying or carried – all were battered and in foul humour. The only man unscathed was Ralph himself.

The earl looked up from his breakfast in some consternation. "Ralph. Where the hell have you been?"

"Chasing the demon! Didn't you get my message?"

His outburst sent a low moan of uneasiness through the hall as Henry's men rotated around the breakfast tables. "SILENCE!" Henry roared at them. "I got *a* message, Ralph. Load of nonsense."

"Nonsense? Look at my men! Ask them if it's nonsense. I tell you, we caught the demon——"

"So where is it, then?" Henry interrupted the tirade.

Ralph deflated. "It... escaped."

"Is it following you?"

"No. At least, I don't think so."

"Why should I call out the guard, then? Honestly, Ralph, and in the middle of my kippers, too!"

"Damn your breakfast, Henry!"

Lord Henry jumped to his feet, shoving his table dangerously close to the edge of the raised dais. "This is *my* castle, Ralph – mind your damned manners! And another thing," Henry waved an accusing finger at his younger brother, "when my men returned last night, they told me you'd hared off after Harry-the-Cough after being expressly forbidden from harming him."

"I was told no such thing."

"Are you saying I'm lying?"

"I'm saying someone is."

It was usually entertaining when the brothers squabbled, but on that dark morning in the great hall, with a red sky outside and talk of demons, the men's mood was hushed.

"Or is it that you don't *listen?*" Henry hissed, aware that all ears were upon them. All eyes were lowered in deference, not daring to look up.

"Alright, Henry, let's hear it. What's so special about this Coughing Harry?"

"Come here." Henry brusquely bade his brother climb the dais. "Look at this." He handed him a torn section of parchment.

Ralph frowned in concentration, following slowly with a finger while he mouthed the words silently. "Where the hell is Shrewsbury?"

"*I* don't know, somewhere near Wales, or in Wales, or some damned place. The Welsh always have their fat eyes on it. Best I understand it, no one even knows *who* owns the place, half the time. Look, you're missing the point. I need Harry——" Suddenly remembering their audience, Henry lowered his voice to a whisper. "All that matters is that the apothecary and the whore be kept safe. So let's not get bogged down, *understand?*" He slapped his younger brother about the head.

"Alright, alright," Ralph agreed tetchily. "Thing is, though, I made a deal, see? That Harry chap was part of the price."

"What?"

"Can we leave that for a moment?" Ralph tugged nervously at his ear, continuing in more normal tones. "You need to know about this demon."

They sat side by side and Ralph helped himself to a kipper from Henry's plate; an act that would probably have led straight to the hole for anyone else, but despite behaving like a couple of brawling bears, no one ever doubted that the brothers loved each other. Albeit in a violent, no mercy, no sympathy kind of way.

"It's witchcraft, Henry. No other word for it. That said, it might not be all bad."

"A demon that's not all bad? You should have a word with the bishop – Skirlaw loves that kind of talk."

While his brother was distracted with sarcasm, Ralph stole another kipper. Henry intercepted the theft with his knife, making it a quarter-kipper. "Get your own," he snarled.

"I've been out fighting to protect *your* lands all night, while you've been here doing... what have you been doing?"

"Clearing up the wretched courtyard after that idiot with the fish—— Oh, never mind. Tell me about this demon and his 'not all bad' ways."

"Ah." Ralph leaned in close. "First, tell me, how much do you pay towards the upkeep of those workshy monks at Aynlton Priory, brother?"

"What's that got to do with the price of... *fish?*" He slammed his fist down on Ralph's hand as it wandered back towards his plate.

Ralph blew on his fingers, flexing them. "Just think how much the church would pay *us* should we catch and kill a demon."

"Is that possible?"

"Maybe. If we find the witch who summoned it."

"The witch who summoned it..." Henry repeated thoughtfully, making all the wrong connections.

"Aaargh!" Mad Mab cried out in frustration. She leapt from her makeshift bed among the bushes – the only cover available in that part of the forest. Her cloak was covered in snow, but her anger soon thawed it out.

Insane Alice stirred. "Is he dead?"

"Of course he's dead," she hissed. "What does that have to do with him obeying my instructions?"

Alice stared. "It may be that we're talking cross purposes. Who were you referring to?"

Rather than answer, Mab asked, "Who were you asking about?"

"That wretched Walter Sweet fellow over there, who else?"

Mab glowered. "Oh, him. I don't know. I haven't checked. I understand that freezing to death is very unpleasant, so it seems a fitting end to an unpleasant life. Who cares?"

"Alright. So who were *you* talking about just now?"

Mab stewed in silence.

"Oh," Alice breathed as comprehension dawned. "Lost control of him, have you?" she added with relish.

Again, Mab refused to answer.

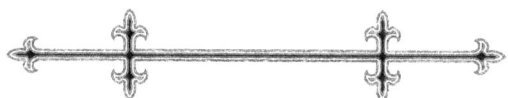

Harry liked nothing better than a freezing cold, red dawn – while he was tucked up in bed. Waking under a bush to a red-grey glow and a sneezing fit figured rather lower down his list. Some may have been tempted to use a phrase like 'there's nothing worse, is there?' but Harry knew better. There was always something worse. For example, on this particular bleak morning, he found that he had also been robbed during the night.

He jumped to his feet, staggered and fell over again with a cry. Lying on his side in the snow, he stared a red dawn in the face. Not all of him had woken up yet. "Pah! Shepherds' warning... They could have bloody well warned me!" He rubbed pins and needles from his semi-frozen leg.

"Good morning," Sister Tick greeted jovially, returning from the stream after her early-morning ablutions.

"Sod off!" was Harry's witty riposte.

"What in the world's the matter?" asked Little Joan, sleepily.

"I've been robbed. Again! Look!"

His bag had been dragged some distance from him while he slept. Several of the medicaments he used the night before, to patch up their many and varied injuries, lay strewn all over the snow. "No!" He fell to his knees. His recipe book, his pride and joy, and sum of all his knowledge, lay on the ground. The pages were too sodden to even flutter any more, but worse yet, something had been torn out.

He picked up his life's work reverentially, all speech failing him.

"Sorry, Harry." Robyn joined them, placing a friendly hand on his shoulder. "Can you save it?"

"If I can peel the pages apart and dry them, maybe." Harry turned each leaf, gently. Made from linen rags, the paper was tough and durable, the common iron gall ink relatively waterproof, but there was one thing he could not undo. "But it's worse than that, I'm afraid."

Robyn knelt at his side. "What is?"

"There's a page missing. It's the spell that I swore to..." he gulped, his emotions overtaking him, "I swore to my father I would never let Mab get her hands on." He shook his head morosely. "I should have destroyed it, but it was the only thing I ever owned that was worth anything." He looked up at Robyn, tears welling in his eyes. "And now I've lost it and failed him."

"I'm still adjusting to the idea that... that *thing* we've been running from was your father."

"He saved us," Harry mitigated.

"He attacked us first, and was particularly unfriendly towards Willa and Mario, back at the priory."

"Yes, but he could have killed us."

Robyn placed an arm about his shoulder. "Harry, he *was* trying to kill us. Trust me, I fought him, remember? Whatever changed his mind, it wasn't our welfare."

"One pure act, and then move on," he muttered.

"What's that?"

"Oh, nothing." Harry let go a shuddering sigh. "Just something he said to me. I can't fail him – not now, Robyn."

Robyn looked uncomfortable. "I'm sorry, Harry. Some of this might be my fault."

He turned his gaze upon her as a tear dropped.

Robyn felt terrible, but perhaps this was not yet the time for the whole truth. "You see, Insane Alice told me to look out for you. She said you were a good man, but too soft to see through people who might be up to no good – that you needed protection. After all that's happened, I…"

"What? Robyn, *please?*"

She wiped his tear kindly, before it froze. "Look around, Harry. Someone's missing."

Matty, Lott, and especially Bodges, rose stiffly. Matty stretched to bring life back to her limbs. "That's a night I won't forget."

Lott grinned. "Thought that was every night for you?"

Her eyes narrowed. "Watch it!"

"I don't, erm, think I'll survive another, erm, one like that," Bodges groaned, weakly.

Matty and Lott shared a look of concern. Last night had been incredibly tough, even with youth on their side.

"Bodges, come here," Matty invited. "Lott, you too."

Together they embraced, attempting to warm one another.

"This feels a little, erm, *awkward*," Bodges confessed.

"You got the 'erm' in the right place," Lott pointed out.

Matty clipped him around the head. "I'm warning you."

"Ow! My ear's burning now."

"Good," Matty bit out. "Bring it over here so I can warm my hands on it. We need to find Alice. Any ideas, anyone?"

"What do you think we spent all day yesterday doing?" Lott replied tersely, rubbing his ear.

"I wouldn't know. I had a few problems of my own, what with escaping from the castle and all!"

"Please." Bodges' plea was so weak that they both fell silent immediately, feeling guilty.

"Are you going to be alright?" Matty asked kindly.

"We need to move, or he's going to freeze to death," Lott added.

For once, Matty had to agree.

"There may be a way," Lott suggested. "Insane Alice told me that someone else might come for Harry. It's what I was trying to tell him when you caught me – I really wasn't stealing. I took those things so that I didn't lose my place with L'Éternuement. He steals all his remedies, you see?"

"Fine. Let's say I believe you. How does that help us here?"

Lott was suddenly uncomfortable. "I wasn't to mention this to another living soul, but seeing as things are..." He tailed off, taking in the remains of Alice's burnt-down house.

"In the midden. Yes, I know. You were saying?" Matty egged him along.

The street-boy turned apothecary's assistant sighed. "She taught me a rune – a sigil, I think she called it."

Matty frowned. "What's that?"

"I'll show you."

Bodges coughed. "Wait. Are you sure about this, young man? Dabbling in the dark arts might get us all burned alive."

"You'd prefer to freeze to death?" Matty asked him, reasonably. "Go on, Lott. Show us."

He stepped within the burnt-out dwelling and found a likely stick. A few days ago, it would have been part of the wattle within the daubed walls, but now it was a mere charred remnant. Just outside the building sat the large, flat stone Alice used as a base for her quern, where she ground the small amount of grain she needed to bake her weekly loaves. He wiped the snow from its surface, rubbing it clean. Satisfied, he began to draw.

"Wait," Bodges called again. "You haven't told us what it'll do."

Chapter 19
Crossed Line

Mab stared. "Looks like you've got a call coming in, dear." As she said it, the pendant around her own neck began to vibrate. She reached into the folds of her dress and pulled it out – it glowed.

"You too, dear," Alice countered, taking her own pendant in her hand. The small stone bore a runic sigil and was suspended on a fine leather strap. "Interesting."

"Are you going to answer it?"

"Are you?"

Impasse. The wary sense of shared interests that bound the witches was tenuous at best. It was by no means an alliance. They simply observed, benefiting from their combined strength, while each waited for a weakness to present itself in the other. Alice recruited Lott to watch over Harry-the-Cough, giving him strict instructions never to summon her under any but the direst of circumstances. She could only imagine that whoever summoned Mad Mab would have been placed under similar restrictions. Furthermore, she might even know who that someone was, and if she was correct, they were in trouble.

She felt confident that Mab's outburst the previous evening heralded her loss of control over the golem – Alice could not bring herself to think of the creature as Hugh, her deceased husband. Whether off on a jolly of his own, or dead – again – she had no way of knowing and saw little point in asking. The problem she faced now was whether to find Lott or follow Mab. She could see only one reason why Mab's spy would risk summoning her like that. He must have Harry's spell. Should he successfully hand it over, unchallenged, it would be a disaster for them all, and for countless others down the centuries.

Mab studied Alice in turn, wondering who she might be working with. She could almost hear the other's thoughts. After the event that left him orphaned, she had taken Harry in, had groomed him for this very day. The body of his father, Hugh, was found immediately after that Scotch raid across the border – buried conveniently near the village for her complex death magic to reanimate several years later. The village men gave chase to the raiders, but though they failed to retrieve any of their stolen cattle, they did come back with disturbing tales about Harry's mother, Maud, and toting a blue headscarf as evidence – evidence Mab now knew was either completely bogus or accidentally misleading. If the men did find a ravaged and disfigured body, it had clearly not been Maud. The real Maud, a peasant farmer's wife, had disappeared, before returning to England many years later as Insane Alice, a witch of some ability. Mab wished to know more of that transformation. Although, in a sense, all that really mattered was that Alice knew enough about how the spell worked to try to stop her. Add to that the fact that Alice's only son, latterly known as Harry-the-Cough, was also in the firing line, and she might react *unwisely.*

Mab often wondered why Insane Alice, having secured her freedom by whatever means, had not returned to her son as Maud. Of course, everyone knew that slaves taken in cross-border raids were not treated well – whichever side they ended up on. Consequently, she may have suffered considerably during her time north of the border, so there was always mental instability to consider, but Mab doubted that. She knew better than anyone the projected persona of the cackling crone. It was a powerful folk image and what the peasants expected, but it was marketing, nothing more. Designed to create an aura of fear and respect. No one truly insane could carry such knowledge and work it effectively. Perhaps Maud, or Alice, simply wished to avoid causing the boy any further damage – she had certainly been keeping tabs on him from a distance.

This seemed to be one of those situations where Mab always felt slightly disadvantaged, and more than a little bewildered. The idea of sacrificing one's own interests and well-being for another made no sense to her. They called it 'love' but that was just a word – what did it *mean*?

"So, how's it going to be?" Insane Alice broke into her thoughts.

"Parting of the ways?" Mad Mab suggested.

They stared intently into each other's eyes.

They waited, but for what, no one was really sure. "Lott, why did you fake your own death and disappear, getting Harry accused of your murder?" Matty asked.

"It wasn't quite like that," he replied defensively.

"Quite how was it then?"

"I met with Insane Alice. She explained to me about how Harry was in danger of losing his business, his home, and possibly even his life, in the middle of harsh winter. Everyone knew L'Éternuement was responsible for what was being done to him, so Alice told me how to set him up."

"Harry?"

"L'Éternuement."

"Ah."

"Yes. What I had to do was pretty unpleasant, I can tell you."

"And brilliantly executed, too. They completely exonerated L'Éternuement and hunted Harry instead. Good job!"

"Alright, alright, calm down. Alice foresaw that possibility, too. One of the reasons I needed to see Harry so desperately before all this happened was to warn him. I wanted to tell him to make sure he was somewhere with lots of witnesses, who would all swear he could not have murdered me. When I found out he was at the castle with Lord Henry himself, I thought, perfect! Time to act."

Matty's eyebrow rose with her ire. "That would be the alibi your master ruined by getting Lord Henry to throw Harry out, giving Harry a whole new grudge against L'Éternuement that the earl witnessed for himself? Perfect timing."

"Well, I didn't know. Alice told me to tell Harry to get himself somewhere with witnesses – he did, all on his own – that was all there was to it. The other thing she asked me to tell him was to leave town for a few days afterwards, because someone was searching for him, some sort of creature. I didn't really understand."

Matty considered. "That seems to fit," she admitted grudgingly, "but why bring Bodges into all this?"

"You do know I'm, erm, *Doctor* Bodges, don't you?"

Matty hid her smile as she recalled what Harry thought of Bodges' skills as a physician, and the title he gave himself. "Of course, Doctor. Well?" she asked Lott.

"Dr Bodges was to be kept out of the way for a while." He looked at the old man, quickly adding, "Safely, of course. He was to stay with Alice. I got the impression, Dr Bodges, that you were happy to be out of there?"

Bodges shrugged. He was still extremely cold and had been largely uncommunicative since they awoke.

"Very well," Matty continued. "But *why* was Bo—— *Doctor* Bodges to be kept out of the way?"

"It was all part of Insane Alice's plans for her..." He suddenly clammed up.

Matty frowned. "For her what?"

"Nothing. I can't tell you. Really, Matty, I can't. I'm sorry."

"Damn it! I knew I couldn't trust him." Harry jumped to his feet. "He's really crossed the line, but working for Mad Mab... I mean, *why?*"

"I think of more immediate concern, is where?" Robyn corrected. "And *how* – come to think of it. We had a watch, didn't we? I know I took my turn."

"Dick took his, as well," Mario supplied dourly.

Robyn placed her head in her hands and groaned. "He was left on watch alone?"

"You may not have noticed," Mario continued, "but he was the only one not involved in some way with that fiasco last night. Harry was being strangled by that thing, and we were all fighting for our lives. We're lucky none of us were killed. Dick, on the other hand, was like a leaf in a gale, never landing in one place long enough for anyone to take a pop at him! Of *course* he took a watch. The rest of us were all beaten up and knackered. If there was some reason we shouldn't have trusted him, it would have been nice if management had shared it with us. We might have had our throats cut in our sleep!"

Harry rounded on Robyn, snapping his fingers and pointing accusingly. "That was it, wasn't it? What Insane Alice warned you about. When we left her by the campfire. Just before we went to the priory. She told you something, didn't she? Not that hogwash about me being too soft. She told you not to trust Dick, am I right?"

Mario got to his feet, too. "You knew this and didn't warn us?"

Robyn sighed and nodded. "So much has happened. I was exhausted, too, remember? I'm sorry, everyone. Sorry, Harry. Alright, Insane Alice told me she recognised Dick, or Bobby – whatever his name was – from back in the village where you grew up———"

"Hang on," Harry interrupted. "How did she know he was going by Dick these days?"

Robyn snorted sardonically. "A rabbit really did tell her. The furry little devils were actually spying on us in the forest – can you believe that? You really can't tell any more, can you? I mean, they look friendly enough, with their little twitching whiskers and flappy ears, but can you really trust them?"

Harry raised his hands to forestall her. "Perhaps we should leave the soundness of bunnies for another time. Back to Dick, what did she tell you about him?"

"Not much, only that Mab was likely to send more than one servant after you, because what you carried was so important to her. Alice found it very suspicious that Dick simply popped up out of the blue, after ten years, with a new persona and just happened to bump into you. She also said that when he was a boy – that was when he was called Bobby – he tended towards lying and stealing."

Harry mulled it all over. So many things were suddenly clicking into place. His dead father, Dick – or Bobby – but then there was Insane Alice. What was her interest in all this, and in him especially? He paced for a while, deep in thought, and then stopped dead.

Slowly he turned to Robyn. "How long have you known Insane Alice?"

She shrugged. "Couple of years. Why?"

"Who is she?" he asked, quietly now.

She shrugged again, sensing something else may have just gone wrong.

Harry stepped close to her. "*How* did she know Bobby as a boy in our village?"

Robyn had no answer.

They both turned when Willa called to them. "Look here. Tracks."

Seven miles west – beyond the boundaries of the known world for most Warmstirrup folk – lay the small village of Hwitaham. Another mile west lay the even smaller village of Twyford. A few short years previously, Twyford's population, though small, had been three times the size before the sweating sickness came and carried so many prematurely to their rest. Now, the few who remained worked harder still; especially the serfs, who had their masters' quotas to fulfil.

Houses and barns decayed.

Two of Twyford's peasants were absent. However, not being indentured serfs themselves, the local powers did not care. For the last month, they had been locked in the cellars of Hwitaham's west pele tower[1]. Both in their fortieth year, the couple were entering old age by the standards of AD1399 peasantry. They suffered greatly from the cold, damp conditions and had no idea why they were there. Three men had simply come for them one night, and that was the last time they had seen the sky. They were thrown food of the poorest sort once a day and provided with small beer. All pleas to speak with the priest went unanswered and despair settled on them.

With no living family, but for a son not seen since before the sickness came to their village, they had little hope of rescue and could have no way of knowing that their current predicament was linked with his. Mother cried. Father tried to comfort her. They waited, in the dark.

Dick made his way south-east through the forest, his destination, the ford, just east of Warmstirrup Abbey's new gatehouse. The abbey was a Premonstratensian house and not directly associated with Aynlton Priory. Of all the places to cross the River Aynl, it was one of the safest in early February. The monks, under their lazy, wealthy abbot, occasionally gave low quality alms at their gates, but rarely stirred without their walls before spring.

Mad Mab pre-arranged this meeting place because it lay on the opposite side of Warmstirrup to Harry-the-Cough's workshop and was well outside

---

1. Pele towers (pronounced peel) were small, square defensive structures built along the Anglo-Scottish borderlands during the later Middle Ages up until circa AD1600. Often built next to, or associated with, a church, they provided villagers with a refuge during the cross-border raids of the period. Happily, they now stand within some of the most peaceful landscapes to be found in Great Britain.

and away from The Sprawl.

Dick was afraid, and with good reason. Heaven knew what Harry and the others would do if they caught him before he met up with his protection. They must surely know by now that he had stolen the spell. He had hoped to find it in Harry's workshop a few days earlier, but that was not to be. As children they had been friends, and as such, Dick had no wish to harm Harry, but what choice did he have?

When he first caught Harry, in Cutthroat's Way, he intended to take his life and relieve him of his goods – such a crime would hardly have drawn attention in that place – but he simply had no will to do it. Even with what was at stake, and despite living by the seat of his pants for the last few years, he was not a killer, he was a singer. Of course, when the money ran out, he was often a thief, too, but never a killer. Mab, on the other hand, was most definitely a killer, and she had his parents. They may have been estranged, but he had to try to save them. It was only a piece of paper, after all. Harry would just have to live with it – or rather, without it. At least he had not taken the option of *living* away from his childhood friend.

In that way, he convinced himself that his actions were justified, and perhaps they were, but he still hated himself for them. Regardless of the item's value, he knew Harry had all sorts of problems just now. Having heard much of the exchange between Harry and his long-dead father, the night before, Dick knew that the last thing Harry needed was to be robbed by an old friend taken on trust.

Before he even realised it, he was at the treeline. All he could do now was wait and hope he had not done too much damage.

"He's been, erm, staring at us for a while, erm, now," Bodges noted cautiously. "I don't think he likes, erm, the fire."

"I'm not sure it's that," Matty replied, thoughtfully.

"Oh?"

"No. I think he wants us to follow him."

Lott stood, carefully, turning to face the hart, who was indeed showing quite unnatural patience while waiting for the two-legs to gradually work out the obvious. He lowered his young but already majestic head, and gestured north.

The three humans shared a look of rising concern.

"Does anyone else think that this is a bit, well... *odd?*" Lott asked.

"Could calling up, erm, deer be a result of your, erm, magic sigil, erm, thingy." Logic was against him, but Bodges nevertheless beat the bushes heroically, searching for any kind of rational explanation.

Lott shrugged. Turning to Matty, he blew out his cheeks, nervously. "Shall we?"

Matty returned his shrug. "We can't just sit around here for another day. We'll catch our deaths." It was bad timing, but while evaluating the hart, she innocently added, "I'm *starving,* too."

The deer gave her a cold stare, showing his square, front, nipping teeth.

"They know we eat, erm, meat – on the occasions we can get it," Bodges spoke out of the corner of his mouth.

"Oh, of course, I mean – that is to say, what I meant was – a few nuts or some fruit would be nice," she tried again, carefully. "I wasn't suggesting, er..."

The hart snorted two plumes of steam into the cold silence and pawed at the ground.

"So you're no longer after him, you're after his dinner?" Lott suggested.

She gave up. "Perhaps we'll set breakfast aside for now."

They set off through the snow after the hart, who proved an excellent guide; never trotting too far ahead, always making sure his small herd could see him. This was because his thought processes were much simpler than those of a human being. A smaller mind is easier to fill, which is why animals are so often mindful of our needs, whereas thoughtlessness requires intelligence.

Sir Ralph was on his feet, bawling down the great hall. "You! You caused me no end of trouble yesterday, Mr Bloody Sneezy!"

Felix L'Éternuement crept cautiously towards the high platform. Desperate to leave, yet drawn irresistibly onwards, the fearful apothecary somehow contrived to move forwards while appearing to move backwards – a similar dance would not be seen again until the 1980s.

"My lord?" was all he could say.

"That sub-creature gave my men a right hiding."

"But, my lord, I didn't want you to pursue the..."

"Are you saying it was my fault?" Ralph was red in the face.

"No, my lord. Never. I merely came to see how our *other* business was proceeding. I must plan my move, you see..." Again, his words withered under Ralph's furnace glare.

One storey up, in the keep's chapel, Lord Henry was on his knees receiving a blessing from the castle priest, Father Michael. At least, that's what he believed was happening. Always an interminably long-winded affair, the familiar highfalutin ceremonial Latin favoured by the Church always seemed to go on forever, though he had absolutely no idea what the man was talking about. While his small group of tame monks sang for the glory of God, and the health of their patron's soul, Lord Henry caught snatches of an altercation taking place below. He had an unusually loud and easily recognisable voice – an asset on the battlefield. One he shared with his brother. Henry sighed, shoulders slumping.

"We'd better skip to the end, Mike."

Father Michael was nonplussed. "That's the second time this week, Henry. If anything happens to you, you'll have more to worry about than the state of your undergarments, you know."

"I know, I know. I'm sorry. You'll just have to give me two, erm... wossnames, next week. I'd better see what this is all about."

"Very well, Henry. You know best." Michael crossed the kneeling magnate, flicked some holy water at him and pronounced him fit to leave.

Henry rose from the 13th century encaustic tiles that had decorated the chapel floor for more than a century, bowed to the altar and left. Taking the spiralling steps two at a time, he descended quickly, happy in the knowledge that he had at least placed a down payment against his sins.

He burst from the stairwell into the great hall, roaring, "By Christ, Ralph, what the hell is going on? You *knew* I was in the chapel, and you, better than anyone, know how long it takes to confess everything, damn you!"

At the heart of a private storm that flung everyone out of his path, the earl whirled towards the raised dais and Sir Ralph. "I have a royal deputation arriving today. They'll want to turn us from supporting Bolingbroke. God knows I'll need to be shriven before meeting with those leeches!"

"Forgive me, brother. The Sneeze, here, was just about to explain why he sent me on a fool's errand yesterday."

Henry beckoned the apothecary approach. "Well, L'Éternuement?"

L'Éternuement climbed the dais as though it were the scaffold. "My lord, I simply struck a bargain with Sir Ralph——"

"Ah, yes. About that..." Henry interrupted, glaring at his brother – who suddenly looked shifty.

"It's a minor affair, Henry." He waved his hands, disingenuously. "Nothing to worry about."

"Sir Ralph promised me a knighthood, my lord," L'Éternuement explained. Seeing his patron on the ropes, he wanted to make sure he did not back out of their deal.

Henry's eyes widened, aghast. "Did he now?"

Ralph mumbled something about bringing useful learning, not to mention products and services, within the remit of Henry's nobility. No one believed him.

Henry nodded in a friendly manner, also false. "And this *apothecary* will provide me with military service and men-at-arms, will he?" he asked his brother.

"Well, yes. I mean, no. That is, not in so many words, perhaps——"

"My intention is to leave this shire, my lord," L'Éternuement contributed, before Ralph could dig his hole any deeper.

"Really?" Henry asked, sarcastically. "While bringing essential skills within the remit of *my* nobility, eh?" The second question was directed pointedly at his brother, who was industriously wiping away crumbs left on the table from his breakfast. Henry turned back to L'Éternuement.

"What about your shop and business—— Ohhh." He spoke slowly, as realisation dawned. "So, Felix gets his knighthood. I *lose* my apothecary, and what do you get, Ralph? Hmm?"

"Just a small piece of property," he mumbled.

"That wouldn't be the fine townhouse and workshop just outside my gates, would it?"

"My lord, your noble brother did promise to rid you of a thorn in your side, too."

Ralph gestured desperately for L'Éternuement to be silent.

"Did he?" Henry's pleasantness was more terrifying than his bark. "Well, Ralph. Do tell, what is this great service you're about to render unto me?"

"To dispose of the murderer, outlaw and all-round nuisance that is Harry-the-Cough, my lord," L'Éternuement stated confidently.

Ralph placed his head in his hands, voice muffled through his fingers. "Imbecile!"

"WHAT?" The earl was on his feet, the long table across the dais turning over to fall from the platform amid a clatter of pewter plate and crockery, not to mention a few surprised screams. "You're aware of my orders to bring Harry-the-Cough to me – safely and *alive*?"

"I am now, brother. I wasn't then," Ralph placated.

L'Éternuement suffered the horrible realisation that his statement to ingratiate had only served to infuriate. "B-but he's a wanted outlaw, my lord."

"Shut up," Ralph spat. "You're already over the Rubicon, you horrid little man!"

"SILENCE!" Henry roared. "I'll make this clear, once and for all, to everyone, shall I? Get out of here – *all* of you – and find Harry-the-Cough. The man who brings him to me in one piece stays alive!"

There was a terrific scraping of benches and shuffling of booted feet as the soldiers left the great hall en masse. Lord Henry was not known for hyperbole.

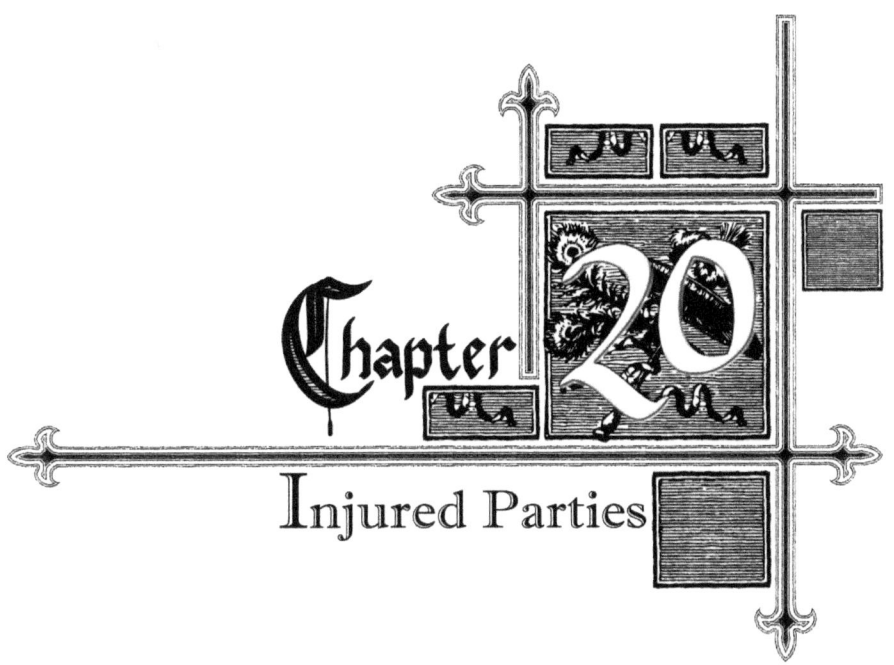

Chapter 20
Injured Parties

Mad Mab was hurt and bleeding badly. Her battle with Insane Alice had been short but brutal. She may have left the clearing, but whether she walked away the winner was still in the balance.

She stumbled again, crying out. Breathing hard, she took a moment before forcing herself back to her feet with another cry. She would need to tend her wounds soon, or all would be for naught. Grim determination kept her going, but she regretted setting up a meet near Warmstirrup Abbey. She was certainly in no condition for any further altercations that day. Assuming that the comfort-loving, lazy monks would never walk abroad in the dead of winter was all well and good, but as a witch, Mab also knew it was bad luck to trust in luck.

Bodges felt his fear growing once more. The powers of good and evil are rarely in balance, they merely slosh from high point to low point, describing the mean over time. As selfishness plays a huge part in bringing both sides down, the *mean* average is a mathematical irony. When the tide is in along one beach, it is out along another. Indeed, there are almost as many metaphors as there are ways for things to go wrong. Spikes occur everywhere, offering proof that, whether one is in government or in groceries, we all need help from time to time, and about the only thing any mortal can decide is whether we try to attract that help or buy it[1].

Bodges sensed something was wrong. He always found that, no matter how paranoid he became, it was never quite enough.

The hart kept going, though obviously nervous. He sensed it, too.

Matty sniffed. "Anyone smell smoke?"

The old physician whimpered.

Presently, they came upon a clearing in the forest. Whether it had always been a clearing was hard to tell because of the scorching. Their guide released a coughing bark and ran back into the trees, leaving them behind. Matty called uselessly after him.

"He's not a dog," Lott hissed, tugging at her sleeve.

"But we don't know where he was meant to—— oh."

---

1. Good or evil, goodwill or hard cash, the one thing both sides agree on is that help, if it arrives, will be less than you need and after you need it. Which is why most fill the little boat they sail through life with as much booty as they can fit – some even acquire enough to buy a bigger boat. It also explains why we spend more time rowing than rowing, and why the waterfall always comes as a surprise. However, despite the hole in his boat, Bodges instinctively knew that when the river runs quickly, the ride is short.

They both ran into the clearing with Bodges creakily bringing up the rear. Near the centre, and lying on the blackened earth, was Insane Alice, her rough clothing also blackened from burning.

"Alice!" Matty screamed, as she bent frantically to check on the older woman. Unsure how to help, she slapped her friend's face to revive her.

"Let me see. Let me see." Lott knelt beside her.

Tears streamed down Matty's cheeks as she looked him in the eye. "Can you help?"

"I don't know. I've been learning..."

"From a fake!" she snapped harshly.

He shrugged uncomfortably. "Fair enough."

"Let me, erm, see." Bodges caught up with them, colour returning to his cheeks both from exertion and from having something useful to do.

"Oh, Dr Bodges, please help her," Matty implored.

Bodges bent to listen to Alice's chest. Straightening, he turned the crone's face this way and that. "Hmm."

"Well?" Matty asked, anxiously.

"She's alive, but she's had a beating. It's a wonder she wasn't burned to a crisp, looking around at the ground here. Can't make out how she survived. Lott, do you still possess the ammonia salts you used to revive me?"

Lott handed him the small phial. Bodges removed its bung distastefully and wafted the small container beneath Alice's nose. "Wake up, dear lady. Come back to us."

Matty noticed that, while working, Bodges seemed to have lost his twitch and nervous habit of dropping 'erm' inappropriately into every sentence. Harry's opinion of Bodges was low, but now Matty pitied him, wondering what kind of man he might have been, had he not lived so many years in fear for his life.

Insane Alice coughed. "Take that away, for the love of... Oh. It's Bodges, isn't it?"

"Alice!" Matty hugged the older woman fiercely.

"Let me breathe, girl," Alice chuckled weakly.

Matty diverted her attentions to Bodges, throwing her arms around him. "Thank you, Dr Bodges. That was miraculous."

Lott was nonplussed, but before he could explain that he had had a thing or two to do with Alice's recovery, something caught his eye. "Matty," he muttered quietly. When she failed to notice, he repeated more urgently, "*Matty.*"

She stopped mothering Bodges to see what was wrong. Once everyone was still, they heard laughter. Thoroughly unpleasant laughter. Matty looked to Alice, who seemed to have lost consciousness again. She turned, dreading what she might see, and there stood Sergeant-at-arms Walter Sweet, grinning.

Mab fell again. This time, she was unable to get up. It was time to look to herself. Knowing that all the power she would ever need waited just at the bottom of the valley taunted her, but it remained out of reach. She lay on her side, opening her cloak. A stick that could only be described as a stake stuck out from her chest, just below the heart. It was a near miss. Insane Alice had proven a most worthy opponent.

If she removed the stake, she might bleed to death. If she left it where it was, she would die anyway. Mad Mab knew well that the vast majority of what people called magic was actually knowledge – a science that, for most, was lost in the mists of time. Much of witchcraft was reputation and fear rather than action or power, but then there was the real magic. The spell she had entrusted to Harry, when combined with other knowledge gained on her long journey, would unlock its secrets at a level few ever experienced. Yet, for the first time, she doubted she would live to wield that power.

Having no choice, she grabbed the stake with both hands and pulled. Her scream rang down the valley. Dick heard it, as did others.

"Can you track him?" Harry cycled through his emotions all the way from anger to a sense of betrayal and loss, and back again. Anger seemed best – it kept him on his feet.

Willa huffed.

"That means yes," Robyn translated.

"Well, come on then! What are we waiting for?" he shouted angrily.

Willa crossed her arms, stubbornly.

"Alright," Harry lowered his voice to a cold fury, "let me spell it out for you, shall I? If that missing page ends up in the hands of Mad Mab, it will be very bad for everyone. Possibly worse yet, if it found its way to the authorities, they would hunt us down and burn us at the stake——"

"We understand, Harry." Robyn placed a calming hand on his shoulder.

"Oh, no! I'm not done yet," he disagreed. "Dick pinched those coin stamps, too. If he gets caught with them – because, let's face it, he's not that bright – he'll spill his guts and the authorities will hunt down everyone involved and hang us all first! Whichever way we go down, it will not be pleasant."

"Calm down, Harry," Robyn spoke more forcefully. "Willa, track him. Come, let's move out."

Willa led them through the forest, occasionally stopping to check for a footprint or a broken twig. At one point she found a few fibres from Dick's coat, snagged on a barb.

"He's heading towards Warmstirrup Abbey. Why would he go there?" Harry wondered aloud.

"It would be pretty cheeky to seek sanctuary from the abbot," Sister Tick offered, breathless from their brisk walk.

"He's got no shortage of cheek," Harry fumed. "He can talk out of all four of them!"

"This way," Willa interrupted.

They followed. The ground was sloping downhill when she stopped again, abruptly, holding up a hand for silence. They all heard the scream.

"That was close," Robyn whispered.

Willa nodded. "A woman."

They drew swords and knives, in readiness for whatever lay ahead. Little Joan hefted her bow like a staff, its string kept in a pouch, safe and dry from the weather. Checking everyone was ready, Willa led on once more.

Mad Mab almost blacked out from the pain; only a deep focus on the healing spell she wove kept her conscious. The blood in her mouth made the Brittonic tongue even thicker. She was dying. She must act quickly. The spell would stabilise her for now, as long as she remained still. She clutched the stone about her neck and chanted a summoning charm.

Dick cried out in alarm. Something was going on in his trousers that was most unwelcome. He jumped to his feet, hopping in circles as he retrieved the stone from an inner pocket he had sewn in for concealment, or some might have it, stealing. It was suddenly burning red and too hot to hold, so he let it fall, hissing into the snow.

He stooped. It still glowed. Gingerly, he touched the back of his fingers to it. Warm, but no longer burning. He picked it up once more, turning towards the river crossing and the abbey. The stone grew dimmer. His eyebrows shot up in surprise. He turned back the way he had travelled. The stone grew brighter, but no longer hotter. Dick blew out his cheeks. A warning would have been nice.

Not knowing what else to do, he set off uphill, retracing his steps.

Mab heard someone approach. No, not someone, several people. She closed her eyes, sensing the world around her. Falling deep into nature, a further presence snagged her attention. Human beings were too complicated to sense this way. This was a creature who belonged to the world – was part of it. She began yet another incantation, rocking with the words as she lay on her side in agony. With a psychic jab, she sent the other mind off at a run, terrified.

Willa knew they were close to the source of the scream. In addition to Dick's trail, she had also picked up another, where they crossed. The second individual was easier to follow because they were trailing blood. She sniffed and held up her hand once more for them to stop. Listening intently, she suddenly cried, "Scatter!"

Knowing Willa as they did, the Merry Women – and Mario, who belonged in neither camp – dove for cover among the bushes, leaving Harry alone and wondering what was happening. It did not take long for him to find out. The crashing and snuffling through the trees could only be one thing, and it was heading straight for him, at speed.

He cried out and leapt to the side as a huge wild boar lunged through their group, tusks sweeping from side to side with lethal intent. One second later and Harry would have been gored. As it was, he was caught up in a thorn bush, terrified to move and terrified not to. "Heeelp!" he cried out as he hung from its barbs.

Dick froze. He heard the cry. Worse yet, he recognised the voice. Shaking his head, he turned to flee when the stone in his hand glowed hot once more, making him cry out, too. Clearly, flight was not an option. He groaned and set off uphill again, almost immediately stumbling across Mad Mab on the floor.

Though terrified of the witch, he was also relieved. Harry's cry, and so near, gave away the presence of other, more immediate enemies at hand. While he served her, she would protect him – at least, that was what he hoped. Getting back up after his misstep, he realised she was in a bad way. *Oh, no. Just my luck!* he thought, some might say, selfishly.

Her eyes snapped open, glaring up at him and at that moment, he truly saw the madness within. "The spell!" she rasped, holding out her hand, demanding.

Dick reached within his coat and drew out the stolen page, handing it to her.

Mab clutched it to her heart, closing her eyes again in silent prayer to the old gods. Unfolding the spell, she scanned for the passage she needed at that moment. Hands and voice shaking as her strength failed, she read.

Dick felt lightheaded. More than the fear and the worry, something was suddenly very wrong.

Mab grabbed his leg and her touch seemed to burn. He cried out and fell again, but her grasp could not be broken. The wooziness in his head was spreading through his whole body; he could no longer feel his extremities. The pain in his leg ebbed as all feeling left him, like ripples on a pond fleeing a splash. His thoughts were sluggish, becoming muddied. Perhaps it was delirium, but he fancied his life force was travelling away from him. Was he dying?

A crash from the trees brought his focus back to the here and now, as bodies ran for them. He recognised Robyn and her followers, but though aware, he could no longer move.

Matty put her arms around Lott and Bodges, pulling them both behind her protectively, though with no idea how she might defend them against a beast like Walter Sweet.

"Time to pay, little trollop." The sergeant-at-arms moved closer, leering at her as he drew his sword. "Have me thrown in the hole, would you?"

"It was no more than you deserved," Matty answered with a courage she hardly felt.

He chuckled nastily. "I'll soon break that spirit of yours. Teach you some respect, I will… before the end. And it's going to be a painful end, little trollop – you can trust me on that."

"Sergeant-at-arms," Bodges greeted, shakily. "You wouldn't dare, erm, molest Lord Henry's, erm, physician. Lay down your, erm, sword. That's an, erm, order!"

"Sorry, Bodges, but you see, this little strumpet has to pay for what she did to me. Trouble is, the earl wants her and Harry-the-Cough alive and intact. Now, if I disobey him, he'll have my head, but if I just happen to find this girl's corpse in the woods, well… that's just the way it goes."

"I'll, erm, not allow it! I'll tell the, erm, earl."

"Of course you would, Bodges."

"I think that means he's going to find *your* corpse in the woods, too, Dr Bodges," Lott explained.

"Now, you see, the lad's clever, he's got brains – pity they're going to be all over the forest floor in a minute. It's a funny old world, isn't it?"

"Hilarious," snapped Matty. "What are you talking about?"

"I mean that I lay here – just over there, as it happens – all night, paralysed. Couldn't move a muscle. Thought I was done for, I did. Would have been, too, if the witches hadn't set about each other."

"What happened?" asked Lott, playing for time.

Sweet shrugged. "I heard something about glowing stones and messages from somebody or other, and then the other witch, the one who got away, attacked this one with burning fire."

Matty and Lott shared a glance, both feeling sick as they recalled the sigil Lott had drawn on Insane Alice's quern stone. "We caused *this?*" Matty asked, the distress evident in her voice.

"Really?" Sweet's demeanour was almost sunny. "So I've you to thank, have I? Well, isn't that special, because without that massive fire those two crones set blazing, I'd have frozen to death before I ever got chance to regain any feeling." He stretched his neck left and right, then rotated his head to relieve the stiffness. "Thought I'd broken my neck. Turns out, I was only stunned, after the fall from my horse." He laughed again, raising his sword in threat.

Lott screamed and ran at him, grabbing Sweet's sword arm and thrusting it up into the air. The experienced soldier gut punched the youth with his left, but although winded, Lott hung on like a limpet, just long enough for Bodges to also grab Sweet's arm.

"Gerroff me, you old fool!"

Matty was as frightened as she had ever been in her life. This man absolutely intended to kill her, but she screwed up her courage and piled into the fray, grabbing Sweet's other arm to prevent him from punching Lott again in the stomach.

In the confusion, Sweet dropped his sword and glared down at Matty with murder in his eyes. She had no fighting skill, but she hung on, for herself and for the sake of the others. Sweet had no compunction about dropping his head, butting her in the face.

Matty cried out and fell.

Sweet kicked her, doubling her over in so much pain she could barely move. Free to focus on the men, he swung his powerful arm around them both, dragging them off their feet.

Lott and Bodges shouted in bantam fury but could do nothing to stop themselves from being thrown to the floor. Sweet laughed again, as he took a kick at Bodges' face. The old man's nose exploded. Covered in blood, he cried out nasally, bringing his hand to his face.

Lott scrambled to his feet and ran at Sweet's midriff, spinning the soldier around but not off balance. Laughing merrily now, the sergeant-at-arms swung the boy off into the trees. Despite having time to raise his hands, Lott hit a tree trunk side-on and hard, breaking a rib and knocking the wind from his chest. He fell to the floor and groaned as he turned one last time to face their enemy. He was in agony, but he had done enough. His last feint, though doomed to fail, had been undertaken quite deliberately. Holding his side, he staggered back to his feet, grinning bloodily through broken lips.

"Now *that* is sweet," he wheezed painfully.

The boy's reaction brought a look of confusion that turned immediately to shock, and that was the last expression Walter Sweet's face ever wore in life. The blade of his own short sword erupted from his belly, red with gore. He grasped it and fell forward, the hilt sticking out of his back.

Lott smiled painfully at Insane Alice, who stood like an avenging angel, glaring down at the bully's corpse. "I should have made sure of you last night," she said with finality.

Chapter 21
Second Wind

Dick's eyes fluttered open. Everything seemed somehow dulled, his vision and hearing less sharp than he was used to. He lifted his arm with a groan. His hands looked different, too – older.

Mad Mab was on her feet with her back to him, studying something. Giving no warning, she screamed. It was bloodcurdling and Dick feared for his life. He had fulfilled his promise; what could be wrong with her now?

Turning onto his side, he could see bodies all around him. From the ground, it was hard to tell if they still lived. None of them moved. Every effort pained him, but he managed to raise up onto an elbow. Robyn, Tick, Mario, Willa, Little Joan – they were all there, but as far as he could tell, no Harry.

Mab straightened and turned slowly. She approached Dick, who held up his hands hopefully.

"Can you help me up? Please? I don't feel right."

"You fool!" she hissed. Her expression changed from angry to vindictive. "Mummy and Daddy are going to pay for your failure here, little Bobby."

"I don't go by that name... any more." Dick was struggling for breath. "I've given you what you want. Why would you harm my parents?"

Her hands curled into claws, and she screamed again, inhuman as she loomed over him.

Dick covered his head, waiting for an attack. "What have I done?"

Mab was not sure if the question was direct or rhetorical. Dick was not even sure himself as he blacked out again.

Harry had to admire the courage of Robyn's band, but that would not help him if they got themselves killed. As soon as the boar vanished into the forest, they had jumped to their feet and shot off after their quarry. Whether it was Dick or another, Harry could not say, but whoever it was, they were losing blood, as evidenced by the trail left through the woods.

Unfortunately, in their haste, his friends seemed to have forgotten about him, and he was left hanging from a thorny bush, frightened to move for the risk of damaging himself further.

Sounds of an altercation reached him from a little way off, and then nothing. The awful scream that followed chilled his blood. Whatever was going on ahead, it was nothing good. With no choice and no help, he slowly extricated himself from the thorns. Almost immediately, his hands and face were scratched and bleeding. In the end, he simply lunged back towards the track they had been following.

Rolling over in the snow, he groaned miserably. "Ohhh, that's a lot of pain." He hated to think what he might look like. Crawling, he dragged his bag over to a tree and sat against its trunk. He was hurting from myriad cuts. The leap and fall had winded him, too, leaving him close to vomiting.

Taking shuddering breaths, Harry reached into his bag, feeling around for a phial prepared just a few days ago, before his life had been turned upside down. It contained imported liquorice sticks mixed with elderflower, camomile and sliced ginger – a tonic he used chiefly to treat colds. It also worked as a pick-me-up, something Harry suddenly needed more than he ever thought he would.

A horrible suspicion gnawed at him, that his friends were incapacitated – or worse. Whoever was out in the surrounding woods, he doubted they were any friends of his. The tonic soothed his stomach and throat, relieving the pangs of sickness. He took a deep breath and coughed.

Replacing the phial, he noticed something sticking out from the bottom of his badly mistreated recipe book. Taking it carefully from his bag, he opened the cover and leafed through the pages, just thankful they had not yet stuck together. He really needed to take care of it before he lost all his work, but while he was pondering how he might dry it out in the middle of a winter forest, he reached the last page.

Upon discovering the theft, he had been too angered to look closely. Now, he could see that a fragment remained of Mab's spell. It was only a corner, still attached to the binding where the page had been carelessly torn out. Maybe Dick had been in too much of a hurry, or perhaps it was simply too dark to see properly, but if he *had* returned the spell to Mab, it was not the *entire* spell.

Hope rekindled within him. Might he yet avoid catastrophe?

A second scream cut through the forest, freezing his blood. "I need to get out of here." He struggled to his feet, but where to go? Should he follow Robyn and the others? Maybe he could help them? *Or maybe I could take this remnant right to Mab,* he thought darkly. Reaching a decision, he set off uphill and west, hoping his friends were alive but unable to help them at that time without making matters worse.

"FOOLS!" Henry bellowed, loud enough to shake the floor above. His men had returned empty-handed after searching all morning and much of the night. "Incompetent fools!" He strode down from the dais and his great chair. "Bring me my armour! Ralph, you can come, too. To make up for the mess you've made of things!"

Ralph followed, hangdog; even he knew when it was best to keep his mouth shut as far as his brother was concerned.

"Jack!" Henry bawled. "Where *is* that boy? Jack!"

"Henry," Ralph spoke cautiously, "a fire was reported earlier. The smoke was spotted at first light – down near Warmstirrup Abbey. Perhaps we should begin our search there, wouldn't you say? Bit unusual for this time of year, a forest fire."

"How big a fire?"

"Big enough. It was no campfire, but it didn't last long." Ralph shrugged. "As it went out by itself, the guards on the walls didn't think any more about it. Perhaps it *was* just a campfire that burned out of control, but what do you think?"

Henry pondered in silence, then spotted his master-of-hounds and began shouting again. "Ah, Jack! I want my hounds ready and hungry. I wish to leave right away. Saddle the horses!"

The great hall, and by extension the whole of the inner ward, erupted into life as the earl prepared to ride out from Warmstirrup Castle.

Insane Alice batted Matty's attempts to help her away. "Don't fuss, girl. I'm alright."

"Are you, erm, sure, erm, dear lady?" Bodges asked with some concern.

Alice opened her mouth to speak but thought better of it. She looked to Matty. "Don't I look alright?"

Matty, Bodges and Lott shared a glance, each clearly waiting for one of the others to explain. "You... er, you do look a bit mad," Lott tried. "I mean, with the blackened face and burnt hair and..."

Alice glared, silencing him. "And? They don't call me Insane Alice because I enjoy parties, boy!"

"Yes, but there's insane and then there's..." He chuckled nervously, to cover his sudden embarrassment. "Oh, God," he tailed off again.

Alice continued to glower and then bent to scoop a double handful of snow. She rubbed her face, vigorously, smudging soot everywhere. If newspapers had existed in 1399, and one were to be screwed up into a ball, painted with two brightly piercing blue eyes and topped with a badly singed mophead, that would have been the effect. The fact there were no newspapers made the look no less arresting. "Better?" Alice challenged.

They glanced at one another again.

"Definitely."

"Absolutely."

"Most, erm, assuredly, dear lady."

Alice's expression soured. "Alright, don't overdo it. We need to find Mad Mab. She must not get that spell."

"Get what?"

"A spell?"

"Erm, erm?"

"I'll tell you all about it as we go," Alice assured them. "Come on. And somebody grab the sword out of that brute's back. Better give it a wipe, too. You never know. There might be outlaws about."

"You alive, Robyn?" Mardy Mario enquired after his wife.

She moaned. "Not sure. I feel like I've been run down by a horse. How are you?"

"Feel lousy – not that anyone cares."

Robyn rolled her eyes, but that just made her headache worse. "What happened?"

"I think that was the witch," Sister Tick explained in subdued tones.

"Which witch?" asked Little Joan.

"Oh, come on," the others groaned.

"Get some new material," grumbled Willa.

"Whoever it was, she's gone now. And taken Dick with her," Joan continued unabashed. "He didn't look in a good way, did he?"

"I don't know," Robyn countered, stretching her back in the snow. "I was too busy not being in a good way myself to notice. Where's Harry?"

"Dunno," replied Willa.

"Do you think *she's* got him?" asked Tick.

Willa huffed. "She's welcome to him – too needy, that one."

"Oh, come on, that's hardly fair," Tick pointed out. "He has got a witch, a demon and all of Lord Henry's army after him."

"And his landlord," added Mario. "If I heard right."

"Ha! He's really in trouble now, then," Robyn stated with finality.

The others laughed, painfully, holding their heads. They felt hungover, but also drained, like they had heavy colds, just without the sniffles.

Robyn rose experimentally, to see if she could stand, wobbled a little, and hung on to a low branch to steady herself. "Why do we always seem to be cold and wet?"

"Because we're outlaws," Mario answered grumpily, "and therefore homeless. This robbing's harder work than people realise."

"*And* because we keep helping people," Willa added, "instead of just taking their money and leaving them in a heap by the side of the road."

Their appraisal of her leadership left Robyn torn between upset and fascination. "Willa, I do believe that's the longest sentence I've ever heard you utter."

"Cobblers!"

Robyn sighed. "Ah, back to basics. Good."

"You shouldn't talk to our leader that way, Willa," Tick leapt to Robyn's defence as was common within their little group.

"Why not?" asked Willa, belligerently.

"Because it might catch on, and where would that leave us? Chopping the heads off kings and hurling abuse at our leaders in the streets?"

Willa considered a moment. "I like that idea."

"Republican![1]"

"Royal slave!"

"Enough!" Robyn interrupted, before the future could gain an early foothold. "Come on, we should find Harry. Remember what Insane Alice told us? If anything happens to him, or if Mad Mab gets what she's after, we're all for it."

"Mad Mab's already got what she's after," Sister Tick complained. "That's how we all woke up in the snow."

"She's right," agreed Joan. "We're lucky the witch didn't kill us."

"God was with us," Tick assured them.

That sparked another row about bended knees, distant kings and the lot in life reserved for England's poor.

"For the love of... Alright, *alright!*" Robyn raised her voice. "Let's see if we can pick up their trail."

Harry thought furiously. Continuing uphill, he knew he was headed roughly south-west, but once at the top of the rise it would become increasingly difficult to discern direction in the forest. He suspected Dick had delivered the spell to Mab. By now, she would have realised it was incomplete – that may even have been the reason for the furious shrieks he heard earlier. If he stayed within the trees, he had a chance of remaining hidden; several parties might wander the forest all day and never bump into

---

1. Simon de Montfort's attempt to turn England into an early republic died with him in AD1265, at the Battle of Evesham, where he was surprised by the royal forces of Prince Edward (later Edward I). Sister Tick's appraisal was perhaps a little unfair, because had Willa been present, she would probably have taken a swipe at anyone who came near.

one another. The problem was what to do next.

Unlikely or not, should he be unlucky and actually bump into Mad Mab while she searched for him – and he felt sure she was searching for him – it would be the worse for everyone if he still had the remnant of her spell on his person. So, he decided to hide it, but where? He could hardly risk burying it in the woods – he may never find it again. Worse yet, it may be found by someone else. He could burn it, but he had nothing with which to start a fire, and everything was soaked, including the thing he intended to burn. No, he needed a secure hiding place that only he knew about or could find. An idea struck him. There *was* a place that fit the bill. A place that, firstly, no one would ever think to search because it had already been thoroughly turned over; and secondly, no one would ever think to search because it was a stupid idea. Stupid and dangerous. Harry sighed. "Sounds about right."

Insane Alice inspected Bodges' face, gently feeling the bridge of his nose. "It's broken, dear. Here, why don't I…" Giving no indication as to what she was about, she grabbed it between her first and second fingers and yanked it back into alignment with a loud *click*.

Bodges' eyes were mostly whites. Only Alice's other hand slapped across his mouth muffled his scream and prevented him from giving away their location.

She eyed her work carefully and gave a nod of approval. "Good. Who's next?"

"I'm actually feeling a lot better," Matty lied.

Lott winced, releasing the side he had been nursing to stand up straight. "You know, it's funny, but I've never felt so well. Honestly."

Insane Alice summoned him with a crooked finger. "Come here, boy. I heard that rib crack when you hit the tree. It'll be worse for you if it sets badly, or you have internal injuries."

Lott approached gingerly, with the air of a puppy caught crouching in the house and given no time to hide the evidence. "Really, it's not that ba——"

"Here," Alice cut him off, pointing the same finger straight down at the ground, right in front of her. "I need to make sure you're all at least functional, and those ribs need binding. I suspect the worst is still ahead of us, and..." She tailed off as a horn sounded from Warmstirrup.

They all turned towards it. "Oh, no," Bodges moaned thickly through his broken nose.

"That's the castle, isn't it?" Matty asked, though she already knew the answer. "Lord Henry setting off on a hunt?"

Bodges nodded painfully.

Alice sat heavily on a tree stump. "Oh, *God*. That's all we need, that oaf charging around the forest with everything else we've got going on."

Matty was suddenly ashamed. "He will probably want to, er... that is——"

"Burn me at the stake?" Alice completed for her. "I've already been set on fire once today. I'm getting used to it."

"I'm so sorry, Alice. I never thought they'd find you under Old Tom. When I found your house, I... I..."

"Don't worry, lass. It was brave of you to send them off on a fool's errand, even if it did lead them right to me. Still, at least that devil, Sweet, won't be a problem any longer."

"My, my, what do we have here?" Mad Mab mumbled to herself as she inspected the fresh corpse of a soldier in the woods. Finding the body in the same burnt-out clearing where she had despatched Insane Alice led her to two separate conclusions. Firstly, Alice had obviously *not* been despatched, and secondly, she must have killed the man on the ground before her. She recognised Sweet from the previous evening. Somehow recovered from his fall, he would have been a strong adversary, which surely meant Alice was relatively uninjured, too.

That was unsettling, especially as Mab had checked her corpse before leaving. Alice must have used some kind of illusion or trick to fool her. She knew little of Sergeant-at-arms Walter Sweet, but she did know he had been no friend to Insane Alice, and that gave Mab an idea.

"Hello again, my pretty," she rasped.

Though no longer painful, her injuries remained, her voice sounding strangled, almost choking to her own ears. The spell had certainly taken its toll on Dick; he looked twenty years older, at least, but she was greatly concerned that it had not healed her outright. The magic knocked down the group of outlaws that pursued him, too. They had fallen like the ancient game of ninepins – or more precisely, fivepins – and for two pins, she would have made sure they stayed down, too, but things were in motion, and she needed to find Harry.

Only the missing remnant of her spell mattered now, and it was surely still in the possession of Harry-the-Cough. She yearned to unlock its secrets, but that would have to wait – she needed help, first and foremost. Dick looked half-dead, so there would be little from that quarter.

A horn cried from the town. Mab turned. She would need to move quickly, too.

Alice raised a hand for them to stop. They could hear the thunder of hooves not far away, leading from Warmstirrup's northern gate towards the River Aynl and Warmstirrup Abbey. She turned to them. "We should split up."

"Good idea," agreed Lott. They all looked at him and he looked down. "Sorry. That was sarcasm. What's your plan?"

"To find Harry, what else?" Insane Alice stated coldly. "I suggest Matty comes with me. We're the ones they want to execute, after all. Lott, if you take Dr Bodges with you, you should both be relatively safe."

"And if, erm, we find him, erm, first, dear lady?"

Alice turned once more to Lott. "Make the sigil. We'll find you."

"And if you find him?" asked Lott. "How do we find you?"

"You don't, lad. Both you and Dr Bodges would do well to stay clear of us from here on out. Hopefully, we can all meet up again at some better time. Good luck to you both. Now go."

"You'd better have this, then." Lott handed Matty the short sword he had removed from the dead sergeant-at-arms.

She took it gingerly, sceptical about how much use she could make of it. Hiding it in the folds of her cloak, she nodded thanks.

Bodges held out a shaking hand. "Dear lady, erm, Matty."

Insane Alice gave a nod.

Matty took the hand and gave them both a hug. "We'll see you soon. Take care."

"Right." Alice straightened. "We'll take the east and work our way around to the south of town – you gentlemen take west and do the same."

They parted ways.

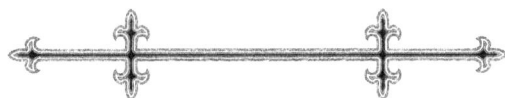

Harry walked for half an hour, eventually stumbling across the main road that led south-west past Edcase Castle towards the market town of Strewthbury. Looking both ways, he crossed the road and headed deeper into the forest on the other side. Retracing his steps as best he could, he made his way back to the place where Robyn's misanthropic malcontents had first kidnapped him. It was not far, and much easier without the confused magics of two witches focused on him.

He soon came to the place where he had run across the fields, narrowly escaping a mauling from Jack's dogs and being skewered by Henry's men-at-arms. It looked deserted. Taking a deep breath, he stepped out from his cover and strode as quickly as he could through the slushy snow back towards the southern sprawl outside Warmstirrup's walls.

He reached the copse on the other side without incident. As far as he could tell, he was hitherto unseen. The brooding sky gave little away, but he assumed it was around noon as he made his way along Dark Lane.

The gentle snow was gaining in strength again. He looked up and sighed, as flakes landed on his face and melted, proving that the sky had more to give away than he originally guessed. By the time he passed Cutthroat's Way, the flakes were large, building on a fresh blanket of treachery underfoot. Hundreds of feet had left marks in the slush over the last few days. Now all the prints were vanishing to leave just one set – Harry's.

He rolled his eyes and swore as he cut through to New Row. He was just about to cross when he froze. On the opposite side of the staggered junction that cut across New Row lay a small passageway, leading to the rear burgages that backed onto Harry's hovel in Scrubber Alley. The passage was short, and at the end of it, Harry could see the Red Baron strutting about like a sentry.

He cursed under his breath. The cockerel had developed a vendetta against Harry. Having his legs and nether regions pecked at by a squadron of yard hens led by the dawn avenger was bad enough, but if they drew attention to his whereabouts, he might be in far worse peril. What should he do? To go around would be to use The Sprawl's main road and someone would be bound to recognise him. Poisoning the little so-and-so would take too long. Might he try bribery?

"Sir William, you take the north road – Ralph, the Parkworth Road," Lord Henry barked. "I'll take the Strewthbury Road. Where the devil is that rogue, Sweet?"

"He never came back last night, my lord," one of Henry's men-at-arms stated. "Some of the men are saying he found the witch, my lord."

"And?"

"And that was the last anyone saw of him, lord."

"What the hell is going on in this town?" Henry demanded, furiously.

Ralph held up his hands. "I'm just a visitor," he offered by way of apology.

"Alright," Henry bellowed. "I'll make this clear. I want Harry-the-Cough captured and brought to the castle alive and in one piece. If you come across that little... If you come across Matty from Scrubber Alley, bring her too. And *unmolested* – everyone hearing me at the back? Any harm comes to either of them and I'll have something *inventive* in store for those responsible."

"What about the apothecary?" asked Ralph.

"The who?" Henry looked down from his destrier to see a dishevelled-looking L'Éternuement in the hands of his guards. "Oh, just get him out of my sight. Let him go."

Henry turned in his saddle to face his brother. "And, Ralph, should anything, shall we say, *unexpected* befall the fellow, the town charter states that all his goods and property come to me."

L'Éternuement and Sir Ralph looked at each other. It was hard to say who was the more scandalised. "Since when?" Ralph found his voice.

"Since now," Henry shouted. "Everybody hear it?"

"Aye, lord," his men called out, loyally.

"There go you," Henry winked to his brother, "it must be law then. Move out!"

Jack cried out, for upon hearing Lord Henry's command, five savage dogs dragged their master-of-hounds down Line Street towards the town gates, snapping at their leashes and one another in their eagerness for the hunt.

Henry Warmstirrup let go his own bark of laughter at the spectacle and set off after them.

Chapter 22

Playing Chicken

B*ribery, bribery, bribery,* Harry thought ferociously, and then the idea came to him. *No. Not bribery. Bilberry. Of course!* He knew chickens loved bilberries and he just happened to have some in his bag. They were dried, left over from last year's season, but would be no less of a treat for that. He rummaged and found the small pot he was looking for. Removing the string that held the cloth lid in place, he whirled the berries around with his finger, unfreezing and unsticking them from one another.

His eyes narrowed. *Right, here goes – back to the mission.*

Harry strolled nonchalantly along the passageway and popped out into the large allotment that backed onto his own meagre yard, shared with three other tenants. The Red Baron turned and saw him. He watched the cockerel's chest inflate as he opened his beak to squawk for an attack.

"Look!" Harry hissed. "I have a gift for you and your me—— er, wom——, er, hens. Look, you, you... bloody bird!" He scattered a few of the berries.

Like all good commanders, the Baron sent in a patrol to reconnoitre before committing his main force. When they began happily pecking at the ground, he stormed in furiously to shoo them away, strutting his demands before Harry.

Harry had no choice. He popped a couple of berries into his own mouth, scattered the rest, and ran for it, during the confusion. Squeezing once more through the broken planks in the fence, he looked around his yard. At least the weather was keeping his nosy neighbours indoors. He ran for his own back door, tugged it open, dashed inside, slammed it shut behind him and leaned against it, panting.

His eyes adjusted to the semi-darkness quickly and he froze. So did the room's other occupant. Harry gawked. "What the hell are you doing here?"

Lott and Bodges were only minutes behind Harry, although they had no way of knowing it until they came across the tracks in the snow. A lone man, trekking across the fields towards the sprawl. They shared a glance.

"You think?" asked Lott.

Bodges shrugged. It was not as though they had anything else to go on. "Alice and Matty probably, erm, won't dare to, erm…"

"Enter the town," Lott finished for him, bored with Bodges' delivery. He blew out his cheeks. "Come on, then."

Together, they crossed the field. The set of prints they followed was disappearing under the snow, but they deliberately confused them anyway, just in case they did indeed turn out to be Harry's. Almost at The Sprawl, they heard shouting and the tramp of heavy horses. "Quickly," Lott encouraged, dragging Bodges into the copse just outside the town.

They could not see anything yet, but the horsemen certainly made no attempts to hide their passage. No one ever accused Lord Henry of hinting.

Lott turned to Bodges. "You don't think The Cough went back to his own lodgings, do you? Surely no one's *that* stupid?"

"I always found, erm, young Harry to, erm, be very clever…"

Lott relaxed. "Of course."

"Erm, with herbs."

Lott stiffened. "You think he *is* that daft?"

"Not, erm, natural spy material, erm, that one."

"No. Seriously, I can't believe anyone would be that stupid."

"Care to, erm, make a wager, erm, young man?"

Lott placed his head in his hands and took a deep breath before looking up. "Those soldiers we can hear charging up and down the streets think Harry's a man of learning. That gives us the advantage."

Bodges looked doubtful. "How so?"

"Because only we know he's a complete idiot. Just maybe, we can get to him first."

Insane Alice froze. "Some evil is afoot here."

Matty took her arm, making the older woman flinch in surprise. "What's wrong?"

"Something…"

Matty released Alice and made a rolling gesture with her hands. "Can you be more specific?"

"Dark magic. Mad Mab is up to something very nasty. I can feel it. It's sickening."

"Can you tell where? Should we run?"

"Probably."

"*Will* we run?"

"Probably not." Alice smiled weakly, showing hardly any teeth. "But *you* should."

"No. I'm staying with you."

Alice grabbed the younger woman's arm, gratefully, and for the first time

Matty realised her friend was afraid. It was unthinkable. How powerful must Harry's spell have made Mad Mab for Alice to react so? The fear was more infectious than one of Harry's specialisms and Matty needed reassurance.

"How did you survive Mab's attack in the forest?" she asked.

"Simple. I cheated." Alice was lost in thought, but eventually noted Matty's impatience. "Alright, I'll tell you. I learned everything I could about fire protection from the wise woman who taught me. In our line of work, you might call it insurance. My protection was enough – at least, for a little while, but Mad Mab is strong. Very strong. I knew she would overpower my charms eventually. So I waited until she was fully committed, in the middle of a complex incantation, and used the opportunity to strike back."

Matty listened, open-mouthed. "What did you do?" she asked in an awed whisper.

"I hit her with a stick."

"Oh."

"Don't knock the simpler solutions, my girl." Alice grinned. "The stick broke, so I rammed the sharp end into her chest. That should slow her down."

"Slow her down?" Matty was horrified.

Insane Alice shrugged. "I know, but I'm sorry. I fear it will take more than that to kill her."

"So, back to my question – if we don't run, what *do* we do?"

Alice fell once more into deep thought. Eventually, she muttered something about needing help and sat in the snow, chanting.

Harry could not believe the nerve. Despite everything, he was furious. L'Éternuement, in his home. "Well?" he demanded.

"Y-you're a murderer." L'Éternuement attempted deflection, but Harry was having none of it.

"Rubbish. I had nothing to do with your servant's death and you know it."

"Prove it!"

Harry's mouth opened, but he found no answer. How *could* he prove it? It seemed half the town believed him guilty. It would take nothing short of a miracle to prove his innocence – especially in the eyes of Lord Henry. Lott would practically have to…

"Well?" L'Éternuement demanded in return, interrupting Harry's thoughts. "You chopped his head off and fed him to *my* pigs, you, you swine!"

Something gnawed at Harry, something he had considered odd at the time. "Don't you think it strange that the murderer removed the head, *then* fed him to your pigs?"

"You tell me, executioner!"

"Look, what do you want me to do, bring him back from the dead?"

L'Éternuement huffed. "You won't get away with this, Harry-the-Cough. I'll find the evidence I need, if it takes me——"

Harry's back door crashed open. Lott and Bodges barrelled into the room. Harry and L'Éternuement screamed in spite of themselves.

"You're dead!" L'Éternuement managed, almost tearful in his terror.

Lott straightened his jacket, scornfully. "Relax, will you?"

"Ha-*ha!*" Harry voice was strangled but he did his best to present Lott like something L'Éternuement had just won at a fair. "There's your proof, damn you! Innocent as proved. So what do you say to that?"

"Witchcraft!" L'Éternuement hissed. In a flurry of movement, he forced open Harry's front door and ran out into Scrubber Alley, screaming, "Witchcraft! Witch—— *Ugh!*"

"Ew… Sorry, dear," Mrs Pigden apologised from her upper storey window, opposite. "His Nibs back here has an upset tummy. You got anything for it, Harry?"

Harry missed her request, as L'Éternuement barely noticed the ordure streaming down his face and into his clothes. He was too busy screaming 'witchcraft' from the middle of the alley for the whole town to hear. Knowing his neighbours only too well, Harry watched from the safety of his doorway.

"Make way! Make way, there!" cried old Mr Tanner, the tanner.

Harry had barely plucked up the courage to play chicken with a chicken – although he would never have used the word 'plucked' within the Red Baron's hearing. He could only suggest to L'Éternuement that playing chicken with Neil the pony was a far worse proposition, but his competitor was no longer listening, to anyone.

The warning died on Harry's lips as L'Éternuement went down, under the hooves and wheels of Mr Tanner's commercial vehicle. "Maniac!" the old man roared as he went by. "You'll have an accident one of these fine days, my boy!"

The cart trundled on to disappear around the corner.

Harry could barely look. He shared a glance with Lott and Bodges before stepping gingerly out of his doorway, nervous of further biological attacks from the air. "L'Éternuement?" he asked, gently. He knelt to give his nemesis a gentle shake.

L'Éternuement neither moved nor made any sound. Added to the filth already on his face and in his hair, there was now a good deal of blood.

Lott stared down at his former master stoically. He took no pleasure in what he saw, but felt no sympathy, either. "Is he dead?" It was all he could bring himself to ask.

Harry felt for a heartbeat. "No. Help me. Let's get him off the street and see what we can do for hi——"

"Harry-the-Cough?" A man bawled the question from further up the alley. "This way, boys. It's The Cough. Get word to Lord Henry. I saw him first!"

Harry looked desperately to Lott and Bodges. "Don't let this idiot die. They'll blame me for that, an' all!"

He turned and ran.

Mad Mab's last undercover underling had undergone a change of heart, leaving her understaffed and understandably underwhelmed by the undead. However, she had high hopes for her latest acquisition. A born killer, she doubted he would mind the destruction of his soul – not if it brought him back from hell.

Sergeant-at-arms Walter Sweet, deceased, stood up from the freezing muck left in the wake of last night's blaze.

Dick backed away, terrified. "Mistress, I take it you will no longer need my services now you have the spell?"

Mab turned coolly. "You don't look well, Dick. What if I were to release you and you weakened further? How would I ever live with myself?"

"I-I can take my chances, mistress. C-could you p-perhaps see your way clear to give me the letter that will release my p-parents? Please?"

"Feeling the cold, Dick?" she smiled. "You'll catch your death."

"I'm f-fine, mistress, honestly. I just d-don't want to b-be near *him*."

Sweet looked at Dick, but gone was the mirth he always experienced when confronted by others' misfortune. He felt nothing. He simply was, whereas just minutes ago, he was not – at least, not any more. He carried no memories of hell. It never worked that way – up or down. The only difference between Sweet and Not Dave, was Not Dave's sense – like an unscratchable itch – that he might be missing something. Sergeant-at-arms Walter Sweet was fairly sure *he* was missing something and was only too glad of it.

Mab toyed with the idea of letting the boy go. No... not boy. He looked forty years old – and a hard forty at that, since she had drained him to save herself. Letting him go now and releasing his parents would be the fair thing to do. He *had* stolen the spell as per their bargain, but no, he had not secured all of it. As for fair... *Ha!* she concluded.

"You can go when I have the *entire* spell, and not before."

Dick hung his head in shame and despair. "And if we get it, you'll let me and my parents go then?"

"Of *course* I will." She smiled again.

Mab had no idea what a nice smile looked like, yet she tried. Dick did know what a nice smile looked like and was equally certain that was not it. He had played a game of chance with the Devil. It was no surprise he had lost. All that was left to him was to wonder what he could do to address the balance, before it was too late.

Chapter 23

The Also Rans

Harry ran away from the soldiers, ducking around the corner at the bottom of Scrubber Alley. Just two doors further on, Mr Tanner's cart blocked the way while he made a delivery. Harry leapt into the cart, grabbed Neil's reins and shouted for the pony to giddy up. He had absolutely no idea if that was the correct command, but Neil, feeling the light tap of the reins on his back, dutifully obliged anyway.

Fortunately for Harry, old Mr Tanner never went anywhere slowly. Neil was young and willing, and enjoyed terrorising the neighbourhood, so when Harry shouted for a second time, slapping the reins with more vigour, Neil took off.

The sounds of pursuit from behind diminished with every step Neil took. Scrubber Alley was L-shaped. Having already taken the corner, Neil galloped towards the T-junction with Struggler's Road. Opposite, and on the junction itself, was Harry's local tavern, The Struggling Man, that gave the road its name. He saw its landlord – and by unlucky coincidence, his own landlord – throw open the doors to greet the lunchtime crowd, already clamouring to get inside out of the cold and the snow. Harry had never before been in charge of a horse, and as Neil drew nearer the junction, he realised he had no idea how to get one to stop.

Scrubber Alley was barely wide enough for Neil's cart to pass and Struggler's Road was little better. There was absolutely no way they could make the turn at speed. Harry looked forward, despairingly, locking gazes with his landlord. In high-stress situations, the details that stick in the mind are often surprising. For instance, in the remaining seconds before Harry reached the end of Scrubber Alley, he noticed the tavern had a new, freshly painted door and frame. It looked rather cheerful.

"Harry-the-Cough?" the landlord cried. "I hope you've got your rent money, canny lad, because I..." he tailed off. Seeing Harry aboard old Mr Tanner's cart was a surprise, but seeing that he was clearly not in control of old Mr Tanner's cart came as a worse one.

"Get out of the way!" Harry screamed, diving into the back of the small cart.

In either sense of the idiom, Neil saw no problems going forward. After all, there was a doorway open right in front of him, easily big enough to allow passage for a dexterous young pony. Harry's landlord, and several of his most loyal and enthusiastic customers, dove for their lives as Neil galloped, flat out, through his front door. The pony passed through without incident. The incident came when the cart followed. Harry cried out again as the heavy oak chassis and its solid oak, iron-hooped wheels smashed through the new door and frame, taking a sizable chunk of the front wall with them.

The wattle and daub disintegrated with a bone rending *snap!* Harry pulled his greatcoat up over his head to protect himself from the falling debris and thatch as they passed under the eaves. He glimpsed out into a whirlwind of sparks as the building's central fireplace exploded under Neil's iron-shod hooves. Harry almost bounced out of the cart as the wheels took off, over the raised flags of the hearth, to crash down again on the other side.

The fire terrified Neil, who was already heading for the back door, which, fortuitously, was directly in line with the front. Though it would have been more fortuitous for being open because, sadly, Neil was unable to stop, even if he wanted to – which he did not. Harry ducked again.

The landlord sprang to his feet, shouting. He darted through the hole in his wall, fists raised, ready to take his damages out on Harry's head. When he saw a large portion of his rear wall vanish to leave a horse and cart shaped hole, he screamed, tearing at what remained of his hair. Fury was quickly twinned with terror when roof timbers began falling all around him. He dove for his life again, rolling out into the muddy slush of Struggler's Road, coming to a stop at last, against a soldier's boot.

"What the hell's going on here?" the man asked.

The landlord was unable to speak. He watched from the gutter as his tavern collapsed into a pile of thatch and timber. Fortunately, snow on the roof smothered the fire before the thatch caught.

Harry heard the *creak* and *crash* behind as he burst out of the ruins to escape along Hangman's Avenue on the other side. The irony of the grisly road name was certainly not lost on him. If the authorities caught him now, his only solace would be that he could only die in excruciating agony once. He dared not look back to see what Neil had done. Of course, no one would blame Neil, he was only a pony, and with that thought came a second, stark realisation – he was driving a stolen horse and cart, too.

Harry burst into tears. All he had ever wanted was to earn enough to pay his rent, buy some food and maybe have a little left over. Now he owed one month's rent plus a whole tavern, and if L'Éternuement died from his injuries, he would undoubtedly pay for that, too. No one would ever believe L'Éternuement's was an accident of his own making, so despite Lott's remarkable recovery – after being beheaded and eaten by sows – he would find himself accused of murder all over again.

"Got anything else to throw at me?" he bellowed furiously, glaring up into the heavens.

At the end of Hangman's Avenue, The Sprawl was bisected by the main south-west road to Strewthbury. Harry climbed back into the driver's seat and pulled on the reins, not really sure what he was doing, or which commands Mr Tanner used. Neil slowed dutifully, nonetheless.

Finally! Something's gone right, Harry thought, tetchily.

He was wrong, of course. Neil slowed not for Harry, but for the horsemen blocking his way at the junction. However, the heavens had indeed taken up his challenge, because at their head was Lord Henry Warmstirrup.

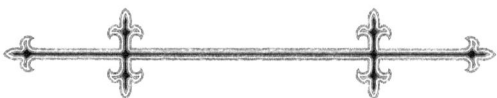

Alice and Matty forded the Aynl where it shallowed and widened. The water was bitter cold, but they pressed on, working their way south around the castle and town walls all the way to the bridge that carried the Parkworth Road back over the river towards town. The south-east bridge was guarded, but not heavily, not yet; a situation that might change if civil war did break out. The token duo on guard that day were there to gather Lord Henry's tolls from all who crossed the bridge.

Needless to say, the soldiers collecting the tolls were less than enthusiastic on such a filthy day. The weather kept almost everyone else at home, meaning there was very little traffic to tax, but at least that meant fewer arguments with the locals. The collected taxes paid for the upkeep of the bridge. However, given the overall condition of the bridge, taxpayer scepticism remained high.

Matty distracted the guards. It was a task for which she was more than qualified and more than satisfactorily endowed. Meanwhile, Insane Alice sneaked under the bridge to approach them from the other side, whereby she administered a nightcap with a large bulk of timber found washed up on the riverbank.

Heavy, billowing snow made their task easier, obscuring the view of anyone along the town walls. Rather than risk another challenge, they turned west before reaching the south-east gate, and headed into The Sprawl along Dark Lane.

"Alice," Matty began warily, "what was that chant for – back in the forest, I mean?"

Alice grunted. "Never mind. It didn't work, anyway. Wait." She drew up suddenly. "Before we go into town, there's something I need to do, lass. This won't be easy, but we need to build a fire."

"Out here?" Matty's disbelief was understandable. Everything was sodden and covered with snow, but that was not the extent of her concern. "What if someone spots it? You did just knock out two of Warmstirrup's finest."

"Can't be helped, dear. If we're to stand any chance against the power Mad Mab now wields, I must make this preparation."

"Would any fire do? Like, for instance, a fire*place?*"

"Yes. That would do fine. You're not suggesting going back to your own hovel, are you? Only an imbecile would——"

"No, no. I have an idea." Matty smiled. "Come on."

A few minutes later she knocked at Dora's door.

"Who is it?"

"Matty. Can we come in, please?"

The door opened a crack. "We?"

"Just me and Alice."

Dora's eyes widened. "Insane Alice, the wise woman?"

"That's me, dear. May I?" Alice did not bother to wait for a response; she simply strode in like she owned the place. "Right, now let's get this fire built up. You can barely feel its warmth. You must be freezing, dear."

"I don't have much firewood left and I can't afford——"

"Dora's been ill," Matty explained. "Don't worry, we'll see you alright, pet."

Alice was already unpacking various ingredients from the folds of her rags. She grunted, straining. "Ah, there you are."

Dora screamed. "Is that a bat's wing?"

Alice grinned. "Quite ubiquitous, your average bat's wing, dear. Useful for all sorts of——"

"Oh, Matty," Dora pleaded. "Not witchcraft. I thought those soldiers were going to kill us last time."

"Soldiers?" Alice turned to Matty, questioningly.

"Yes. It's been quite a week," Matty explained, wearily.

Alice rummaged some more. "Ah, here we are. I knew I had it safe."

"What's that?" both girls asked together.

"This, my dears, is hair. More specifically, hair snatched from Mad Mab's head when she blew up my home – knew it would come in handy. I have you now, Mab. Name and body, wherever you are, I have you." She had spoken those words at the time, but *this* time she did cackle, heartily.

Lott and Bodges turned what was left of Harry's workbench the right way up, propping the right-hand end with what remained of his broken chair. L'Éternuement lay on top of it, while Bodges melted some snow using a pot found in the back yard, the remains of much that Harry owned providing fuel for the fire. With relatively clean, warm water on hand, Bodges cleaned the filth from the wounded man's face and hair.

One of Neil's iron shoes had struck L'Éternuement right in the centre of his brow. He was lucky to be alive. Bodges cleaned the blood away. Head wounds often bled copiously, though the damage to the skull seemed superficial. "He's a thick head. Good for him. Try the ammonia crystals again, lad," Bodges instructed.

Noting again how Bodges' tic and speech impediment vanished while he worked, Lott drew the small phial from his scrip and unstoppered it. Wrinkling his nose, he wafted it in front of L'Éternuement's face.

L'Éternuement woke with a start, staring up into Lott's apparently still attached to his shoulders and not in any way dead face. He screamed and jumped to his feet.

"Whoa!" Bodges called out as the work bench collapsed again.

"You're dead!" L'Éternuement cried. "Witchcraft!" He stormed out of Harry's front door once more and, unimpeded by falling sewage or carts driven by cranky old men, ran for his life.

Neil trotted meekly to a complete stop, right in front of Lord Henry's huge, armoured warhorse. Of the most aristocratic of stocks, both horse and rider stared disdainfully down long noses at the commoners before them. Though of one mind, it was Henry who spoke. "*You* are coming with me."

Harry visibly wilted.

"Don't you know, I've been searching high and low for you and the girl, Matty, for days? Well? What do you say, fellow?"

"Sorry, my lor——"

"What's *that?*" Henry bellowed. "Speak up, damn you!"

"Sorry, my lord," Harry tried again, his voice quaking with fear. "I was, er…"

Henry leaned forward in the saddle. "Yes?"

"On the run, my lord," Harry finished, quietly.

"I know that, you damned fool. But there was no need. The whole matter has been dealt with. I've pardoned you for that chap's murder."

Harry's eyes were perfect circles. "Pardoned?"

"Yes," Henry drawled, aristocratically. "Days ago."

"But he… h-he's not dead, my lord. The lad, Lott. He's alive. He's back in my…" Harry tailed off as he turned in the driver's seat to see the collapsed ruin of the tavern, just a few hundred yards directly behind him.

"*Really?*" The earl was genuinely astonished. Rallying, he added, "Well, like I said. The matter's been dealt with." He frowned. "Is that Old Tanner's cart?"

"I didn't steal it, my lord," Harry snapped. "I, er… borrowed it."

Lord Henry raised a wry eyebrow. "With or without Tanner's permission?"

Harry gulped.

Henry rolled his eyes. "Return the pony and cart to Old Tanner," he ordered one of his foot soldiers.

"His name's Neil," Harry explained, guiltily, as he handed over the reins.

Henry leaned down from the saddle. "*You* will now come with me. And do try not to get lost again, won't you?"

"Yes, my lord," Harry agreed. It was not as though he had a choice.

Chapter 24
Dues

Lord Henry led his men, and Harry-the-Cough, through the south-east gate along Line Street. Almost at the castle gates, they were greeted by a battered, bruised and rather crazy-looking L'Éternuement. "My lord," he cried. "Harry-the-Cough is not only a murderer but a witch! He took me prisoner and forced me to commune with the dead. He, he, he..." Breathlessly, he ran out of words, possibly due to the severe blow to his head.

"What's this about, now? Cough?"

Harry was thrust through the fighting men to stand next to the earl.

"Well?" Henry pressed.

"My lord, this is news to me. I don't know what he's babbling about."

"He stuck Lott's head back on and made him talk, my lord. He's a witch! I saw strange writings, my lord, in his hovel – scratched onto the underside of his workbench. He's working with the Devil, my lord!"

A low, dangerous moan went through the soldiers.

"Quiet!" Henry barked. "Cough, I thought you said that young chap wasn't dead?"

"He isn't, lord. I didn't need to stick his head back on because he never lost it. Gave me a right start when he walked through my door, though – I'll not deny that. I didn't make him talk, my lord. He does it all on his own, on account of him not being dead."

Henry soured. "What's this about, L'Éternuement? Sour grapes because I called off the manhunt on your main rival?"

Harry was surprised; he had not credited the earl with such perceptiveness.

"No, lord." L'Éternuement dropped to his knees in the fresh snow. "I swear, he's a devil. He must burn, lord. At the stake. Both secular and Church law demands it – burn him!"

"Don't dare issue orders to me!" Henry began, when a messenger galloped along Line Street, catching them up from behind, his horse throwing clumps of snow into the air as he heralded the earl.

Skidding to a halt, the man spoke without preamble. "The Scots, my lord. Reivers attacking from the mountains to the west. I've ridden south from Chilly Castle to bring warning from my Lord Grey."

"Where are they now?" Henry demanded, urgently.

"The last we heard, lord, they were camped in the ancient hill fort at Old Spewit."

Henry lost no time in sending riders to recall Sir William and his brother, Sir Ralph.

"The witch, my lord, he must burn," L'Éternuement tried again to regain his lord's attention. There was something manic in his manner. "Justice, my lord. I demand justice."

"*Demand?*" bellowed Henry.

Startled and annoyed by all the sudden shouting and movement, Lord Henry's destrier took a bite out of the messenger's mount, nipping the animal's rump. The horse reared, throwing its rider and coming down hard on L'Éternuement, who still knelt in the snow. For the second time that day, he was knocked to the ground by heavy hooves.

"Get that horse under control," Henry barked to his men.

Harry dragged L'Éternuement out of danger and checked him over.

"Is he dead?" asked the earl.

"No, my lord." Harry stood. "Not yet, but this time, he might wish that he were. I'll do what I can, my lord." He said nothing about justice called for and summarily dispensed by a higher power; it would gain him no favour with Lord Henry, who saw justice as his sole prerogative.

Henry studied him. If he saw irony in L'Éternuement's predicament, he kept it to himself. "You would help him? Even after that little tirade?"

"I don't think he's in his wits, my lord. I'll help him – if help is possible. And I'll be here when you return victorious, lord, should you have wounded."

Henry smiled slowly. "And *I* will ride to save our people, young Harry Bones, Apothecary. I'll hold you to your word."

Harry bowed. "God go with you, my lord."

Mad Mab watched with interest as a large group of armed and well-mounted men rode into Warmstirrup at the gallop, only to ride back out again as part of a much larger group a few minutes later. She smiled slyly to Walter Sweet. "That was Lord Henry Warmstirrup, wasn't it?"

The walking corpse nodded.

"Along with most of his force and all of his notables, if I'm not mistaken."

He nodded again.

"Well, well, well, it seems the gods do help those who help themselves. Gentlemen, our time has come. Let us enter the town, and Dick, that means you, too."

Lott and Bodges appeared, as if by magic, the moment Lord Henry left. Harry rounded on them. "You two were supposed to be helping him." He gestured towards L'Éternuement, on the ground with a crowd gathering around him. "What the hell happened? And why didn't you get here sooner? He was obviously out of his wits, ranting like a lunatic in the street like that."

"Was he out of his wits? Or do you just have that effect on people?" Lott shot back. "How did *you* get here?"

"I was... detained," Harry admitted quietly.

"Yes, well, in answer to your question, it took us a while to get here because we had to take a circuitous route, and Bodges isn't as quick on his feet these days."

"*Doctor*, erm, Bodges."

Harry and Lott shared a secret look.

"Why the circuitous route?"

Lott moved in close, to avoid being overheard. "*Because* a very angry group from The Struggling Man turned up at your place and smashed the front door in. I didn't ask who they were, but I'm pretty sure they weren't the darts team[1]. Something about a demolished tavern?"

Harry straightened. Looking around, he noticed L'Éternuement's front door was still ajar. "Quick, let's get him inside before he dies in the street. We'll just get him home, where he can rest," he added for the benefit of the crowd.

The three men carried the fourth easily enough to lay him down on his own kitchen table. "So what happened?" Harry prompted.

"You were there. Didn't you see?" asked Lott.

"Not to L'Éternuement. I mean, what happened at home – *my* home, in Scrubber Alley?"

"I barely caught the gist of it," Lott admitted, while Bodges inspected L'Éternuement's dented skull with professional interest.

---

1. That would have been impossible. The early 14th century military pastime of darts would not become a pub sport until the early 20th century.

"Go on," Harry pressed.

Lott sighed heavily. "Let's just say, I wouldn't go back there if I were you. They started getting quite rude as we were leaving. One man was like, 'The Cough's got no money, so I'll settle for his head'. It all got a bit nasty after that."

"Tell him, erm, about the, erm, chickens," Bodges interrupted. Remarkably, the man seemed to hear everything without ever giving the impression that he was listening – behaviour converse to many of his profession.

Harry shot Lott a questioning look. "Chickens?"

"We had to run out the back door, obviously. Once in your yard at the rear, there seemed to be nowhere to go. That was when an old cockerel showed us the way."

Harry frowned. "Hang on, what?"

"Aye, he jumped up and down, drawing our attention to a broken plank in the fence. Once we were through, he squawked at all the other chickens to get them out of the way and cleared our path to a passage at the far end of the burgage. Amazing."

Harry was struck dumb. "That evil-eyed old sod *helped* you?" he managed at last.

"Aye. I've always had a way with animals." Lott shrugged his success away.

Harry sat heavily on the bench seat at L'Éternuement's table. "Why does literally everybody have it in for me?" he asked everyone and no one.

"I don't think this one will recover from this," Bodges noted, analytically.

"No. I'm just in shock, that's all," Harry replied, lost in self-pity. "The law, witches, business rivals, chickens, ponies… even rabbits line up against me."

"Actually, I meant *this* one," Bodges tried again.

"Oh." Harry stood, remembering L'Éternuement and the job in hand.

"Harry," Lott moved around the table, sidling up to his request, "would *you* teach me the apothecaries' trade? I'd work hard, honest."

The request took Harry completely by surprise, leaving him speechless.

"Please?"

"Er... Well, I suppose I could."

A mad cackling from the door made them all look around sharply. "That might just be the shortest apprenticeship on record," Mad Mab noted drily.

"I'm sure," Willa confirmed. "They've gone into the town, three of them."

Robyn frowned. "Three? They've picked up another?"

Willa nodded. "A man, and quite large by the size of his tracks."

"As big as Mario?"

"No one's as big as that wuss."

"Oi! Don't get me going again," Mario snarled. "I'll ring your scrawny little——"

"Yeah, you and your wife," Willa bit back scornfully.

"Stop!" Robyn snapped. "You may not have noticed but we're in considerable danger here. For one thing, we're hunting a witch. For another, it looks like we're going to have to follow them into the town – not a great move for outlaws."

"Maybe we could disguise ourselves," suggested Sister Tick.

"Go on," Robyn encouraged.

Tick shrugged. "As men, maybe?"

Willa rolled her eyes.

Little Joan sighed. "And I thought that might be going somewhere for a moment, too."

"Well, have you any better ideas?" Tick rounded on her.

"Actually, you may have a point." Robyn considered the idea. "The rumours about us, you remember, the ones *we* started, tell of the return of Robin Hood and his Merry Men to the forests of England."

"And?" Little Joan prompted.

Robyn gave a half-smile. "Well, we don't *exactly* fit that profile, do we?"

Joan leaned on her long*ish* bow. "I don't follow."

Robyn kneaded her brow impatiently. "Perhaps we should just walk into town, in ones and twos, and not draw attention to ourselves."

"But you're dressed as a man." It was always the same when Little Joan got her teeth into something; she would never let go.

"We still have skirts in our packs, don't we? For subterfuge – times like this, perhaps?"

Joan moved her bow staff from one side to the other, to get a better look at Robyn. "You're going to wear a skirt?"

"What of it?"

"But you look like a man. Won't they think you're a Scot, and shoot you?"

"I look like a—— Thank you! Thank you very much. Look, I'll tell you what. I'm going into the town to see what I can find out for Insane Alice. You lot follow me, in pairs, in whatever manner you like, just keep it *quiet*."

She unwrapped a long, shapeless dress from her pack, threw it over her clothes, adjusted her cloak to hide her sword, and set off for the north gate.

"It certainly seems to have quieted outside," Dora noted. "All the soldiers have gone, as far as I can tell, anyway."

"This could be our chance to find Harry," Matty suggested. "Alice?"

The crone was still half in a trance state, as she sat on Dora's three-legged stool by the fire. Matty placed gentle hands on her shoulders. Alice jumped.

"The soldiers have all gone," Matty explained.

"We must go. Now." Insane Alice was on her feet in an instant. "I think I know what Mab has done. The help I called for hasn't arrived, so we'll just have to do what we can. I know where she is – and if I'm not very much mistaken, we'll find Harry there, too. Everything is about Harry. I've sensed it all along. He's the convergence."

"What does that mean?" asked Dora.

"It means that, of all the people in the world, everything's going to fall on him. Come on, Matty."

"Do you want me to come with you?" Dora offered valiantly.

Matty embraced her. "You still need to get your strength back."

"I'm feeling better."

"Yes, you look it, too, but you've a way to go yet. Thanks for the offer, Dora, but this will be dangerous. Best you stay out of it. Besides," Matty smiled, "I may need somewhere to stay over. Who knows what's happened to my place while I've been away."

"Be careful, Matty."

They embraced again. Alice opened the door to the street and they stepped out into the falling snow.

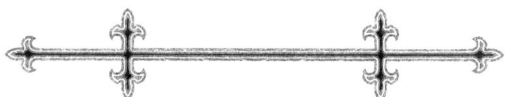

"You have something of mine, young Harry," Mab stated simply.

Harry stood, keeping the table between himself and his old guardian. "Aside from your winning bedside manner, I'm not sure what you could possibly mean?"

"You have my sunny sense of humour, too. That's three things of mine. The spell, boy. Where is the remaining piece? Give it to me. *Now.*"

"I don't suppose you'll believe me if I say, what spell?"

Mad Mab folded her arms and smiled.

"Didn't think so. What do you want it for? Can you at least tell me that?"

"Nothing that concerns you, my boy. Give it to me and you'll be free to go."

"Free to go and hang, more like," Harry retorted bitterly. "Half the town thinks I'm a murderer, the other half thinks I'm a witch, and now I'm consorting with one. What exactly do you think I'll be going free to... if I help you?"

"That's not really my problem, is it?"

Harry thought quickly, trying to come up with anything that might stall his enemy or allow him to come through everything with some kind of a life at the end of it all. "Could you at least help *him?*"

Mab looked down at L'Éternuement on the table. "You want me to help the man who's spent the last several months trying to destroy you? Did that horse knock you on the head as well?"

"You saw that, did you?" Harry smiled, weakly. "No, it's just that if I cured him, it might go some way to proving that I'm a healer and not a killer, or a monster."

Mab snorted. "And you think my healing him with witchcraft will, what, *exonerate* you?"

Harry's shoulders slumped. "Good point, well made," he conceded.

Mad Mab cackled madly. "Give me the spell, boy. You can sort your own problems out after that." She circled the table, bunching Harry, Lott and Bodges together as they, too, circled the opposite way. "And don't try to run, dear. I have a… I'll go with *man* at the back door, and the front door is guarded, too."

As if summoned, the kitchen door swung open to reveal Dick in the hallway.

"*You,*" Harry roared. "You thieving little git! You wait 'til I… Whoa." Harry recoiled when he saw the condition of his faithless friend. "Dick? Is that really you?"

"What do you mean?"

"It's just that you look *old*. Really old. Forty, at least."

"I-I've not been well," Dick admitted, sadly. "I'm sorry, Harry, she forced me to do it. She wanted me to kill you, remember? In Cutthroat's Way?" He glared at Mab. "But I'm not a killer. Not for anyone."

"Why, Dick?" Harry asked, the pain of betrayal clear in his face and voice.

"She has my parents, Harry. They're prisoners in Hwitaham's west pele tower. In this weather, they'll be… they'll be dying. I'm sorry, whatever that spell is capable of, it's still just a piece of paper. I had no choice."

"So that's what all this has been about," Harry muttered, almost to himself, the final pieces falling into place.

"We could charge him," Lott suggested in his ear. "He looks half-dead already."

With a last sad appraisal of his childhood friend, Harry dashed for the door.

The fast riders Lord Henry sent on ahead had woken the land to the approaching danger. Men soon converged on the Old Spewit Road, ready to defend their fields, their stock and their homes. Henry smiled to Sir Ralph and Sir William at his side; waking within *him* was the battle joy. "To me! To me, men of Warmstirrup," he called, enthusiastically.

Ralph and William shared a nod of approval, grinning, too.

The newcomers joined the column and Henry shouted down the line, "Footmen, bring up the rear and mop up any who're left. Horsemen, with me. Come on, my lads, we'll teach them to raid our lands[2] by killing every last one of them. Onwards!"

With that, Lord Henry Warmstirrup turned his mount and set off at a gallop, hotspurring fearlessly towards peril in defence of his people, men of the north charging loyally after him, to a place where history meets legend and great names, and great deeds, live on forever.

---

2. Raids across the border were common in both directions. However, irony would not enter the English language as a figure of speech for another 150 years – as evidenced by the suggestion to kill everyone as a teaching aid.

Chapter 25
A Bad Day in Warmstirrup

The gathering outside the entrance to Warmstirrup Castle was breaking up. Aside from a small garrison, left behind to man its walls and the town gatehouses, almost every soldier had flowed through the north gate to follow Lord Henry in search of glory and booty.

Matty, wrapped closely in her stolen cloak, hat pulled low to disguise her features, questioned a few townsfolk as they headed back along Dispensary Street for the shelter of their own homes, there being no more drama to be had.

The weather dispersed them quickly, leaving the street suddenly empty but for a few raggedy beggars with nowhere else to go. The unnotables hovered, biding their time before taking up what shelter they might in various doorways. Each knew that, should they move in too quickly, the residents would drive them away to die of exposure, and to men, women and children caught in a blizzard, a freezing cold doorway was nothing to be sniffed at.

"Poor wretches." Alice spoke with feeling. "Even a damp gaol cell would be preferable in this weather."

As it happened, Alice was wrong. Gaol cells held prisoners only until they were sentenced and punished. They would not be used as a punishment in themselves for another two hundred years. Beggars putting their hand up for a crime in Warmstirrup, to escape the cold, would find themselves severely disadvantaged when trying to put that same hand *out* a few days later, once justice had been served. Matty saw a one-handed beggar staring longingly at a doorway and wondered whether he had already tried Alice's approach once, and decided to quit while ahead.

"Are you sure it's a good idea for us to be here?" Matty asked, nervously.

"Mad Mab is close. The tracking spell I cast into Dora's hearth won't last the day – that's why I saved it until it really mattered – but while it lasts, it cannot be fooled."

They heard shouting – a sudden commotion to the rear of L'Éternuement's house and shop. Alice gripped Matty's arm. "This is it. Be ready," she whispered, unspecifically.

One man, to whom the idea of a gaol cell 'in this weather' was no comfort at all, was the recently minted Dick Richard. Mindful of his terrified parents locked away in the dark, he stood his ground, but Harry never moved on him. Instead, he ran for the back door. "Harry – no!" he called.

Shoving the drawbar aside, Harry launched himself through and out into L'Éternuement's back yard, Lott and Bodges hot on his heels. They all slipped and fell to the floor, stunned, as Sergeant-at-arms Walter Sweet clotheslined them, banging their heads together.

"My ribs," Lott wheezed, agonised.

"My dose – *again!*" Bodges cried out from the bottom of the pile. Tears may have obscured his view, but they failed to dampen his ire.

Sweet would have taken great satisfaction in watching the three men struggle painfully, and especially in having Harry prostrate before him in such a fashion. He would have, but no longer. He felt nothing, knew nothing, but the commands of his mistress. It was so simple, so *freeing*, and as long as her instructions coincided with his natural *unnatural* predilections, he preferred it to being alive.

L'Éternuement's yard backed onto the blacksmith's workshop. Mr Tommy Bullock's property was not as fine as L'Éternuement's, but was still a quality premises befitting his standing within the town. Situated to the rear of his townhouse, his workshop's western elevation was open, making it easier to bring horses and vehicles nearer the forge. The smoking chimney signified he was working that day. Harry could also hear repetitive hammering of metal on metal. A red, almost welcoming glow lit the gaps around a badly fitting back door. Scrambling to his feet, he ran for L'Éternuement's pigsty, lying between the two properties, and leapt the fence. A loud smash came from behind. Not looking back, he leapt again, high enough to clear the rearmost fence, when his collar was caught in an iron grasp that snatched him from the air. He cried out in shock and anger.

Three sows ran from their shelter and began snuffling around, checking out the newcomers in their search for food.

Lott limped forward, holding his side, his broken rib agonising, as he stepped into the sty to grab Sweet's arm again. He was experiencing an almost paralysing sense of déjà vu – how could the man possibly have survived Alice's stab in the back? Bodges followed, holding his nose in one hand, while pulling ineffectually at Sweet's leather jerkin with the other.

Sweet swung Harry back over Mr Bullock's fence and threw him down into the sty. The pigs squealed and ran back into their shed. Fortunately, the fresh snow was settling thickly, sparing Harry another drenching in filth. Sweet ignored Lott and Bodges in his pursuit of Harry.

Mad Mab stepped out into the yard from L'Éternuement's back door, followed by Dick.

Snatching Harry from the ground, Sweet threw him back towards the house. Smashing what was left of the pigsty fence, he came to a rolling stop at Mab's feet. The undead sergeant-at-arms came on coldly, as only a murderous walking corpse can, reaching for Harry once more.

Dick shouted, "No!" and leapt for Sweet himself.

Mab raised an eyebrow, her lip twitching in mild amusement and surprise at the sudden heroics from her doubly treacherous colleague.

Harry watched in horror as Sweet grabbed his severely weakened friend by the head and twisted. The crack of neck bones brought bile to his throat, causing him to retch.

Dick fell into the snow beside him, eyes staring, but no longer seeing.

"Bobby!" Harry shouted the man's childhood name, his emotions raw. There was nothing he could do but stumble back to his feet. Sweet caught him a glancing blow for his trouble, sending him sprawling again.

"I want him unharmed," Mab demanded, reedy voice squawking at her creature.

"As do I," Insane Alice called across the yard, appearing out of the passageway that led around the back from Line Street.

Mab cackled. "You want to challenge me *again?* Third time lucky, perhaps?"

"Lucky?" Alice retorted. "I've not done too badly, so far."

"Indeed," Mab drawled. "And you simply *must* let me know who does your hair. The singed look becomes you."

Sweet picked Harry bodily from the ground and looked to Mab for instruction.

"On second thoughts, dear," Mab spoke to Alice, "perhaps I don't need him. Indeed, perhaps the *world* no longer needs Harry-the-Cough."

Alice stepped quickly forward. "You leave my son alone!"

Harry stopped struggling against Sweet's grip at his throat to stare at her. "Your *what?*" he asked in a semi-gargle.

Mad Mab cackled again. "Yes, Mummy came back from the dead, Harry. She never bothered to reclaim you, though, did she?"

Alice returned Harry's gaze. "I'd been dead to you for more than five years by the time I escaped and was taken in by a local wise woman – rather like your own story, but with one exception – Murderous Meg was the kindest soul I ever met, apart from your father. She taught me how to protect you from afar. What good would it have done to turn your world upside down again?"

"What she means is," Mab elucidated, drolly, "she couldn't be bothered – didn't want you getting in the way of her profession. Intoxicating, isn't it, dear? Hard to give up so much power. What's a son compared with that? Especially a long-lost son."

"I did what I could for you," Alice spoke directly to Harry. "I had to keep my distance. You know what Lord Henry would have done to me, had he caught me. I didn't want that life for you, Harry."

Mab cackled creakily. "*Liar*," she spat.

Alice looked to the bag hanging over Mab's shoulder. "The spell – in there, is it?"

Mab's fingers tightened unconsciously around the strap. "That's none of your concern, dear."

Alice nodded, but not to Mab.

While Alice went around the back, Matty entered L'Éternuement's house through the front door, just to the right of his shopfront. Finding the kitchen door ajar, she simply followed the sounds of trouble all the way to the back door, removing Sweet's sword from the folds of her cloak on her way through. Hearing the full exchange, and burying her shock deep to work through later, she watched Insane Alice for a signal.

As soon as the crone nodded, Matty struck. Sneaking up behind Mab, she grabbed the handle of her bag with one hand, while using the sword's edge with the other to cut its strap.

Mab shrieked in surprise and alarm.

Matty was gripped by terror and desperation once more. Before the witch could react, she screamed and plunged the sword inexpertly into Mab's back from the right side.

Shock forced Mab to her knees, though she did not fall all the way.

Sweet dropped Harry to land heavily on his backside. Turning to help his mistress, he reached for Matty.

Matty ducked the swing and threw Mab's bag to Harry, who caught it, somehow getting his feet back under him.

Mab reached around to pull the sword out of her own back, making a hideous, keening cry as the blade slipped free.

Alice winced, imagining the excruciating pain of drawing steel at such an angle from one's own back. She was awed by Mab's strength and marvelled at how she remained upright. When, with a gargantuan effort, she got back up off her knees and turned on Matty, Alice cried out in alarm, "Matty, run!"

Matty struggled to process all that was happening, let alone what she had done. Staring at the blood on her hand, she was frozen in place when Mab raised the short sword to strike back with vengeance.

Alice ran across the yard, shouting, "Harry, burn it. Burn the bag, burn all of it!"

"No!" Mab shrieked, granting Matty a moment's reprieve. She turned to face Alice, who was performing an incantation as she came on to help Matty. Mad Mab leapt for her nemesis and sank the blade into Insane Alice's chest, dropping the other witch to the ground instantly.

"Alice!" Matty cried.

Harry was paralysed. Insane Alice, his mother? Back from the dead, like his father, and now lost to him, *again?*

Matty, seeing Harry's danger, recovered enough to pull him away. "Harry, do as she said. Burn it!"

"Where?" He spun around in fear and confusion. "Oh, no."

Sweet was on the move again – and heading straight for him.

Harry threw Matty roughly to the side to save her life and ran for all he was worth, towards the forge. Sweet crashed after him, smashing everything in his path. The squealing pigs escaped and ran into L'Éternuement's kitchen.

Harry made it to Bullock's back door just ahead of Sweet and crashed through, sprawling across the floor.

Tommy Bullock, though not tall, was an immensely stocky man, with massive arms and shoulders. It was little wonder L'Éternuement had thought twice before meddling with his daughter and oldest child. With a glowing rod in his left, hammer in his right, he worked at his anvil like a Norse god, sending sparks flying with every blow. As with all blacksmiths, his hearing suffered greatly for his craft, so he did not notice Harry's arrival until he skidded into him, almost taking Bullock off his feet.

"What the hell? Harry-the-Cough? What's going on?"

When Sweet ripped the forge's door from its hinges and whirled in like a fury, Tommy Bullock was a little put out.

"Sergeant Sweet, you'll pay for that door, damn you! The new blades aren't finished yet. I told his lordship——"

Harry never found out what Tommy had told Lord Henry, because Sweet launched the blacksmith through the air to smash through the wattle sidewall of his forge as though he were no more than a child.

The extraordinary language coming from the new hole stood testimony to Bullock's continued survival, and for that Harry was grateful, yet it did not help him. He lunged forward with Mad Mab's bag, reaching for the forge, but once again, Sweet snatched him out of the air.

Harry could not even turn to face the end he knew must be coming. Surely, there was no way he could survive this, not after Matty had stabbed his hated guardian. She would want him dead now more than ever. His mind worked, quick as light, as he went through everything that had been and everything he might have done differently. So many questions. The first being: why was Lord Henry's sergeant-at-arms working for Mad Mab? Apart from creating a nightmare scenario for Harry, what was in it for him? There was definitely something very *off* about him, too. Sweet was well known about town, and one of life's natural gloaters, yet through all this pandemonium he had not uttered a word – not even a sound, despite his prodigious physical efforts. Slipping from Harry's torrent of final thoughts, one in particular snagged at the banks to stand out from the flow. *No... He couldn't be, could he? Another like his father?*

As Harry pondered Sweet's mortal state, he felt Mab's bag being twisted from his hands as he was thrown to the flagstones. He turned to look up at what must surely be his approaching death, when a deep, percussive *thud* filled his ears instead. Eyes wide in the red light, he saw Sweet fly into Bullock's small forge, crashing through its stone plinth in the middle of the workshop to spread sparks and fire everywhere.

Amid the turmoil, Harry could barely make out what was happening, at first. A figure had stormed in and collected Sweet, taking the villain off his feet and plunging them both into the fire. "Tommy?" Harry called, his voice shaking. "Tommy? Are you alright?"

Smoke and sparks flew everywhere as a terrible combat raged in the confined space. "Tommy, you can't beat him. He's not a man. Not any more. *Tommy!*"

"I'll take your word for it, lad," said a voice by his ear.

Harry felt himself being lifted bodily once more, but this time by the entirely natural means of powerful muscles and a strong back. "Tommy?"

"Aye, lad. Quick, let's get out of here. Woman's in t'house wi' t'bairns. Help me get 'em out!"

"Of course." Harry followed Bullock back through what remained of the forge's doorway. They turned right, and right again, around the side of the forge to enter the back door of the abutted family home. Quickly finding Bullock's wife and two young sons, the blacksmith and Harry each bundled a child into a blanket and carried them out into the street on the far side of the house. Once outside, Bullock bellowed, "Fire at the forge! Fire at the forge!" at the top of his lungs.

Harry handed the child to its mother. "Where's your daughter?"

"Out, a-working," replied Bullock.

Harry nodded, glad she was safe. "I have to go back."

"You can't go back in there," the blacksmith argued. "They're devils – monsters!"

In no time at all, people streamed from their houses carrying buckets and tools for ice-breaking. A fire in town was *everyone's* problem.

"I have to," Harry explained. "There're people who need me."

"Don't—— Harry. *Harry!*" Bullock shouted after him.

Harry ignored him and ran back through the house out into the yard at the rear. The forge's thatch had caught and the whole workshop was engulfed in flames. Harry made his way around the side as quickly as he dared, slowed, rather bizarrely, by the risk of slipping over in snow – snow that was melting fast in the heat.

He was almost to safety, when two figures smashed through the forge's wall, blocking his route. They were both fully on fire and Harry screamed unashamedly. One of them turned to him, and through the flames, just for an instant, he saw his father's face. Harry reached out instinctively, but immediately pulled back from the heat. "*Dad,*" he cried.

His father nodded, just once, before throwing himself one final time at Sweet. Both men vanished into the inferno, never to return. Harry took two steps forward, but the fire was so intense it singed his hair. Having no choice but to retreat or be destroyed, he ran for L'Éternuement's yard, fences no longer providing any obstruction. What he saw made him sick: a small group, around a pathetically tiny figure lying in the snow. He ran the last few steps to join Matty, Lott and Bodges, as they looked down on Insane Alice, still with the sword embedded in her chest.

"Harry!" Matty cried, tears streaming down her face as she leapt into his arms.

"I'm alright, lass. I'm alright. Is she…?" He could not bear to finish the question.

"Not yet," a quaking voice replied from the snow.

Before Harry could deal with that, he had to know. "Where's Mad Mab?" He looked from one to another.

"She's just *gone,*" Lott admitted, baffled.

Matty shrugged, hopelessly.

"Erm, erm…"

Harry sighed, shaking off his irritation. It could wait – hopefully. "Insane Alice." He spoke gently, kneeling at her side, taking her hand in his. It was freezing cold. "We should get her inside. Bodges, Lott, help me——"

"No, no," Alice overruled him. "I can't move, lad. Not now."

"Alice." His voice broke.

"Actually, my name is Maud – as you might remember – but just this once, I think I'd quite like to go with Mum." She coughed, blood trickling down her chin.

Harry lifted her head gently, cradling it.

"Mum," he repeated quietly.

"Ah, that's better." She smiled weakly. "I see your father turned up again, in the end. I thought he'd ignored my summoning." She took a sharp, painful breath. "Always had a sense of timing, my man," she added proudly.

"Mum." Harry reached into his jacket and untied a blue scarf from around his neck. "This was all I was given. All the men brought back after the raid, when they took you. I kept it. Here."

He placed it in his mother's hand and wrapped his own around it.

"I always loved that scarf. You're a good boy, Harry. Now, listen to me. You keep working hard and make a name for yourself, and most important… ly…" She was fighting for breath.

"Mum, don't leave me. Not now. Not after all this…"

"Shut up." Insane Alice fired up one last time. "Listen. This is important. Is Matty there?"

"I'm here, Al—— Maud." Matty knelt at her other side, while Bodges drew Lott away respectfully.

Maud took Matty's hand. With all her remaining strength she placed it into Harry's and wrapped the blue scarf around both. "Mark my words, my son. You should marry this girl. Don't let her get away. You can worry about money later..." She coughed again, a horrible, squelchy sound. "I have a feeling that money will find you both, and soon enough, but it won't change you." Her breath rattled in her throat. "Let's just say, I've foreseen it. And Matty... something blue?"

Matty nodded, tearing up. She got the reference, even if Harry missed it.

With a gentle hand, Harry turned her face towards his. "Matty, will you———"

"Yes!" She cut him off in no uncertain terms.

Maud cackled one last time, just like Insane Alice. "I love you... son, and daughter. I'm pr... oud..."

"Mum? *Mum?* Noooo!" Harry screamed at the black skies overhead.

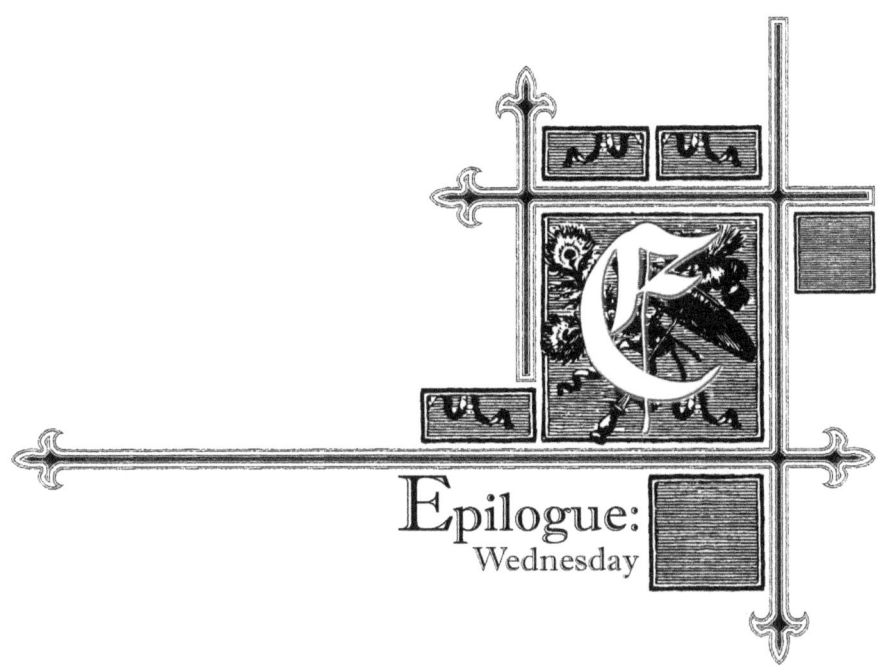

Epilogue:
Wednesday

Harry woke with a start, an edge of panic slicing through his woolly thoughts. What had he forgotten? After so many years where anxiety and worry were his go-to emotions, it took a while to get his bearings. Returning quickly, his memories poured back like soothing liqueur. He had not forgotten. He was not in trouble. He had not missed a thing. He had, he realised, as he stretched languidly, plenty of time.

The door to his bedroom almost shook off its hinges, making him jump.

"Harry! Come on, Harry. They'll kill me if you're not ready. I swore I wouldn't let you oversleep. Harry?"

Harry groaned and threw his legs over the side of his bed, rubbing his face tiredly.

"Harry!" *Bang, bang, bang.*

"Alright, alright." He stood, dropping his blanket to the floorboards and took a step towards the door. His bare foot unerringly found his belt buckle, eliciting a most unmanly cry. Holding his foot and hopping the rest of the way, he opened the door to see his new apprentice, waiting with arms folded, foot tapping impatiently.

Lott rolled his eyes. "Look at the state of it. Come on. I've got some warm water here for you. You can wipe all that off your face. What the hell is it?"

"Huh? What day is it?"

Lott shook his head sadly. "What an honour, to think that I should be in the presence of such questing intellect. It's Wednesday – as in *the* Wednesday, you know, the day, remember? I've got a gift for you – and Matty, of course. Something tells me I should give it to you now, though."

"A wedding gift, already?"

"Yes. It's *Wednesday*."

Harry's panic returned in a rush. "Wednesday?"

"Now he gets it. Now he makes his move," Lott mocked him, excitedly. "Here, look, I picked it up just this morning from Tommy Bullock. Don't worry, he let me have it cheap, after all the hours I put in, helping him rebuild his forge after you destroyed it. Trust me, Harry, you need it *now*."

"*I* destroyed it?" Harry retorted, groggily. "What is it?"

Lott handed him a steel plate, two feet long by a foot wide, with beautifully hammered tracery around its edges, the whole burnished to a perfect shine.

Harry took the mirror reverentially. "It... it's gorgeous. Wow. Thanks, Lott. It really is absolutely... Oh, God. Is that me?"

"'Fraid so, Harry. Hot water?"

Stripped of the previous evening's facial decorations – artefacts of a mostly forgotten stag night – Harry looked almost human in his best clothes. Indeed, he still marvelled that he *had* best clothes. The changes wrought on him in the last couple of months were hard to describe, and beyond all his expectations.

Felix L'Éternuement, Harry's one-time nemesis and all-round pain in the backside, never fully recovered from his second hoof to the head. Consequently, his arrangements with Sir Ralph were never realised, much to Sir Ralph's consternation – knighthoods cost nothing, after all. The murder of a peasant, followed by a quick tap on the shoulder for

L'Éternuement, and he would have gained a fabulous new townhouse to rent out for top whack.

Fortunately for Harry, Lord Henry's word was indeed law in Warmstirrup. Once it was clear that L'Éternuement would never reclaim his wits, the property reverted to the earl. Harry's kindness in caring for the man who tried to have him killed – even moving in to help L'Éternuement survive the early days of his convalescence – impressed Henry. Not to mention Harry's skill and commitment as he tended the soldiers after the Scottish raid was repelled. The earl therefore decided he liked the idea of having a talented apothecary right outside his gates. Particularly while the size of his retinue reflected the troubles of the moment. Illness was indeed rife among his encamped men. All that, and Bodges' recommendation, persuaded him to lease L'Éternuement's premises to Harry-the-Cough, Apothecary to thee Nobility – and his business had hit the ground running.

It turned out that L'Éternuement also kept a moneybox under his bed; a remarkable treasure trove of silver pennies, jewellery and no less than thirty Henry III gold coins, minted a century and a half earlier. Harry dutifully submitted the fortune to his lord, flabbergasted when the earl allowed him to keep it as a 'lifetime's rent' for L'Éternuement.

Harry tripped fondly down memory lane, while chewing on the deliberately plain oatmeal breakfast Lott provided to settle his rebellious tummy.

"You intend to care for Old Felix-the-Sneeze, do you?" Lord Henry had asked him on that fateful day.

"He'll die otherwise, lord. Besides, he's actually quite pleasant once you remove the guile, dishonesty, cowardice and selfishness – a simple soul, lord. He's keen to work, too, fetching and carrying, you know, simple tasks. I... *like* him."

The earl had laughed at that. "You're a singular fellow, young Harry. I'll tell you what. You keep his money. That should pay for his board. Perhaps you each need the other, after your fashion. The thirty pieces of gold can be the traitor's price for the debt he owes you."

"Thirty pieces of *gold*, lord?"

"Aye, should be silver, I know. We'll call it interest, shall we? Besides, I understand you've yet to make reparations for driving a horse and cart through the Struggling Man Inn."

Harry remembered reddening. A rebellious soul himself, Lord Henry had actually winked at him.

"Furthermore, I wish to present you with a gift for your upcoming nuptials, Harry."

"My *lord*." Harry had knelt then, his lord's gesture just so unexpected, so overwhelming.

"Aye. Let all here bear witness – I hereby transmute Harry-the-Cough's rent to a mortgage, payable for ten years. Scribe, take this down. As long as the monthly payments are met, and on time, then from the first of May, in the year of our Lord 1409, the freehold for the house and workshop that shall henceforth be known as *The Apothecaries',* in Dispensary Street, shall pass in its entirety to Harry Bones Esquire."

Just eleven weeks later, and despite his banging headache, Harry was munching away happily at his own kitchen table with everything to live for. The earl's was perhaps not the last word in generosity, considering he had simply granted himself someone else's property in the first place, but it was nonetheless a huge show of favour to a peasant, raising him, and his future wife, right then and there to the ranks of town gentry.

May 1st, AD1399 was an unusual choice, being a Wednesday, but Matty had been insistent. She wanted everyone to celebrate the rebirth of their lives from the ashes, and what better day was there than May Day? The

Maypole erection[1] took place the day before in Miller's Field, alongside the River Aynl. There was a real air of celebration, befitting a spring fair, and the field was already filling up with excited partygoers.

A voluminous canvas marquee stood alongside – courtesy of Bavol's sail-making business. Harry-the-Cough had recently saved Bavol's son from the sweating sickness, and since then, nothing had been too much trouble for 'Harry's big day'. Though the title of maitre d' was yet to be coined, Bavol was all set to play host for the happy couple, introducing their guests and providing a story to get everyone into what he described as the party spirit.

Harry had lived with the dread of what might come out in that story for weeks, now. Still, today was his wedding day, so he tried to put all worries aside, and it promised to be quite an event. Most of the town would be there by afternoon, whether they knew the couple or not. Harry only prayed the Scots weren't spying on them. Should they invade this Wednesday, there would be no one left within the town walls to defend them. A few drunken punch-ups were to be expected, of course – it was a wedding – but he most certainly did not want to go down in history as Harry-the-Cough: the man who caused one of England's most northerly towns to fall to the Scots, having lured its inhabitants to an unlicensed rave two miles away.

He shuddered. Having lived with hurt for so long, he had very little defence against dark thoughts when they circled his troubled mind. Even when happy, his emotional response was always the same – anxiety. He

---

1. A direct description, as no narrative sleight of hand was going to find its way around that one. Every single pun there ever was, has already been spoken, written or thought – in many cases by Shakespeare himself. Reworking the prose to allow for 'upright' or 'standing proud' would hardly have helped, especially in a highly charged environment where even 'sleight of hand' was likely to set someone rocking. There are times when an author must simply employ straightforward prose and ignore the mire of euphemism, no matter how hard it is... Oh, damn.

took a deep breath. "Things are better now. Things couldn't be any better. Get a grip, man." It was a line he had practised often of late – now he even had a mirror to provide focus – but with so much damage done, it was not easy, forcing him to really concentrate if he wanted to turn the frown upside down.

Lott popped his head around the scullery door. "What's that?"

"Nothing, just giving myself a talking to."

"Can I help?"

"You've already given me a talking to today, thank you."

Lott grinned. "Ready?"

Harry stood, took another deep breath, and straightened his tunic. "Of course I'm ready. What could possibly go wrong?"

Harry, Lott, and the confused but latterly ever-smiling Felix L'Éternuement, strolled out of the north gate to raucous cheers and catcalls from the few town guards still on duty. It was a beautiful day. Harry was no expert, but he was fairly sure he had never felt happier. The walk along the river Aynl was glorious, the warm springtime sun twinkling from every ripple across its gentle waters. Ducks thrashed about, quacking aggressively at one another; whinchats and redstarts sang their melodious death-threats high in the branches; rabbits watched him pass, disapprovingly, from their hiding places within the treeline; hedgehogs shushed one another to prevent the two-legs from hearing their latest song. It was, actually, perfect.

Out in front, neither Lott nor Harry noticed L'Éternuement hop off the road behind them, holding out his hand in the hope that a robin might perch upon his finger. The robin decided to fly away instead. They heard the splash from behind and Harry stopped, closing his eyes.

When he could bring himself to turn, he saw L'Éternuement doggy paddling near the bank but unable to climb out. Lott and Harry glared beseechingly, each to the other.

"I'm the best man," Lott complained. "I can't get covered in mud."

Harry stared at him in disbelief. "Of course. I'll do it, I'm only the groom!"

"Yes, but I promised... I mean, I... Oh, for crying out loud, together then?" Lott suggested, weakly.

Harry bowed his head. "If this goes wrong, I will personally hang the pair of you from the maypole."

"It's not *my* fault!"

"As best man, I thought you were keen on managing everything around me today. I mean, what about him? Does he look like he's managing?"

"No. He looks like he's... *drowning*. Harry – quick!"

A few minutes later, Bavol rode by on a beautiful chestnut mare. "Morning, Harry. All set for the big d—— What in the world are you up to?"

"Washing my cuffs in the river. We've had a bit of an incident."

"Is everything alright?"

"Don't know about alright. Everything is absolutely true to form – I *can* tell you that."

"What happened to poor L'Éternuement?"

"He was after a bird."

Bavol's eyebrows shot up. "Good Lord – couldn't he wait 'til the dance?"

Harry sagged. He just could not find it within himself to explain. "We'll be along anon. Thanks, Bavol."

"Righty-ho, Harry. I'll see you there, then." With a cheery wave of his expensive cap, Bavol replaced it onto his bald pate and spurred his mount to a merry canter.

Presently, Harry and his companions arrived at Aynlton Priory and were greeted by a beaming Prior Augustus. Harry shook hands warmly.

"Why, Harry, you're all wet," Gus noted, drying his hand on his vestments. "Come in. We expected you half an hour ago. The wedding vehicle will be here any minute."

"Wedding vehicle?" Harry asked, suspiciously.

"Yes, yes. Never mind about all that. Brother Luke will take you and your, erm... *best* man?"

Lott glared, offended, and Harry laughed. It was like medicine, unlocking the secret to health and happiness, while infecting all around him. Well, almost everyone. Sub Prior Robert glowered at them for laughing inside his church, his stare somehow suggesting that Harry's disrespectful mirth had brought his prior low. Unfortunately for Robert, this only made Gus laugh all the harder. A strangely cynical optimist, Harry remembered just why he liked the old man so much. In Harry's mind, there had never been any choice about who he wanted to marry them.

"She's here!" Brother Luke shouted from the rear of the priory church.

"Brother Luke!" hissed Sub Prior Robert, scandalised.

The diminutive monk flushed red and ran from the nave, to find anyone who might take his confession and eliciting further laughter from the guests, including Robyn and her – for once – *merry* not-all-men.

A large crowd gathered outside, not wishing to absent themselves from one of the year's big events and it was standing room only in the church when Matty entered.

The whole congregation took a breath as she walked down the aisle in the blue dress, initially stolen from, but later granted by, Lord Henry. Harry turned to watch his bride approach on the arm of Dr Bodges, who wore his very best coat to give her away. Harry knew he was not supposed to look, but decided he *was* meant to see, and upon seeing, his heart almost burst. The ceremony was a blur for him after that.

He vaguely remembered Lott knocking an urn of wildflowers all over the floor. Foot still wet after the rescue of L'Éternuement from his dunking, he slipped up the well-worn steps to the altar when handing the ring to Prior Augustus. The laughter barely penetrated Harry's world, and before he knew it, he was kissing his new bride and bustling out of the church.

Once outside, he saw the wedding vehicle for the first time. That, for him, was when the laughter came.

Neil the pony stood waiting, beautifully groomed and shiny-hooved – if a little put out by the ribbons tied into his mane and tail. His little cart, also draped in a riot of ribbons and flowers, had been scrubbed and scrubbed again.

Old Mr Tanner smiled broadly. Stealing a cheeky kiss from the bride, he placed the reins into Harry's hands. "You will take him steady, won't you, young Harry? He's used to going steady." Mr Tanner was completely oblivious to the amusement his words drew from the crowd.

"Harry."

He turned at his name, to see a very attractive lady he completely failed to recognise. She wore a fine green dress. Matty drew her new husband close to whisper in his ear. "It's Robyn," she helped him out.

Harry blinked. "I knew that," he lied, unconvincingly.

Matty and Robyn laughed.

"I have something for you, Harry." Robyn held out a small, wooden toy horse. "Dick's – or should I say, Bobby's – parents said you would remember this. Apparently, you always loved it as a boy?"

Harry could not speak, could hardly breathe past the lump in his throat.

Matty answered for him – there really was only one word to ask. "How?"

Robyn drew them aside for a little privacy. "You remember we came into the town to help on... *that* day." She looked regretful. "Too late, I'm afraid. There was nothing we could do for you or Alice, and with the return of Lord Henry possible at any time, we had little choice but to leave. However, we did bump into Mad Mab on her way out."

"She escaped, then." Harry spoke tonelessly.

"No. She was losing a lot of blood. It looked like she'd been..."

Harry and Matty exchanged a glance.

"Well," Robyn changed tack on this happy day, "she was gabbling – ranting even. Kept going on about Dick and how he'd betrayed her and if it was the last thing she ever did she'd make sure his parents rotted in the cell under Hwitaham's west pele tower. She tried to use her witchcraft on us again. Perhaps you weren't aware of how she knocked us all out before? She did something terrible to Dick. Anyway, for whatever reason, she must have been too weak to do it again by the time we caught her. Sister Tick was able to catch her squarely under the chin with her ass' jawbone, to send her over the side of the bridge into the Aynl. She broke the ice as she went in."

"She's dead, then," Harry stated, lifting slightly.

"No. After taking a vote, we all decided we owed Mad Mab for what she'd done to us, and to you. So, after we fished her out, we gagged her and took her back to Hwitaham. Turns out, the people there remembered her well – once we'd re-introduced them. They were most unimpressed to find out she was still alive and up to mischief again. Apparently, she had a deal with the local priest, but we never found him."

Harry's memories travelled back to the village ducking stool – a shared asset with Twyford. He had a suspicion no one ever would find him.

"Anyway, we found Bobby's parents," Robyn continued. "They were in a bad way, yet both recovered. We told them about their son, and all he had been through to try to save them. It was a shame, what happened to him. Naturally, we spared them some of the details. Some of what he did was..." She tailed off, not wishing to speak ill of a young man forced to do evil to save his family. Especially as he had turned on his dark mistress in the end. "Anyway, they're not yet well enough to travel far, so they asked me to deliver this wooden toy horse to you as a wedding gift."

Harry shook his head, ruefully. "I don't know what to say."

"We left Mab," Robyn continued, "in the cell Bobby's parents were no longer using. I don't know if she's still there."

Again, memories of the ducking stool came irresistibly to Harry's mind, but he kept his suspicions to himself. "Thanks, Robyn. I'll have to make time to go and see them." He helped Matty up onto the cart's bench seat and hopped up after. "Thank you, everyone." They waved and set off.

Matty and Harry's short drive along the bank of the River Aynl to Miller's Field passed mostly in silence. Reeling from events, all they could do was smile at each other, and at what fate had provided them.

A little calmer now, Harry noted his mother's blue scarf tied at Matty's wrist. "You wore it, then?"

"Of course. My dress is blue, so I went with something old, instead."

Harry had no idea what that meant but grinned anyway.

Presently, they arrived at what was already a healthy gathering. John Miller greeted them at the little bridge over his leat. "Hello, Harry. Hello, Matty. Congratulations, my friends. Just wanted to make sure you didn't fall in this time."

Harry laughed. "I've already had one slip in the river this morning. Hey, John, I have something for you." Harry called the miller to him, close and confidential as he leaned down from the cart. "You may want to get these back to your friend."

John's eyes widened as Harry dropped the coin minting stamps into his palm. "Sorry it's taken so long to get them to you. I was waiting for the dust to settle after I removed them from... from the person who took them from you. Didn't think it would be a good idea for the earl's men to find them." He winked.

The look of panic on John's face was almost comical. "Not here," he hissed. "Harry, please, could you keep them just a little longer for me?"

Harry was confused but took them back without comment.

"There are people here who might..." John looked around nervously. "Look, this is far bigger than I ever realised. I wish I'd never... I'm sorry, Harry. Perhaps this is a story for another day. You wouldn't believe the trouble those have caused me – especially since they went missing, but thank you, for bringing them back, and for hanging on a little longer. Now come, the wedding feast is almost ready." With obvious effort, the miller shoved his cares aside. His sudden grin was broad and infectious. "Take your seats at the head table, and as soon as the other guests arrive from the priory, we'll eat!"

Bavol managed a reasonable job of introducing everyone, although his memory, not to mention his speech, did suffer after his third flagon of ale. Eventually, the moment Harry had been dreading arrived – Bavol's story. He recruited a helper in the form of Jack, Lord Henry's master-of-hounds, and they delivered the story from the top table as a double act. Their tale brought back to life a bleak winter's day, not so long ago, when a pack of extremely disobedient dogs stole a giant fish from a prominent local tradesman, only to drag it into the castle's inner bailey, where all manner of shenanigans occurred.

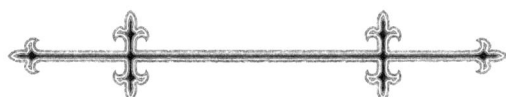

Later that evening, Harry and Matty strolled along the river, hand in hand. The revels, in full swing behind them, filled the lands with sounds of joy and laughter. As the sun sank in the west, the blue deepened in the east and the North Star winked at them. Everything was perfect – only they were not alone. Not truly.

"Our boy's done well," said Hugh.

"He has," Maud replied, proudly. "Good turnout, too. Lot of people here. You're looking better, by the way."

"Yes, since I stopped being Not Dave, my soul has almost regained its full weight of 21.3 grams – or so I've been told."

"What's a gram?"

"No idea. Don't think they've been defined yet. Amazing, the things you learn after you're dead, isn't it?"

"Aye."

"Aye."

"I'm glad you're not Not Dave."

"Me too. He took it well, though."

Maud turned to her ethereal husband. "Who?"

"Dave."

"He didn't mind what you did to him?"

"No. Well, I *say* no. I doubt he enjoyed it at the time, and he was a bit put out that I lost his cart, but…"

"But what?"

Hugh shrugged. "His life was awful, anyway. 'S what he told me – all turds and rags. *Upstairs* have promised him another go in a few hundred years. Says he's going to work for the Cow 'n Sill?"

"What's that, a tavern?"

"Dunno. Reckons he's going to drive a giant, horseless cart that eats rubbish, or summat. He can't wait."

"Really?"

"Aye."

"Aye."

Felix L'Éternuement wandered innocently beside the river towards the bride and groom, mumbling hellos to every bird and woodland creature he met along the way. He approached Harry and Matty with his usual, slightly puzzled smile, but also with a bowl of succulent early fruit. "Harry." He offered the fruit as a gift – 'Harry' and 'hello' being among the few words he could still say.

Harry was about to thank him for the gift when he froze. "Matty, can you hear singing?"

"From the party?"

"No." Harry tilted his head. "Listen carefully."

They all listened, Matty's eyes widening in surprise. "I can now."

Harry could not quite believe his ears. They were way too far from the priory to hear the monks singing over all the carousing from the celebrations – notwithstanding the monks singing drunkenly *at* the celebrations. "That's *Gaudete*."

"Isn't that a carol?" asked Matty. "But it's spring."

Harry turned sharply. "Dick? Dick Richard, is that you?"

"The name's Bobby, remember?" replied the ghost of Harry's childhood friend. Mab's evil magic reversed by his good deeds, he now looked like a twenty-year-old once more.

"They can't hear you, lad. They never hear us," Maud assured him.

"They heard my singing, Alice."

"Maud."

"Sorry, force of habit."

"They only heard it because they weren't expecting to. From here on in, you'll find you're talking to yourself, just like the rest of us. But don't worry. My son's a good man – he'll be along, in God's good time."

"You sure? He married a prostitute."

Maud slapped him around the head in a characteristically Insane Alice kind of a way.

"Ouch! I felt that. How come I felt that?"

"Because you were meant to. It's called telekinesis. Insane Alice knew a lot of things, remember? Watch this..." She gestured towards L'Éternuement's fruit bowl. It lifted from his hands, emptying all over his head. The ghosts of Harry's loved ones almost laughed themselves to life.

Harry-the-Cough will return in
MINTED

Author's Notes

As stated, the setting for 'The Apothecaries' was inspired by the real medieval market town of Alnwick in Northumberland, England – home to Harry Hotspur.

Harry Hotspur (Henry Percy) predeceased his father, the first Earl of Northumberland, who was also named Henry Percy, and so never actually became Earl of Northumberland. Unfortunately, the real Hotspur failed to receive the warning note from Insane Alice! He did indeed die in a field just outside Shrewsbury on the 21st of July, 1403, battling against King Henry IV (whom he helped to the throne) and his son, the future Henry V.

Like the Henry Warmstirrup in my story, one of Hotspur's brothers was also called Sir Ralph, and they really were both captured by the Scots at the Battle of Otterburn in 1388.

The wedding tradition, Something Old, Something New, Something

Borrowed, Something Blue, actually appeared much later in 19th century Lancashire, but the blue scarf Harry carried as a last link to his mother fitted nicely into the story for any romantics out there.

What's in a name? For anyone planning a trip, quite a lot, I would imagine...

I've played fast and loose with the place names in this story. Most of my fantasy world, and its maps, are loosely based around real locations close to Alnwick and its castle (recently of Harry Potter fame), but are not *actually* Alnwick.

The town walls were in fact built slightly later, towards the end of the 1470s. Dispensary Street is actually located a little further away from the castle to the west than it is in the story. However, the opportunity to place The Apothecaries' building on Dispensary Street was a gift. Weirdly, I didn't realise there *was* a Dispensary Street in Alnwick until after I'd written the book, but it was simply too good to miss, so I had to go back and add it to the story and the maps. The oldest pub in Warmstirrup is known as The Dirty Jugs – this is a rather clumsy homage to The Dirty Bottles, a public house in Alnwick famous for its rather unusual window decoration. The window facing onto the road is sealed and contains several 'dirty bottles'. The story has it that a previous owner, roughly two hundred years ago, tried to remove them and instantly dropped dead. Funnily enough, no one has dared touch them since – hence the dust and the dirt!

The other pub in Warmstirrup – that suffered Harry's early and ill-conceived attempt to combine a drive-by with a drive-thru – I named The Struggling Man. This is the elephant in the room, in that it is not from Alnwick and is in fact a public house from my own childhood that sadly, like so many others, has now gone to make way for a rather less pretty row of house boxes. It was nicknamed 'The Struggler' by the locals, hence Struggler Road. Unfortunately, its total destruction was pre-Google and smartphones, so there are very few pictures remaining of the pub, bowling green and beer garden that overlooked what were then lovely parklands in the middle of the town. We used to play on that park, day and night, but sadly, many are afraid to walk there even in the daytime now. I hope The

Struggling Man retains some small measure of immortality in print from this work.

Aynlton Priory (very definitely pronounced Ant'n!) was based on Hulne Priory, founded in the mid-13th century by the Carmelite Friars who decided that Brizlee Hill resembled a place in the Holy Land called Mount Carmel. There were many monastic orders across Europe in the Middle Ages; I decided to make them Benedictine for the story because that order is probably more familiar to most of us.

Warmstirrup Abbey was based on Alnwick Abbey, a Premonstratensian monastery built in 1147 and, like so many others, suppressed and mostly destroyed during Henry VIII's dissolution of the monasteries in the late 1530s. Sadly, only an extremely impressive gatehouse remains.

The River Aynl is another clumsy play on the River Aln, as the River Foquet (pronounced Foh-ket, honestly!) refers to the locally famous River Coquet (Coh-ket).

In the bow of the Foquet is the castle and town of Parkworth (pronounced Porkworth by Sir Ralph). The real Percy castle and town of Warkworth is pronounced locally as workworth – actually that's an awkward one, too easy to read as werkworth, so let's try walkworth. I love these place names. They present a writer with endless possibilities for bad jokes! Warkworth, like my fictional Parkworth (Porkworth), has a hermitage, too, and it's every bit as impressive as Sir Ralph laments in the story.

Edcase Castle, in the real world, is actually a wonderful ruin named Edlingham Castle, which shares a stunning landscape with an early Norman church and a beautiful Victorian viaduct, all built in stone. Were that not enough, it's also a mere stone's throw from Corby's Crags – for my mind one of the finest viewpoints in the county, looking out towards the Great Cheviot Mountain itself.

Chilly Castle is, of course, the great Chillingham Castle – possibly my favourite of the many Northumbrian strongholds. The gorgeous castle and its medieval church, replete with one of the best medieval tombs you'll see outside Westminster, is a must see. The owner, Sir Humphry Wakefield, makes a great deal of the castle's ghosts. Although, I have not experienced the phenomenon myself, there is certainly a feeling that the previous residents have just 'stepped out' for a moment, when you enter its courtyard and chambers.

Snugly Burn is actually Rugley Burn. A burn is a northern English/Scottish name for a small river or large stream.

Old Spewit is an ancient place, actually named Old Bewick. A small village now, but also near the site of some extraordinary early Bronze Age archaeology, including a cairn and some extremely rare cup and ring marks. The hill fort mentioned in my story really exists and was constructed during the later Iron Age and may still have been occupied into the Roman period.

Strewthbury may sound Australian, but – outside the crazy world of Harry-the-Cough – actually relates to the medieval market town of Rothbury.

Hwitaham and Twyford were small villages west of Alnwick. Hwitaham is now called Whittingham and once had two pele towers, of which only one remains, though other fine examples may be found in the area.

Scotch is an old term (in English) for the Scots, although it is rarely used any more, other than to describe scotch whisky.

Again, Thank you for reading,
Stephen

Also by Stephen Llewelyn
The New World Series
DINOSAUR
REVENGE
ALLEGIANCE
REROUTE
REMAINS
CURSED
COLLISION

Audio books read by **Chris Barrie (Red Dwarf)**

The New World Series, Short Stories
ENGEL
MAPUSAURUS
GHOST
DRUMMOND

Praise for The New World Series:
"Spaceships, wormholes and dinosaurs! Don't miss it."
Stephen Baxter – The Long Earth, Doctor Who

"Epic! Full of big ideas! A thrilling read told on a huge scale."
Simon Guerrier – Primeval, Doctor Who

"If, like me, you love time travel and prehistoric beasts, you'll relish this."
Nigel Marven – Walking With Dinosaurs

"This series gets more intense with each offering. Gobsmacking!"
Wordz

"Action, science fiction and adventure, all topped off with a wonderful garnish of humour, these books should be on the shelf of any sci-fi and history fan. Truly stunning."
Amazon Purchaser

STEPHEN LLEWELYN
DINOSAUR

THE NEW WORLD SERIES | BOOK 1

ISBN	eBook	978-1-8380235-1-5	
	Paperback	978-1-8380235-0-8	
	Hardcover	978-1-8380235-6-0	
	Audiobook	978-1-8380235-8-4	Performed by Chris Barrie (Red Dwarf)

978-1-8380235-3-9 ebook
978-1-8380235-2-2 paperback
978-1-8380235-7-7 hardback
978-1-915676-12-2 audiobook

978-1-8380235-4-6 paperback
978-1-8380235-5-3 ebook
978-1-8380235-9-1 hardback

978-1-8382125-0-6 paperback
978-1-8382125-1-3 ebook
978-1-8382125-2-0 hardback

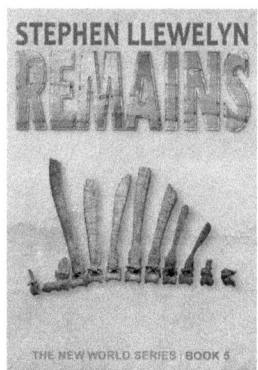

978-1-8382125-3-7 paperback
978-1-8382125-4-4 ebook
978-1-8382125-5-1 hardback

978-1-8382125-6-8 paperback
978-1-8382125-7-5 ebook
978-1-8382125-8-2 hardback

978-1-915676-00-9 paperback
978-1-915676-01-6 ebook
978-1-915676-02-3 hardback

www.ingramcontent.com/pod-product-compliance
Lightning Source LLC
Chambersburg PA
CBHW041135110526
44590CB00027B/4022